Science

into

Policy

Global Lessons from Antarctica

SCIENCE

INTO

POLICY

Global Lessons from Antarctica

PAUL ARTHUR BERKMAN

Byrd Polar Research Center
The Ohio State University

March 31, 2004

David,

It was a pleasure voyaging to Antarctica and exploring the peninsula regions with you.

With best regards

Paul

ACADEMIC PRESS
A Division of Harcourt, Inc.

San Diego   San Francisco   New York   Boston   London   Sydney   Tokyo

Cover photo credits
Clockwise from upper left: Emperor penguins (*Aptenodytes forsteri*) on the sea ice near Cape Washington (74° 39′ S, 165° 25′ E) in Terra Nova Bay, along the northern Victoria Land coast, during January 1999. SCUBA diving in the nearshore marine environment with colleagues from the Italian Antarctic program near Evans Cove (74° 53′ S, 163° 48′ E) in Terra Nova Bay during January 1995. Flags of the Antarctic Treaty Nations at McMurdo Station (77° 51′ S, 166° 40′ E) in 1986. Photos by P. A. Berkman.
Center: Mosaic of Antarctica compiled by the National Oceanic and Atmospheric Administration based on 28 Advanced Very High Resolution Radiometer (AVHRR) images taken by the Tiros-N satellite system.

Academic Press
A division of Harcourt, Inc.
525 B Street, Suite 1900, San Diego, California 92101-4495, USA
http://www.academicpress.com

Academic Press
Harcourt Place, 32 Jamestown Road, London NW1 7BY, UK
http://www.academicpress.com

Library of Congress Catalog Card Number: 2001092779

International Standard Book Number: 0-12-091560-X

PRINTED IN THE UNITED STATES OF AMERICA
01 02 03 04 05 06 EB 9 8 7 6 5 4 3 2 1

To Mom and Dad,
for giving me their strength to explore the world
with family at the center.

CONTENTS

PART I

EARTH SYSTEM SCIENCE: SENSE OF WONDER

1

GLOBAL DIMENSIONS

2

CONCEPTUAL INTEGRATION

PART II

PROGRESS OF ALL MANKIND:
INTERNATIONAL POLICY

3

TERRA AUSTRALIS INCOGNITA

4

AWAKENING SCIENCE

5

INTERNATIONAL STEWARDSHIP

PART III

OUR DYNAMIC PLANET:
INTERDISCIPLINARY SCIENCE

6

SPREADING PLANET

7

FLOWING PLANET

8

BREATHING PLANET

9

LIVING PLANET

PART IV

SUSTAINABLE RESOURCE USE: RESOURCE ECONOMICS

10

ECOSYSTEM CONSERVATION

11

ENVIRONMENTAL PROTECTION

PART V

OUR GLOBAL COMMONS:
PRECEDENT FOR HUMANITY

12

THE SCIENCE KEYSTONE

FOREWORD

It is in the interest of all mankind that Antarctica shall continue forever to be used exclusively for peaceful purposes and shall not become the scene or object of international discord.
—Antarctic Treaty (1959)

Science has been the primary rationale for national activities in the Antarctic region since the International Geophysical Year of 1957–1958. The 1959 Antarctic Treaty (which came into force in 1961) ensures the freedom of scientific investigation as an effective mechanism for maintaining international cooperation throughout the region south of 60° south latitude. The emphasis on understanding the Antarctic environment and its place in the global system, as an international precedent for preserving our world for future generations, is an important theme throughout this book.

From the Antarctic Treaty has grown a complex of Agreed Measures, Conventions, Recommendations, Resolutions, and Protocols, which have become a part of what is now known as the Antarctic Treaty System. This international system includes governments interacting with advisory organizations through the Scientific Committee on Antarctic Research (SCAR), Council of Managers of National Antarctic Programs (COMNAP), International Association of Antarctic Tour Operators (IAATO), and Antarctic Southern Oceans Coalition (ASOC), as well as other stakeholders with interests in the Antarctic region. It is significant that during the year of the 40th anniversary of the Antarctic Treaty System this book becomes available.

The combination of historical and scientific perspectives in the context of environmental and resource policies presented by the author is a valuable approach for understanding the interplay between international science and the political framework that makes such science activities possible. The author's long experience and involvement in Antarctic science together with his experience in research activities involving international cooperation and coordination have provided him with a personal understanding of the materials presented here.

The dynamic role of Antarctica in the Earth system and global climate has become recognized during past decades. The Vostok ice core, spanning the past 500,000 years, has provided humankind with the longest continuous record of global atmosphere variability from anywhere on Earth. The author has presented not only an interesting narrative but an innovative use of tables, diagrams, graphs, data, and concepts that will stimulate the reader to ponder Earth system phenomena across time from local to global scales.

In his personal preface the author has shared some of the background and Antarctic experiences that motivated him to write this book. I urge all users to read this section before journeying into the contents. Not only will the reader have a better understanding of the "why" of the book, but the explanations surrounding the organization and methods of presentation will stimulate inquiry and be very helpful in thinking about the interdisciplinary context of the world we live in.

Robert H. Rutford
President, Scientific Committee on Antarctic Research
Excellence in Education Professor
and Former President, University of Texas at Dallas

PREFACE

The most remote continent—alone at the bottom of the Earth, distant from all civilization—shines as a beacon of international cooperation. Antarctica represents more than a frozen ice cap surrounded by sea ice and giant icebergs with penguins and whales. Antarctica is a land of exploration, not only for intrepid individuals but for everyone venturing into this new millennium with eyes wide open—wondering about global strategies that will nurture our civilization into the distant future.

My sense of Antarctica emerged in 1981 while wintering at McMurdo Station, SCUBA diving under the sea ice throughout the year as a 22-year-old staff research associate with Scripps Institution of Oceanography. For me, this distant perspective of our world was a profound experience. After returning home, driven by passion and a sense of responsibility, I began teaching a capstone course titled Antarctic Marine Ecology and Policy as a visiting professor at the University of California, Los Angeles. I have been teaching the Antarctic course at universities ever since—always with a diverse audience of graduating seniors from science and nonscience majors who are interested in the world we inhabit. Since 1991, more than 900 students from more than 90 majors in 14 colleges have registered for the Antarctic course at The Ohio State University. This book is patterned after the Antarctic Marine Ecology and Policy course.

All of us already are familiar with the natural world because of experiences that began during childhood. Yet, for whatever reason, our innate curiosity about mixing and poking things is not fostered in everyday education. I remember at a meeting, once, the owner of the lodge came up and asked what we were doing. After we elaborated on science education and the many presentations, he inquired, "So what good will these discussions do for my grandchildren?" I asked him to consider his childhood as a time when he had no concerns about asking good or bad questions—when he was just curious about how things worked. Slowly, a big smile came to his face, and he told me of the time as a young boy when he wanted to know how his drum worked—so he cut it in half.

It is this sense of wonder about our everyday Earth—seeing, breathing, touching, smelling, and feeling the world around us—that must be invigorated. Most importantly, creating an educational atmosphere where individuals freely ask questions and explore information instills confidence about their ability to learn on their own. This open, free-form pursuit of information and generation of ideas is central to empowering individuals as full participants in our increasingly technological world.

Beyond the marvels in our everyday lives, science provides a philosophical approach to lifelong critical thinking, problem solving, and creativity. Science develops technologies that open opportunities for resource utilization. Science stimulates continuity in our world—across society over generations—by building on an ever-expanding base of knowledge. Science also provides common ground among nations, independent of their political ideologies. In essence, science provides an educational framework for facilitating the sustainable development of communities across the Earth. In this Earth system context, colored from a palette of natural wonders, Antarctica is an ideal template for teaching about the integration of science, economic, and government policies across the planet.

The organization of this book is designed to promote the integration of diverse topics for each reader. Viewed as connecting rings, two topics have a single intersection; three connecting rings have four intersections; four connecting rings have nine intersections—with the complexity of intersections increasing geometrically as rings are added. To reduce the complexity of integrating diverse perspectives on the Earth system, and to foster information synthesis, learning units are embedded that are generally linked by three elements at each level. This "three-form method" emerged from a Venn-diagram project, quantified from courseware in the Antarctic Marine Ecology and Policy class, where students integrated two or three interdisciplinary elements more commonly than four or more. Venn diagrams also are used throughout this book.

This book has beginning, middle, and end parts that are further divided into related chapters which feature interacting natural and human elements in the Earth system. Each part of the book begins with a summary containing a single unifying figure that synthesizes the materials in the subsequent chapters. Embedded within each chapter are three sections. Titles for each of the book parts, summaries, chapters, and sections are limited to three words with the overall organization presented simply in outline form through the table of contents.

The natural wonders and beauty of Antarctica are introduced in the prologue to outfit you for your journey "on the ice"—looking over your shoulder, feeling the cold winds as the approaching storm races across the dark blue ocean with ice flows careening like shuffled pieces of a giant puzzle; watching the sunsets around the sky for weeks without end, with fiery orange and red changing into purple,

becoming greenish hues of deep blue; staring at meter-tall emperor penguins with
their yellow crescent necks extending toward the ice edge, which is patrolled by
pods of killer whales waiting for their next meal. The prologue is intended to
furnish images that will stimulate your imagination.

The conceptual framework for understanding the Earth as a system of interacting natural and social science phenomena is presented in Part I: "Earth System
Science." Chapter 1, "Global Dimensions," introduces the Earth system arena
where myriad natural elements are interacting across time and space. Chapter 2,
"Conceptual Integration," identifies teaching and learning methods that have
widespread applications for integrating diverse information. Together, the chapters in Part I reflect the interdisciplinary character of our world.

The middle section of the book includes three parts. Part II: "Progress of All
Mankind" characterizes the general sequence of human activities associated with
our expanding civilization. Chapter 3, *"Terra Australis Incognita,"* highlights the
stages of exploration to Antarctica where wild speculation about undiscovered
resources launched voyages where nations competed for priority in their common
quest of claiming sovereignty. On a converging track, the scientific essence of
discovering natural phenomena provided common ground among nations, as
poignantly revealed in Antarctica by the International Geophysical year of 1957–
1958 (Chapter 4, "Awakening Science"). Ultimately, tempered by science, national pursuits turned to international cooperation under the accommodating umbrella of the 1959 Antarctic Treaty as the source of peaceful stewardship across
nearly 10% of the Earth from 60° south latitude to the South Pole (Chapter 5,
"International Stewardship"). Together, the three chapters in Part II reveal the
unfolding history of national perspectives maturing into international policies.

Part III: "Our Dynamic Planet" introduces the panoply of events, entities, and
phenomena coursing across the Earth over its 4.5-billion-year history. At one extreme is the slow incessant movement of continents floating on convecting cells
of molten material deep within the Earth—separating and colliding to form the
oceans and mountains of the world over millions of years (Chapter 6, "Spreading
Planet").

Around 60 million years ago, with the isolation of Antarctica at the bottom of
the planet, vast ice sheets began growing and progressively cooling the Earth's
climate. The development of ice sheets in the Northern Hemisphere, nearly 3 million years ago, brought the Earth into a new climatic period with distinct glacial
and interglacial phases approximately every 100,000 years (Chapter 7, "Flowing
Planet"). These advancing and retreating ice sheets have caused sea level to fall
and rise in a climatic seesaw associated with the Earth's fluctuating orbit around
the Sun.

During the past 1000 years—within a single revolution of the oceanic conveyor belt—the Earth's temperature has fluctuated from the Medieval Warm Period (10th to 14th centuries) through the Little Ice Age (15th to 19th centuries)
into the present warming phase since the industrial revolution. Superimposed on
these global changes of the past millennium are Earth system processes with even

greater frequencies, such as seasonal temperature shifts or water exchanges among ocean, atmosphere, and land (Chapter 8, "Breathing Planet").

During the 19th and 20th centuries, human activities also have affected plant production and temperatures on Earth by enhancing the atmospheric concentration of greenhouse gases (notably carbon dioxide) that insulate and warm the planet. As illustrated by Antarctic marine and terrestrial ecosystems, this variability in the Earth system—which occurs across geological and ecological time scales—ultimately affects the survival, interaction, and evolution of species (Chapter 9, "Living Planet"). Together, the four interdisciplinary science chapters in Part III telescope over time and space, revealing diverse phenomena for interpreting the relative magnitudes of natural and human impacts in the Earth system.

Part IV: "Sustainable Resource Use" focuses on the scientific and policy implications of utilizing resources that contribute to the welfare of humankind. The Antarctic marine ecosystem illustrates the universal pattern of progressively overharvesting the most abundant, accessible, and commercially valuable species, then moving on to the next and the next (Chapter 10, "Ecosystem Conservation"). As one of the richest regions of biological production in the sea, the Antarctic marine ecosystem also symbolizes the foresight required for conserving living resources—especially keystone species such as the tiny krill that nourish the whales, seals, birds, fish, and squid and other marine invertebrates around Antarctica.

Under the Antarctic Treaty System, mineral resource activities are prohibited for at least the next 50 years—embodying global economic issues and the sensitive accommodations that are required among nations in Antarctica and elsewhere across the Earth system (Chapter 11, "Environmental Protection"). Together, these chapters in Part IV underscore the challenge of blending basic and applied science strategies to wisely manage environments and ecosystems along with their living and nonliving resources so that they can be used by future generations.

The book concludes with Part V: "Our Global Commons," highlighting the marriage of science and policy in Antarctica as a precedent of continuity for the sustainable development of humankind. Antarctica is an unique example of nations working together, rising above their differing ideologies, to cooperatively manage a vast region of the Earth for "peaceful purposes only" (Chapter 12, "The Science Keystone"). Antarctica also is vibrant model of continuous interdisciplinary exchanges among scientific, economic, and policy stakeholders that have been fostered throughout the second half of the 20th century.

Throughout the book, information is linked by first principles that are intended to stimulate inquiry and rekindle the curiosity of childhood, when we playfully examined elements of the world around us. Thought questions (identified by ⊛) will be introduced in each chapter for contemplation, discussion, and overall synthesis. Additional readings along with relevant government, international, and education Internet sites are recommended at the end of the book to further stimulate questions that lead to answers and ongoing synthesis.

Sharing international and interdisciplinary perspectives from Antarctica is at the heart of this book and its central objective of facilitating farsighted discussions about protecting the Earth for generations to come. As a region extending beyond the jurisdiction and practical management of any nation, Antarctica symbolizes our common heritage on Earth.

ANTARCTIC TREATY SEARCHABLE DATABASE: 1959–1999 CD-ROM

The integration of science into policy requires a comprehensive understanding of legal documents and regulatory strategies, particularly in the context of managing human impacts on the Earth system. To facilitate this integration for scientists, government officials, and community members alike, information management tools are required that facilitate:

(1) searching numerous documents simultaneously;
(2) identifying only the salient sections;
(3) organizing relevant database elements based on user-defined objectives; and
(4) displaying all search results relative to each other in an easily accessible format.

The purpose of the Antarctic Treaty Searchable Database: 1959–1999 CD-ROM (http://webhost.nvi.net/aspire) is to provide such an information management tool for individuals to freely ask questions about any aspect of the international legal system that governs human activities in the region south of 60° south latitude, across nearly 10% of the Earth.

The Antarctic Treaty Searchable Database project began in 1998 because students in the Antarctic Marine Ecology and Policy capstone course at The Ohio State University were unable to effectively utilize the 1000-page *Antarctic Treaty Handbook* published by the United States Department of State (DOS) for their group decision-making project. Utilizing funds from a grant on Antarctic Science and Policy: Interdisciplinary Research Education (ASPIRE), awarded from the National Science Foundation (Division of Undergraduate Education and Office of Polar Programs), information technology from EvREsearch LTD was used to organize electronic files of the *1994 Antarctic Treaty Handbook* that were generously provided by the DOS Bureau of Oceans and International Environmental and Scientific Affairs. This database project, which is being maintained and updated by EvREsearch LTD, also was implemented in collaboration with the Byrd Polar Research Center at The Ohio State University and Native Voices International. The outcome is the first searchable electronic compilation ever produced with the recommendations, measures, decisions, resolutions, annexes, conventions, protocol, and articles that have been adopted by the international community in furtherance of the principles and objectives of the Antarctic Treaty during the first 40 years of the Antarctic Treaty System.

In contrast to standard search engines, which create long lists of ranked results, the Antarctic Treaty Searchable Database: 1959–1999 produces hierarchal displays (referred to as "Modified Dewey Searches") that can be expanded and collapsed from a single page by clicking the left mouse key on the "+" and "−", respectively, to identify relationships among the relevant database elements. Moreover, these database elements represent separate and unique recommendations, measures, resolutions, or decisions from each of the Antarctic Treaty Consultative Meetings as well as individual articles from the different Conventions and annexes. In addition to the "Search Engine" for generating the hierarchal displays there is a "Document Re-Creation Utility" for assembling the database elements within the highest levels of the hierarchies.

The hierarchal displays for the three "Index Types" are:

Research Centric: year > meeting name > database elements
Year Centric: year > topic > database elements
Document Centric: topic > database elements

The Research Centric mode represents the most comprehensive compilation among the three database types, with information from the *Antarctic Treaty Handbook* as well as subsequent measures that have been adopted by the Antarctic Treaty consultative parties through the 23rd Antarctic Treaty Consultative Meeting in 1999 (scanned from Final Reports provided by the DOS). Additional information is being added to the Research Centric database as it becomes available.

Application of the CD-ROM is discussed in Chapter 2 ("Conceptual Integration") with an illustration of the expanded Research Centric hierarchy with database elements that contain "scientific" (see Fig. 2.4). Additional search criteria are suggested throughout the book by quotes from the Antarctic Treaty System, especially in Chapter 5 ("International Stewardship"), Chapter 10 ("Ecosystem Conservation"), and Chapter 11 ("Environmental Protection"). Other words or phrases for searching the databases can be identified by individual design to learn how the Antarctic Treaty System responds to any issue of interest. Moreover, Boolean logic strategies can be used to construct the search queries. Additional information on the specific operation of the searchable database is provided in the "Help" and "FAQ" menus.

The enclosed Windows-compatible CD-ROM version of the Antarctic Treaty Searchable Database: 1959–1999 contains a replica of the Web site that:

(a) operates with *Microsoft Internet Explorer* and *Netscape* Web browsers that are Java-enabled and installed on the computer, but which do not need to be connected to the internet;
(b) automatically runs, without requiring hard-drive installation of any new computer files; and
(c) functions like any other Web site for printing as well as other features.

The Web site CD-ROM can be displayed in a full-screen (Kiosk) mode or with Windows toolbars. In the Kiosk mode, use the right mouse key for navigating back to previous screens as well as printing and the Alt-F4 button for exiting files.

The Antarctic Treaty Searchable Database: 1959–1999 is central to this book for learning about the integration of science into policy at global to local levels. Currently, this database is being used by:

- *government agencies* from the member nations of the Antarctic Treaty System through the 24th Antarctic Treaty Consultative Meeting in St. Petersburg, Russia;
- *nongovernmental organizations* that include the Scientific Committee on Antarctic Research, Antarctic Southern Ocean Coalition, and International Association of Antarctic Tour Operators; and
- *academic institutions and organizations* that include the Byrd Polar Research Center at The Ohio State University, Centre for Antarctic Studies and Research at the University of Canterbury, American Society of International Law, and Digital Library for Earth System Education.

In the arena of international cooperation, understanding the precedent of the Antarctic Treaty System will reveal insights for wisely and peacefully managing the geometric expansion of our civilization across the Earth.

ACKNOWLEDGMENTS

My Antarctic journey started in 1981 when Ted DeLaca invited me to participate on his winter-over expedition in McMurdo Sound. I especially thank Ted and my winter-over companions, George Preston Shreve and David Marks, for opening the door. I also thank my field companions who have shared in subsequent expeditions and introduced me to many features of Antarctic biology, geology, geodesy, and glaciology: Steven Alexander, Bret Baker, Joan Bernhard, Isidro Bosch, Samuel Bowser, Michael Castellini, Mariachiara Chiantore, Randall Davis, Kazuomi Hirakawa, Marcus Horning, Olafur Ingólffson, Marco Nigro, Michael Prentice, Francesco Regoli, Rob Robbins, Oreal Solecasta, and William Stockton.

Research and teaching go hand-in-hand. Since 1982, I have been fortunate to have had many excellent students in my Antarctic Marine Ecology and Policy courses, and I especially thank them for helping me learn about Antarctic through their questions and creativity. I also thank the various administrators at the University of California, University of Rhode Island, and Ohio State University who have allowed me to follow my enthusiasm in teaching about Antarctica over the past two decades. Throughout, I thank my teachers, colleagues, and friends for sharing ideas about the world we live in.

I am grateful to the National Science Foundation (NSF), in particular the Office of Polar Programs, for providing many opportunities to work in Antarctica and share ideas with colleagues around the world since 1981. I also thank the NSF Division of Fellowships for providing the freedom to begin exploring interdisciplinary perspectives about the Earth system as a graduate student. Support from the NSF Division of International Programs has been invaluable in learning about Antarctica through the eyes of foreign cultures. I particularly thank the NSF Division of Undergraduate Education and Office of Polar Programs for supporting the Antarctic Science and Policy: Interdisciplinary Research Education (ASPIRE) project, which grew into this book.

Access to the Antarctic Treaty documents has been central to understanding how science can be merged into policy. I thank the United States Department of State (Office of Ocean and Environmental Affairs), National Science Foundation (Office of Polar Programs), Marine Mammal Commission, and National Oceanic and Atmospheric Administration (Antarctic Marine Living Resources Program) for providing continuous and easy access to diverse data and information about Antarctica. I especially thank the National Science Foundation and Department of State for providing materials as well as support for developing the Antarctic Treaty Searchable Database: 1959–1999.

Discussions with colleagues have been fundamental in learning about Antarctica, the Earth system, and science in the context of our global society. I thank the National Academy of Sciences for providing the opportunity to interact with the Polar Research Board and view the development of Antarctic science since the early 1980s. In particular, I thank Robert Rutford for providing opportunities to interact with the Scientific Committee on Antarctic Research and for crafting the foreword to this book. I also thank the following people for sharing their enthusiasm and insights about Antarctic science and policy at different times during my education: Raymond Arnaudo, James Barnes, Charles Bentley, Scott Borg, Lawson Brigham, David Bromwich, Harlan Cohen, David Elliot, Sayed El-Sayed, Karl Erb, Guy Guthridge, Robert Hofman, Julie Hambrook, Rene Holt, Clive Howard-Williams, Joyce Jatko, James Kennett, Chuck Kennicut, Dana Kester, Lee Kimball, John Knauss, Richard Laws, Herbert Levitan, Berry Lyons, Yasuhiko Naito, Julie Palais, Arvid Pardo, Dennis Peacock, Dean Peterson, Polly Penhale, Patrick Quilty, Carlo Alberto Ricci, Robert Rutford, Alan Ryan, John Sauer, Kenneth Sherman, Brian Shoemaker, Donald Siniff, Tucker Skully, Todd Sowers, Lonnie and Ellen Thompson, Edward Todd, Warwick Vincent, Gunter Weller, Gillian Wratt, Yoshio Yoshida, Mario Zucchelli, and James Zumberge. I especially thank Tim Baughman, David Bromwich, Dan Farslow, James Kennett, John Knauss, and two anonymous reviewers for their thoughtful and constructive comments, which have significantly improved this book.

The Antarctic Treaty Searchable Database has become a most useful tool, and I thank my friend and partner, George James Morgan III, for being the wizard. I also thank Jeannie Jaros for her excellent assistance with the graphics.

Most of all, I thank my family for instilling the strength and vision to venture confidently into the unknown with a passion for discovery. Thank you for your loving kindness and support in helping me follow my dreams.

PROLOGUE: THE BEAUTY OF ANTARCTICA

The following impressions and insights from Antarctica are taken from my diaries of wintering-over in Antarctica when I was 22 years old—the same age as many of you in various interdisciplinary undergraduate and graduate courses for whom this book was intended. More importantly, these images from Antarctica are presented for those of you pondering the life-shaping experiences that provide passion and direction for contributing to the world we live in.

Envision walking off a cramped silver C-130 Hercules cargo-transport plane—bundled in a bulky red parka with black wind pants and white thermal boots, thick bearpaw mittens, and dark sunglasses—into the blinding brightness reflecting off the sea ice. With the first breath of frozen air pinching your nose, you know you have arrived.

My first impressions and memories on "the ice" began in January 1981 at McMurdo Station, which, at the time, was like a Klondike shantytown with ramshackle buildings and canvas tents sprawled across snow-blown permafrost ground. This was a peculiar community, with no children or elderly people—with scientists and mechanics, cooks and carpenters, pilots and plumbers, electricians, and mountaineers numbering well over 1000 during the summer. The only other facility within thousands of kilometers was New Zealand's Scott Base, with several dozen personnel working around the corner of Ross Island beyond Cape Armitage. For a recent college graduate, fresh from the beaches of Southern California, entering this international land for a year was like stepping off the Earth into another world.

Our fieldwork was in Explorers Cove, on the other side of McMurdo Sound at the base of the Dry Valleys, across the sea ice from Ross Island about 70 kilometers as the skua flies to the Victoria Land Coast. Beyond, the Trans-Antarctic

---

Mountains extend thousands of meters straight into the air with jagged snowbound peaks and a façade seamed with black coal, revealing a giant window into Earth's history.

In the opposite direction, the Ross Ice Shelf stands hundreds of meters over the seawater across thousands of square kilometers—as a bulwark against the immense West Antarctic Ice Sheet. If it ever streamed into the ocean and melted, this ice sheet could raise sea level around the Earth by 5 meters, perhaps within a couple of human generations. Strewn across this windswept white landscape are islands and volcanoes, such as Mt. Erebus with its prehistoric mien and pink plume.

As the summer fades into winter, seasonal change is heralded by an amazing light show that circles the sky for weeks as the sun slowly spirals below the horizon. Not just in a corner of the sky, but for 360 degrees, reds and oranges become pinks, blue-greens, and violets that shade the sky as day turns to night. During the following months of continual darkness, airglow from the aurora australis occasionally appears like giant waving curtains of colored cellophane projecting across the stars.

Tranquility in Antarctica is brief and often punctuated by violent storms appearing out of nowhere. Suddenly, winds can increase 40 knots and temperatures can plunge 30°C—as occurred while I was walking from the aquarium to the Eklund Biological Center at McMurdo Station (less than a half-kilometer distance), when the wind chill factor plummeted 70°C within 5 minutes! During such experiences, there is no protection outside and the icy cold penetrates through clothing like knives.

We were as far from civilization as possible, in an outpost at the bottom of the Earth. Even so, we still were part of the global community, as we were poignantly reminded on 30 March 1981.

The news we received was that President Ronald Reagan had been shot. With information transmitted by shortwave radio, generally filtered and available days later, we could only speculate. I was furious, particularly as childhood memories of President Kennedy came flooding back. In the galley, people were joking about the attempted assassination—which made me even angrier. The next moment, in a blurred rage stomping over volcanic rocks, I was on the top of Observation Hill—overlooking our haven nearly three hundred meters below—huddling near the memorial cross for Robert Falcon Scott and his four companions who lost their lives returning from the South Pole in 1912. I just sat there, looking across McMurdo Sound and the Ross Ice Shelf with the cold wind blowing in my face, fuming for hours until—like a blanket of calm—words came into my head and I understood that *one cannot escape the injustices of mankind.*

As a bridge to home, I read for hours every day: rich imagery and parables from Chaucer, Dante, Dickens, Dumas, Goethe, Ovid, Shakespeare, Tolkien, and Twain; research through biology, chemistry, oceanography, and natural history; and the incredible stories of Antarctic exploration. Cloistered by howling winds, the setting made it easy to imagine joining Ernest Shackleton on his race for survival, traveling with his crew in longboats across ice flows and violent seas after abandoning *Endurance*. It was particularly easy to imagine sledging across Ross Island with Apsley Cherry-Garrard to collect emperor penguin eggs in midwinter at the beginning of the 20th century, as chronicled in *The Worst Journey in the World*.

Antarctica still is a land where survival is a constant consideration, where expeditions just to visit the field are planned over years. Distances that we would normally drive in a couple of hours require helicopters, fixed-wing aircraft, Sprytes, Ski-Doos, cargo planes, and even icebreakers. Field camps require assembly with materials that all come from other continents: prefabricated Jamesways and Scott tents; wooden rock boxes filled with frozen and dehydrated food; generators and solar panels; specially formulated fuels for working in extreme cold; two-way radios and antennas; a couple of stuffed duffel bags with polar clothing and a few personal items; cooking and sleeping gear along with various scientific equipment. We also have sophisticated scientific tools in the field, such as computers and global positioning systems that communicate with satellites for measuring locations on the Earth's surface within centimeters—even in Antarctica. The most important elements of a successful expedition, however, are the members, whose complementary skills and strengths contribute to the welfare of the team.

On one of the expeditions, during a helicopter trip across McMurdo Sound along the retreating sea-ice edge (which the Antarctic marine ecosystem follows *en masse* seasonally southward), we spotted several dozen emperor penguins standing at attention with a pod of killer whales patrolling the water beyond. After turning off the rotors and leaving the helicopter, we began taking pictures of this summer scene. As we knelt on the ice, one of these meter-tall flightless birds began walking toward me like Charlie Chaplin with its orange-yellow neck bobbing as it honked. It had eyes like mine, although its beaked nose, reptilian feet, and paddle-like arms were much different. As we stared eye-to-eye at each other, not more than a meter apart, I realized that this animal was talking to me as though an ambassador trying to communicate with an alien about peace in its land.

Except for the birds and mammals or the mosses and lichens, which are conspicuous in some regions, most of the life around Antarctica is obscured in sheltered habitats. Below the sea ice, diverse plants and animals—from coralline algae and single-celled animals to century-old scallops, meter-tall glass sponges, and supercooled fish—color the sea floor. In the terrestrial oases there are perennially ice-covered lakes with primordial algae and microscopic organisms living in the water underneath. There even are minute green plants trapping water in sandstone rocks with sunlight refracting through the quartz grains. In this polar desert, which is dry enough to mummify organisms, life exists in an environmental extreme. The beauty of Antarctica is at once intense and serene, with images that fire the imagination about all life on Earth and beyond.

PART

I

_____

EARTH SYSTEM
SCIENCE

_____

SENSE OF WONDER

Earth contains land, air, water, and life phenomena with rhythms of
natural variability that are connected over time and space (Plate 1).
For example, continental collisions produce jagged mountains that
gradually erode into rounded ranges. With weathering of the rocks,
minerals are transported into streams that flow into rivers which add
salts to the sea. In the ocean and on land, biological assemblages flour-
ish and disappear with habitat changes that occur during their lifetimes as well as over millennia and millions of years. The challenge
at all scales in this interconnected Earth system is to interpret relationships among seemingly disparate natural phenomena, events, and
entities.

The basic context of the Earth system is the planet itself (Fig. I),
third from the Sun in our solar system, with dimensions from its inner
molten core outward to the edge of its atmosphere (Chapter 1: Global
Dimensions). Earth is unique within our solar system because of liquid water, which is the principal ingredient for life as we know it. The
largest water reservoir is the ocean, which circulates around the continents and interacts with the land largely through precipitation and
runoff. Outside of the ocean—which contains more than 95 percent

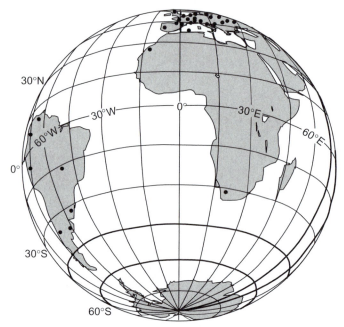

FIGURE 1   The underlying framework for the Earth system is the planet itself and the relative locations of its interacting elements, which can be distinguished over space and time. Orthographic (single view) map projection of the Earth showing the continents and oceans at different degrees of latitude, which parallel each other from 90° north through the equator at 0° to 90° south. Perpendicular to the latitudes are the longitudes from 180° east through the Greenwich meridian at 0° to 180° west (based on the 360 degrees in a circle; longitudes all converge at polar points on a sphere). At latitudes higher than 60° south, Antarctica is surrounded by water at all longitudes. This illustration, which was generated with Xearth Web software (http://ecco.bsee.swin.edu.au/chronos/xearth), is oriented in relation to the 23.5 degree tilt of the Earth's axis. Signatories to the Antarctic Treaty (dots) are shown to illustrate the international dimensions of human interest in Antarctica (Chapter 5: International Stewardship).

of the water—most of the water on Earth is locked into ice, and most of the ice is in Antarctica.

Life itself began evolving in the primordial soup of early Earth nearly a billion years after the planet originated around 4.5 billion years ago. Taking energy from sunlight, plants progressively added oxygen to the atmosphere—making the planet habitable for animals, which consumed the plants and each other. Species' responses to habitat change, like the growth of minerals in rocks, scribe the history of Earth.

Imagine looking at the Earth from outer space. What questions would you ask about the blue sphere underneath, and how would you answer them? Our world is complex, and there are many ways to develop natural and social science perspectives on the Earth system. However, in all cases, educational approaches are based on questions (Chapter 2: Conceptual Integration). Inquiry is at the heart of learning and is fundamental to studying the Earth as a system of interacting natural phenomena that affect and are affected by human civilization.

A common feature of questions involves relating events, entities, and phenomena to effectively address the who, what, when, where, why, and how of things. Symbols such as interlocking circles are often used as simple descriptions of how diverse topics intersect. Similarly, arrows between elements in a diagram often are used to portray pathways connecting reservoirs in systems, such as the Earth.

A most basic first principle in science is the twinned concept of time and space. Each event has an impact that propagates over distance and time as far as its initial magnitude allows. Gradients—which are commonly represented by the axes of a graph—are widely used to describe the relative dimensions of events, entities, or phenomena. For example, a timeline could portray your height at different ages or the Earth's temperature during different millennia.

Hierarchies—which are commonly represented by outlines—can be used to further describe relationships among discrete categories in a system across levels of complexity. For example, your home on Earth can be located in relation to the continents with their nations, states, counties, cities, and streets. Similarly, life forms can be distinguished in relation to their kingdom, phylum, class, order, family, genus and species (mnemonic: "King Philip Can Order Fresh Green Spinach").

The ultimate tool for integrating information is decision-making. Deciding how things work—in the present as well as in the past or future—requires information from different sources. When Sir Isaac Newton's apple fell, he had to know something about the Earth as well as his falling fruit before he could make the leap to a theory of gravity. Decisions also take form through group activities, as in national legislatures or Antarctic Treaty Consultative Meetings, where practical solutions are formulated for society at all levels. In making decisions about the Earth and humankind, progress involves global perspectives and information that are used for designing century-scale policies that will enlighten our civilization into the future.

1

GLOBAL DIMENSIONS

Talk of mysteries!—
Think of our life in nature—
daily to be shown matter, to come in contact with it,—
rocks, trees, wind on our cheeks!
the solid earth! the actual world! the common sense!
Contact! Contact! Who are we? where are we?
                    —Henry David Thoreau (1848), Ktaadn

TOP TO BOTTOM

The Earth system, as an entity in the cosmos, exists within an envelope of gases that are kept from escaping into space by gravitational attraction to the planet below (Fig. 1.1a). Hydrogen, which is the smallest and least dense atom, with a single proton in its nucleus, composes the outermost layer of the atmosphere to a height of more than 10,000 kilometers above the Earth's surface. Underneath, there are distinct atomic layers of helium (two protons) and oxygen (eight protons) overlying a molecular layer that is composed principally of two bound nitrogen atoms (seven protons each). Each denser than the layer above, these different spheres of individual gases collectively comprise the heterosphere from 90 kilometers to the boundary of outer space—beyond the layer of hydrogen atoms rotating with the Earth.

Below 90 kilometers is the thin atmospheric region called the homosphere, where gases are well mixed with a highly uniform composition throughout. By volume, pure dry air in the homosphere is composed mostly of nitrogen (78.084%) and oxygen (20.946%). The homosphere also contains small amounts of argon (0.934%) and carbon dioxide (0.033%) along with several trace gases (including neon, krypton, and xenon). Together, these gases in the homosphere—across one-

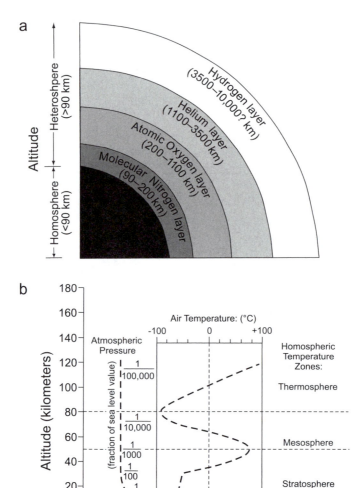

FIGURE 1.1   (a) Gases in the Earth's atmosphere from the planet's surface to the boundary of
outer space, more than 10,000 kilometers above (not to scale). The densest layer of the well-mixed
atmosphere (homosphere) exists below 90 kilometers altitude and is composed principally of a gaseous mixture of nitrogen (N_2 = 78.08%), oxygen (O_2 = 20.95%) and various trace gases including
carbon dioxide (CO_2 = 0.03%). Progressively less dense layers of individual gases exist in the heterosphere above 90 kilometers. (b) Within the homosphere, different atmospheric layers are distinguished by their temperatures at different altitudes (Chapter 8: Breathing Planet). Modified from Strahler and Strahler (1978).

hundredth of the altitude in the heterosphere—exert 99.9999% of the total atmospheric pressure on the Earth's surface (Fig. 1.1b).

Subdivisions of the homosphere are distinguished by temperature zones at
different altitudes (Fig. 1.1b). Above 80 kilometers, temperatures in the thermo-

sphere vary with solar activity and can exceed 1500 degrees Celsius (°C) during sunspot maxima, when the sun erupts in giant flares that can affect Earth's magnetic field. At the boundary between the thermosphere and mesosphere, called the mesopause, temperatures reach an atmospheric minimum. Through the mesosphere, from 80 to 50 kilometers, temperatures swing from nearly −100°C to +100°C and back. Temperatures cool only slightly in the underlying stratosphere, which is where Earth's ozone (three bound oxygen atoms—O_3) shield against ultraviolet radiation exists. Below 15 kilometers, through the troposphere, temperatures warm around 6°C per kilometer in altitude down to the planet surface.

The troposphere is not only the lowest atmospheric layer—it is the principal layer that connects climate, weather, and life across the planet. Moreover, most of the water vapor and other "greenhouse gases" associated with insulating and retaining heat at the Earth's surface exist in the troposphere (Chapter 8: Breathing Planet).

The baseline or zero point for determining altitudes in the atmosphere (as well as elevations on land or depths throughout the Earth system) is sea level. Sea level is an ideal global reference because—like water in any basin—the ocean seeks a uniform level relative to the center of gravitational attraction at the planetary core. For example, consider what happens when you try piling water on one side of your bathtub.

In the same manner that sea level is the zero point for determining vertical positions within the Earth system, the equator is the baseline for horizontal locations across the parallel latitudes from 90° north to 90° south (Fig. I). In the perpendicular direction, longitudes progress from 180° east through the Greenwich meridian at 0° east/west to 180° west. Together, these perpendicular latitude and longitude axes provide the basic framework for pinpointing any location on Earth (Fig. I).

Meridians coincide with the direction of Earth's rotation as reflected by the Sun "rising in the east and setting in the west" across time zones each day. The duration of each time zone is based on the speed of Earth's rotation around its axis, which is approximately 1670 kilometers per hour at the equator. Given that Earth's circumference is nearly 40,000 kilometers, it takes about 24 hours to make one daily revolution. Unlike latitudes which parallel each other across the planet, the meridians converge from the equator toward the poles. Consequently, all time zones coexist at the poles, where days intersect and it is possible to move forward into yesterday or backward into tomorrow before running into today.

Just as Earth's daily period of 24 hours is based on one complete rotation around its axis, Earth's annual period of 365 days (except for leap years) is based on one complete orbit around the Sun. However, during the course of a year, each location on Earth experiences different seasons. For example, at latitudes higher than 66.5° there are polar regions on Earth where there are 24-hour periods of continuous sunlight progressing over the course of the year into 24-hour periods of complete darkness. The reason for these seasons is the tilt of Earth's axis of rotation, which is slanted 23.5° off of perpendicular (90° minus 66.5°)—as indicated by the latitude of the "polar circles" in the northern and southern hemispheres. For perspective, if the Earth's axis was straight up and down (at a 90° angle relative to the plane of the Earth's orbit around the sun) we would have continual night at both geographic poles and uniform day–night cycles at all lower latitudes.

Earth also is not a perfect sphere because its diameter through the equator (12,756 kilometers) is greater than its diameter through the poles (12,712 kilometers). Because this planetary flattening is so slight, north–south distances between adjacent latitudes are nearly constant at 111 kilometers per degree of latitude from the North Pole to the South Pole. In contrast, east-west distances between adjacent longitudes decrease from around 111 kilometers per degree of longitude at the equator to zero kilometers at the poles where all meridians converge.

Extending below the planetary surface, through the crust of the continents and surrounding ocean basins, there are three layers in the interior of the Earth (Fig. 1.2) which are analogous to the gaseous layers in the overlying atmosphere. The outermost layer is the crust, which differs in thickness from more than 40 kilometers through the continents to less than 10 kilometers through the surrounding ocean basins.

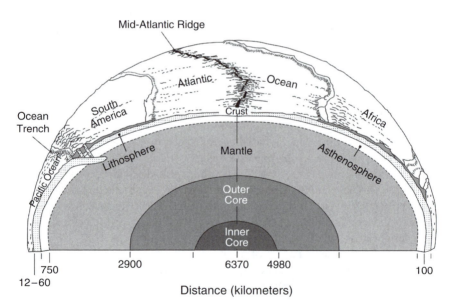

FIGURE 1.2   Layers and regions within the Earth's interior from the rigid lithospheric crusts of the continents and ocean basins through the molten asthenosphere into the dense core toward the center of the planet, 6370 kilometers below (Chapter 6: Spreading Planet). Modified from Wylie (1976).

Although continental and oceanic crusts both are composed of silicate compounds (made up of silicon and oxygen), there are distinct differences between these two crustal types. Continental granite also contains aluminum, sodium, and potassium, whereas oceanic basalt has large amounts of iron and magnesium. The relatively low density of continental granite (2.7 grams per cubic centimeter), compared to oceanic basalt (3.2 grams per cubic centimeter) is the primary reason why the continents stand above the oceans. Similarly, pure water floats on the Earth's crust because its density only is 1.0 gram per cubic centimeter (Table 1.1).

Earth's crust is extruded from the underlying mantle, which extends to 2900 kilometers depth. Temperatures in the mantle range from around 1200° to 3700°C, causing partial melting along with magma formation. With an average density of 4.5 grams per cubic centimeter, the mantle constitutes two-thirds of the Earth's mass and more than 80% of its volume.

Beneath the mantle is the iron–nickel core of the Earth, which extends to the center of the planet, 6370 kilometers below the surface, with densities exceeding 10 grams per cubic centimeter. The molten core of the Earth has temperatures above 5000°C, which is nearly as hot as the Sun. Consequently, even though the core accounts for less than 16% of the planet's volume, it constitutes more than 30% of its mass. As can be seen, from the core of the planet outward to the hydrogen layer at the edge of outer space, all of the concentric spheres in the Earth system are related across a gradient based on their densities.

 Why are there concentric spheres in the Earth system from the outermost regions of the atmosphere to the center of the planet?

TABLE 1.1   Common Conversion Units

Metric	Standard
Length	
1 kilometer (km)	0.62 miles
1 meter (m)	3.28 feet
1 centimeter (cm)	0.39 inches
Weight	
1 gram (g)	0.03 ounces
1 kilogram (kg)	2.20 pounds
Volume	
1 liter (l) equals 1000 millimeters (ml) or 1000 cubic centimeters (cm^3 or cc)	0.26 gallons
Temperature	
Degrees Celsius or centigrade (°C)[a,b]	degrees Fahrenheit (°F) equals 9/5°C + 32

[a] Named after Anders Celsius from Sweden (1701–1744).
[b] Absolute temperature scale in degrees Kelvin (°K), named after William Thompson, Lord Kelvin, from the United Kingdom (1824–1905), is °C + 273.15.

WATER AND LIFE

Relative to the expanse of the Earth system, across more than 15,000 kilometers from the top of the atmosphere to the center of the core (Figs. 1.1 and 1.2), planetary surfaces extend across an extremely thin zone above and below sea level (Fig. 1.3). Actually, from the highest point on land at the top of Mt. Everest to the

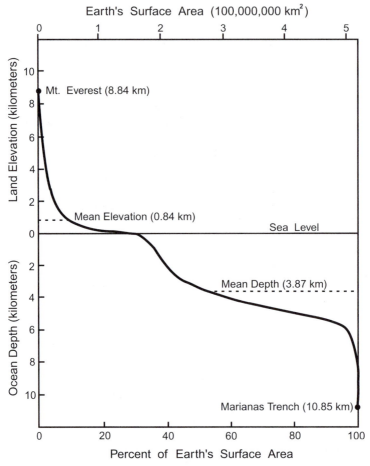

FIGURE 1.3 Hypsographic curve of Earth surfaces today, which illustrates the percentage of the total area on our planet that is occupied at various land elevations and ocean depths relative to sea level. Note that the ocean accounts for more than two-thirds of the Earth's total area with an average depth of 3865 meters and a maximum depth that is deeper than the elevation of the highest mountain. Modified from Thurman (1978).

deepest point in the ocean at the bottom of the Marianas Trench, the vertical range is less than 20 kilometers. Known life exists within this narrow band of surface habitats on Earth.

 How was the Earth system transformed into a habitable environment?

Across the Earth's surface, water is the common environmental feature that makes life possible. Water is the major constituent of metabolizing cells in all known life forms. Water also was the basis for the "primordial soup" in which life initially evolved on Earth and, possibly, other celestial bodies in our solar system. In fact, in his famous simulation of Earth's early atmosphere, Stanley Miller demonstrated in 1953 that merely sending electrical sparks through a gaseous mixture of methane, ammonia, and hydrogen with water will produce amino acids and other building blocks of organic (carbon-based) life forms.

Water exists in all physical states (liquid, solid, or gas) on the Earth's surface; however, only liquid water is capable of supporting known biological processes. Even bacteria frozen into Antarctic lakes or floating in clouds have liquid microhabitats that facilitate their metabolism. Nonetheless, the fact that life is present in these extreme environments gives rise to speculation about extraterrestrial biology on planets, moons, and comets with water in any state.

In the Earth system, the largest water reservoir is the ocean, which covers nearly 70% of the planet's surface with an average depth of almost 4 kilometers (Figs. 1.3 and 1.4). Considering the Earth's surface area is around half a billion square kilometers, a "back-of-the-envelope" calculation indicates that the total volume of the ocean today is between 1 and 2 trillion cubic kilometers—which accounts for more than 97% of the water on the planet. The remaining water in the Earth system cycles among the ocean, atmosphere, and land.

Among the nonmarine reservoirs (Fig. 1.5), nearly 80% of the water is frozen into the ice sheets and glaciers around the world today. Seventeen thousand years ago, when the Earth was in the midst of the Last Glacial Maximum, global sea level was 120 meters or about 3% lower than today. Most of the seawater during this period was locked into massive ice sheets that expanded across the northern hemisphere continents—with twice the ice volume of the Earth system today. For perspective, 90% of the ice on Earth today exists in Antarctica, and if it all melted into the ocean, it would raise global sea level only about 60 meters.

The second largest nonmarine reservoir occurs in the ground, with more than 20% of the freshwater on Earth. Together, all of the other reservoirs—lakes, inland seas, soils, atmosphere and rivers (in order of decreasing volumes)—account for less than 1% of the freshwater in the Earth system today. Compared to the ocean, which has persisted for billions of years, the smaller reservoirs of water are replenished and depleted rapidly over time scales that are proportional to their volumes—underlying their different dynamics and interactions across the planet.

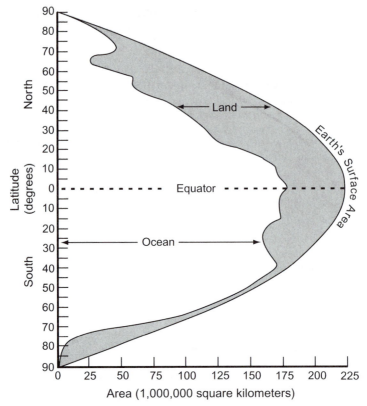

FIGURE 1.4   Relative coverage of land (dark) and ocean (hatched) areas on the Earth's surface at each latitude north and south of the equator (Fig. I). Today, nearly 70% of the ocean exists in the southern hemisphere. Modified from Duxbury and Duxbury (1984).

ACROSS TIME

The concept of time is at the heart of understanding the Earth system as a complex of interacting phenomena, pulsing at different rates since the origin of our planet around 4.5 billion years ago (Fig. 1.6). Earth events and their extension along timelines are analogous to activities which occur during different periods in our lifetime, as riddled by the Sphinx:

> What walks on four legs in the morning, two legs in the afternoon, and three legs at night?

Each of these life stages has a discrete history that is unique unto itself, and at the same time is linked with and often preconditioning future circumstances—as in the Earth system and human civilization.

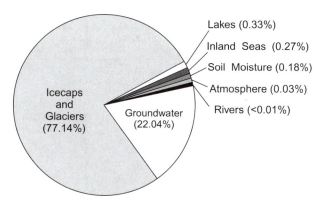

FIGURE 1.5   Water reservoirs in the Earth system today, excluding the ocean, which alone accounts for 97.24% of the nearly 1,360,000,000 cubic-kilometers of water that flows through the various reservoirs in the global hydrological cycle. During the current interglacial (warm) period, the Earth's ice caps have shrunk by more than 60% compared to their volumes in the last glacial (cold) period, which occurred only 17,000 years ago (Chapter 7: Flowing Planet). Today, nearly 90% of the Earth's ice exists in Antarctica, accounting for more than 60% of the freshwater on the planet. Based on data from the United States Geological Survey (http://wwwga.usgs.gov/edu/earthwhere water.html).

 What are the relative space and time dimensions of phenomena in the Earth system?

   After originating around 4.5 billion years ago, the Earth cooled and water pooled on its surface. Primitive life from the "primordial soup" began using the Sun's energy to synthesize carbon dioxide and water into basic sugars and molecular oxygen [Eq. (1.1)].

PLANTS OR BACTERIA
Carbon dioxide (CO_2) + Water (H_2O)
$\Updownarrow$ sunlight or chemical energy $\Updownarrow$ (1.1)
Sugars ($CH_2O)_n$ + Molecular oxygen (O_2)
ANIMALS

With food and an increasingly oxygenated atmosphere (Fig. 1.6), simple cells evolved into multicellular organisms. Eventually, animals evolved that could breathe the oxygen and consume the sugars. As they respired carbon dioxide back into the system, animals also created a feedback with the plant photosynthesizers. These early changes in the Earth system reveal the paired evolution of life and habitats during the Precambrian era—spanning more than 80% of Earth's history.

   Soft-tissue life forms eventually gave way to animals with shelled external skeletons. At the start of the Paleozoic (an era whose name refers to "ancient animals"), around 570 million years ago, there was an evolutionary explosion

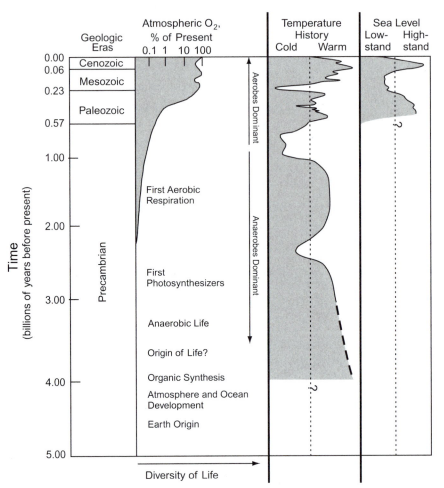

FIGURE 1.6 Earth system history from its origin 4.5 billion (4,500,000,000 or 4.5 × 10⁹) years ago to the present. The vital role of life in transforming habitats around the Earth, commonly known as the "Gaia hypothesis" (Lovelock, 1979), is reflected by the photosynthetic production of oxygen molecules (O₂) by primitive plants that facilitated the evolution of higher life forms (modified from Sumich, 1996). Relative changes in the Earth's temperature (Baron, 1992) and sea-level (Tucker, 1992) illustrate global climatic periods that have been influenced by phenomena that are internal and external to the Earth system (Chapter 6: Spreading Planet).

of species with hard body parts. The Paleozoic extended for the next 320 million years with the appearance of fish and most invertebrate (without backbone) groups, including the ubiquitous trilobites, which inhabited seas around the world throughout this era. The Paleozoic also involved at least two distinct ice ages and the formation of a single supercontinent, called Pangea (all land), which allowed reptiles, amphibians, insects, and vascular plants to extend life's conquest onto land.

Heralding the Mesozoic ("middle animals"), around 250 million years ago a catastrophic Earth system change caused the extinction of more than 90% of Paleozoic marine animals, including all of the trilobites. The Mesozoic saw the dawn of dinosaurs as well as pronounced changes in terrestrial vegetation with ferns, cycads, and the earliest flowering plants. Pangea also began to separate into northern and southern hemisphere supercontinents during this era.

Around 65 million years ago there was another catastrophic global environmental change, possibly from a meteorite impact, which caused the dinosaurs to go extinct. Just as previous eras were distinguished by the appearance and extinction of various life forms as a result of changes in global habitat conditions, the Cenozoic ("new animals") has been recognized as the age of mammals. During this era, the current configuration of continents emerged, including the isolation of Antarctica over the south polar region.

Subdivisions of the Cenozoic, as in all of the preceding eras, provide more refined distinctions among periods of environmental and biotic change. In the Cenozoic, there have been two major periods: the Tertiary (65 to 1.8 million years ago) and the Quaternary (1.8 million years ago to the present). During this latter period, the *Homo* genus began evolving into modern humans (*Homo sapiens sapiens*). The Quaternary also is recognized for its glacial–interglacial variations associated with global climate cooling and warming.

The Quaternary can be divided further into the Pleistocene and Holocene, which represents the current climate epoch from 10,000 years ago to the present. In the same manner that climate periods have been distinguished along the timeline of the Earth system, the "common era" began 2000 years ago following a particular event in the history of human civilization. During all periods, there are shorter intervals—each with their own histories—embedded one within another across time (Fig. 1.6) in the same manner as concentric spheres across space (Figs. 1.1 and 1.2) in the Earth system.

2

CONCEPTUAL

INTEGRATION

It is important that students bring a certain ragamuffin, bare-foot irreverence to their studies; they are not here to worship what is known, but to question it.
—*J. Brownowski (1973),* The Ascent of Man

SYMBOLS AND SYSTEMS

This book is as much about the process of learning as it is an interdisciplinary journey through the science and policy of the Earth system. Rather than teaching by the academic method, where information is presented and restated—where facts are decoupled from the processes that uncovered them—this book will introduce an educational environment where learning occurs by asking both *factual questions* (who, what, when, and where) and *process questions* (how and why). These questions generate answers that in turn provoke new questions and awaken insights as symbolized by "the light at the end of the tunnel" in Plato's *Republic.*

Individual understanding is reflected by questions that are asked rather than through content that is echoed. With independent initiative, this process of learning by asking questions—the Socratic method—evokes curiosity and activates each of us to formulate, explore, and revise hypotheses about our world.

Developing hypotheses—inferences about how things work—in turn, provides the basis for evaluating and integrating new knowledge in the context of what is already known or understood. The challenge is how to capitalize on this immense base of information, which we already possess by virtue of just living on the Earth and experiencing the world around us every day. The integrated character of the Earth system provides a broadly relevant framework for teaching about the open-ended and dynamic nature of inquiry.

Viewing the Earth as an interconnected environmental system clearly is beyond the domain of any discipline. Moreover, the Earth is a community of nations with myriad interests, ideologies, and histories. If we are to understand how to progress into the 21st century and beyond, then we also must develop the appropriate tools for interpreting interdisciplinary relationships. Examples from Antarctica will be introduced throughout to illustrate the events, entities, and phenomena influencing our Earth system across time and space.

Interdisciplinary approaches involve qualitative and quantitative tools for interpreting relationships. Qualitative tools juxtapose phenomena or fields of information for the purpose of illustrating their general connections. Quantitative tools provide pathways for interpreting dynamic links among the sources and sinks of materials cycling through the Earth system.

Venn diagrams, which describe major spheres and the processes that occur at their intersections, are among the most widely used qualitative tools for describing the integration of diverse phenomena involved with the Earth system. Introduced in the late 1880s by John Venn (1834–1923) for mathematical purposes, these circular diagrams elegantly illustrate the three ways in which information can be related: separate, concentric, or intersecting. Moreover, this symbolic logic provides a powerful method for reducing the complexities of interdisciplinary concepts into concise illustrations that are useful in the classroom outward to society (Fig. 2.1).

For example, on Earth, matter and energy are transferred through the atmosphere, hydrosphere, and biosphere. Venn diagrams can be used to describe relationships between these spheres as with the water-vapor intersection of the atmosphere and hydrosphere. Similarly, carbon dioxide could be described as the intersection of the atmosphere and the biosphere (Eq. 1.1). In all cases, such intersections are elaborated by individual design and can be expanded with additional spheres, especially when the human dimensions are considered.

 Why is the Earth considered to be a system?

Models that represent the dynamic relationships between connected reservoirs also can be used for quantifying relationships. An illustration would be two containers of water that are connected by two pipes, one with a valve that controls the outflow and another with a pump that recycles the water. If the rates of outflow and recycling are equal, then water levels in the containers will remain unchanged. If the outflow exceeds the recycling, one of the containers eventually will become empty while the other overflows. The principal advantage of such quantitative models is in estimating actual relationships between reservoirs and their responses to changes in the system.

In a much more elaborate manner, the Earth system also can be modeled as interconnected reservoirs. Water, for example, is cycled between continents through the atmosphere, across lakes, streams, and rivers into the ocean, back into the

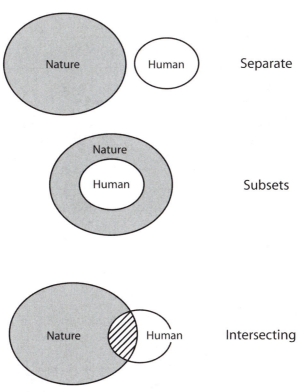

Separate

Subsets

Intersecting

FIGURE 2.1   "Venn diagrams" identify the three types of relationships—separate, concentric, and intersecting—that can exist among events, entities, or phenomena. Different perspectives on the relationships between humans and nature are illustrated to show what can be learned by framing questions through Venn diagrams. Such "thought questions," which are identified throughout this book, provide open-ended tools for interpreting the integrated dynamics of the Earth system and how science is merging into the policies of our society.

atmosphere, and out into masses of ice around the planet. Water volumes in these reservoirs are controlled by evaporation and precipitation along with melting and freezing, as well as by runoff and even sublimation (where water goes directly from the solid to the gas phase). This hydrological system, in turn, is influenced by temperature variations associated with the Earth's weather and climate.

Weather and climate patterns are further influenced by factors that are internal to the Earth system (such as the relative production of greenhouse gases, especially water vapor) as well as external (such as the meteorite that crashed into the Earth and caused the extinction of the dinosaurs 65 million years ago). There also are vital Earth–Sun dynamics that cycle daily through sunrises and sunsets as well as across millennia with the advance and retreat of ice masses across the planet.

The tremendous challenge of characterizing connections among reservoirs in the Earth system—let alone understanding their dynamics—was heralded by the

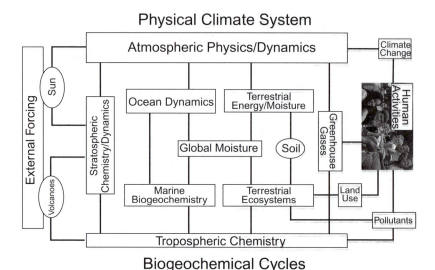

FIGURE 2.2   "Bretherton Diagram" illustrating the complexity of air, sea, and land reservoirs and their dynamic chemical, geological, physical, and biological interactions in the Earth system (Part III: Our Dynamic Planet). Adapted from Earth System Sciences Committee (1988).

"Bretherton Diagram" in the late 1980s (Fig. 2.2). As much an inspiration as roadmap, the "Bretherton Diagram" has become has become a conceptual framework for the International Geosphere–Biosphere Program (IGBP) and other global activities that are studying the Earth system for the benefit of humankind.

 How is humankind related to the nature of the Earth system?

GRADIENTS AND HIERARCHIES

Concepts of time and space are central to science. Consider the impact of dropping a stone in a pond, which creates ripples that expand across time and space. The magnitude of this disturbance and its distance of propagation depend largely on the size of the initial impact (i.e., the size of the stone). In this context, each separate ripple can be related to any other individual ripple at different times and distances away from the initial impact (Fig. 2.3).

Time, space, and matter represent the underlying axes for relating events, entities, and phenomena in the universe. Commonly, these continua contain extremely large and small numbers that can be represented simply by the "power of ten," across exponential scales where "1" is in the center of each axis as the decimal point and zeros shift to the left and right across different orders of mag-

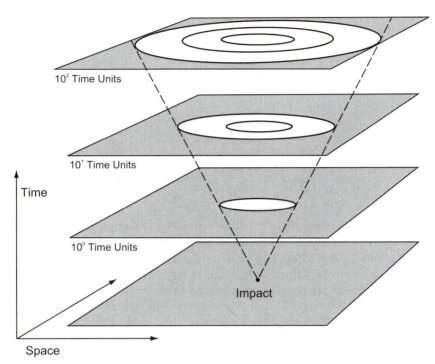

10^2 Time Units

10^1 Time Units

10^0 Time Units

Time

Impact

Space

FIGURE 2.3   Time and space relationships following an initial impact or change in the system, like ripples propagating across a pond after a frog jumps in. Adapted from Hawking (1988).

nitude (from less than 0.001 or 10^{-3} to 10^{-2}, 10^{-1}, 10^0, 10^1, 10^2, and beyond 1000 or 10^3).

With units of space, an ant and the Earth's diameter can be related from millimeters to thousands of kilometers, across nine orders of magnitude. Similarly, with units of time, human lifespans over decades can be related to the Earth's age over billions of years (Fig. 1.6), across eight orders of magnitude. These examples demonstrate one of the most valuable exercises in science—the "back-of-the-envelope" calculation for estimating the relative scale of an impact without actually making the measurements. This process of estimation serves in the process of interpreting the dynamics between human and Earth system events, entities, and phenomena.

Consider the biological impacts from ultraviolet radiation, which is reaching the Earth's surface with greater strength because of the depleted stratospheric ozone. Given that ultraviolet radiation can cause genetic mutations within cells, impacts are direct and potentially much more significant with short-lived single-celled organisms where the entire individual is irradiated than in larger long-lived organisms where cells within tissues will be affected.

Like telescopes and microscopes, focusing across levels of complexity and

TABLE 2.1   Taxonomic Hierarchy

Taxonomic category	Blue whale example	Human example
Kingdom	Animalia	Animalia
Phylum	Chordata	Chordata
Class	Mammalia	Mammalia
Order	Cetacea	Primata
Family	Balaenopteridae	Hominidae
Genus	*Balaenoptera*	*Homo*
Species	*musculus*	*sapiens*

organization, hierarchies provide another useful tool for interpreting relationships among events, entities, and phenomena. One of the most famous hierarchies was formalized during the18th century by Carolus Linnaeus in his 10-volume *Systema Naturae,* which provided the foundation for taxonomic classification (Table 2.1). In this example, the taxonomic hierarchy provides a simple framework for identifying both the uniqueness and commonality of whales and humans.

Throughout this book are figures elaborating the time, space, and matter dimensions of various events, entities, and phenomena. Details in these figures go beyond their descriptions and provide opportunities for integrating information. Consider what is being introduced or compared and why this information is being presented.

- How are entities related?
- Where did events originate?
- What are the underlying causes and effects of phenomena in the Earth system?
- Are there past trends that reflect how phenomena may propagate over time or space in the future?

Asking questions and developing a curious eye about the world, whether from studying figures or walking through the woods, is fundamental to interpreting the complexities of the Earth system and their relevance to human civilization.

DECISION-MAKING

Antarctica exposes individuals to Earth system phenomena as well as a unique international system for maintaining an entire continent and its surrounding seas for *peaceful purposes only.* For all Antarctic issues, the decision-making forum is the Antarctic Treaty Consultative Meeting (ATCM) as established by the 1959 Antarctic Treaty (Fig. 2.4) (Chapter 5: International Stewardship).

The essence of the Antarctic Treaty System (ATS) is continuous consultation.

a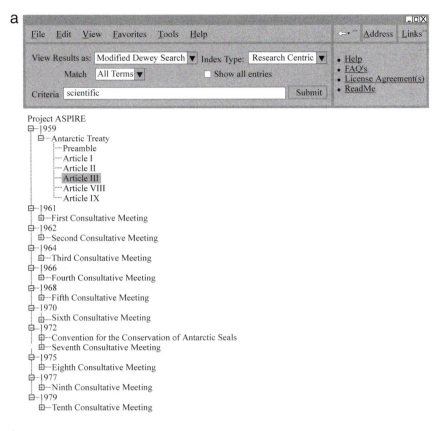

b
ANTARCTIC TREATY (1959)

Article III

[International Cooperation]

1. In order to promote international cooperation in **scientific** investigation in Antarctica, as provided for in Article II of the present Treaty, the Contracting Parties agree that, to the greatest extent feasible and practicable:

   a. information regarding plans for **scientific** programs in Antarctica shall be ex-changed to permit maximum economy of the efficiency of operations;
   b. **scientific** personnel shall be exchanged in Antarctica between expeditions and stations;
   c. **scientific** observations and results from Antarctica shall be exchanged and made freely available.

2. In implementing this Article, every encouragement shall be given to the establishment of cooperative working relations with those Specialized Agencies of the United Nations and other international organizations having a **scientific** or technical interest in Antarctica.

FIGURE 2.4   (a) A hierarchical display of Antarctic Treaty documents that have been organized by their year of adoption (only shown from 1959 to 1979) based on the search criterion of "scientific." This and other collapsible–expandable displays can be generated by the Antarctic Treaty Searchable Database: 1959–1999, which is available on the CD-ROM. Expansion (by clicking the +) and collapse (by clicking the −) of the hierarchical displays can be used to interpret specific Antarctic policies and relationships among legal concepts that have been developed continuously by the Antarctic Treaty Consultative Parties from 1959 through 1999. (b) The Antarctic Treaty Searchable Database: 1959–1999 will identify relevant documents with the user-defined search criteria, which can be read and printed, as illustrated for the search criterion of "scientific" in Article III of the 1959 Antarctic Treaty.

Since 1961, when the 1959 Antarctic Treaty was formally ratified, the Antarctic Treaty nations have been obligated to meet at "suitable intervals" (Antarctic Treaty, Article IX) for the purpose of

> . . . exchanging information, consulting together on the matters of common interest pertaining to Antarctica, and formulating and considering and recommending to their Governments, measures in furtherance of the principles and objectives of the Treaty. . . .

This process of exchanging information, consulting together on matters of common interest, and then formulating, considering, and recommending measures is inherent in decision-making activities.

Information is exchanged and considered at ATCM through plenary sessions, working group sessions, special sessions, and informal negotiations, which may be open or closed to the public and press. Plenary sessions are the principal forums for delegates to share ideas about the implications and interpretations of specific proposals and their relevant alternatives. If agreements on recommendations cannot be reached in the plenary sessions, the delegations often create common-principle platforms that will promote future negotiations.

Prior to most ATCMs, preparatory meetings have occurred in which agreements about agenda items and other factors to expedite effective discussions were negotiated. Circulation of working papers and other forms of communication further facilitate exchanges among the Antarctic Treaty nations. All of the preparatory activities enhance contact among delegations while reducing the risk of surprises that detract from the negotiations through confusion and loss of time.

Through this consultative process, nations consider legal applications of the Antarctic Treaty in view of current world events and perspectives. However, it is the process itself that has been important—bringing the nations together at regular and frequent intervals to work together in resolving issues for the mutual benefit of all concerned. Moreover, common interests considered at the ATCM are general enough to be extended to virtually any decision-making system where scientific, economic, and policy perspectives are involved—from global to local levels (Box 2.1).

The ATCM process also is an ideal negotiating forum that can be modeled in classroom situations to explore creative solutions for mitigating human impacts in our world. For example, in the Antarctic Marine Ecology and Policy capstone course, which has been taught since 1982 (see the Preface), "student ambassadors" represent different Antarctic Treaty nations. As in the ATS, each student ambassador creates a concise recommendation (using actual formats) to resolve a specific human impact of his or her choosing within any category of Earth system policies (Box 2.1). Specific questions are iterated, leading progressively to a synthesis of ideas, logic, and background materials.

- What is the problem/impact that you have identified, and how does it relate to the associated ecosystem(s)? What are the temporal and spatial magnitudes of the problem/impact?

**BOX 2.1 "COMMON" ENVIRONMENTAL
INTERESTS IN ANTARCTICA
AND THROUGHOUT THE EARTH SYSTEM**

(1) *Area Protection* (e.g., Special Sites of Scientific Interest, Specially
Protected Areas, Marine Sites of Special Scientific Interest,
Multiple-Use Planning Areas, Areas of Special Tourist Interest)
(2) *Environmental Assessment* (e.g., baselines, monitoring, or
inspection)
(3) *Legal Status* (e.g., claimant or nonclaimant, acceding or consultative nation, nongovernmental organization or industry)
(4) *Living Resources* (e.g., krill fish, seals, whales, lakes, or marine and
terrestrial ecosystems)
(5) *Non-Living Resources* (e.g., oil and gas, ice, or minerals)
(6) *Pollution Control* (e.g., retrograde, recycling, remediation, or
restriction)
(7) *Population Control* (e.g., tourism, proliferation of stations in accessible areas)

- Why is the problem/impact important to resolve? What are the anticipated
benefits from resolving the problem/impact and anticipated consequences
from not resolving the problem/impact?
- What efforts have been made to mitigate the problem/impact? What types
of legal documents have been previously developed to solve the problem/
impact?
- What solution(s) are you recommending? What types of information or
procedures will be required to implement the solution to the problem/
impact?
- What groups (nations and other interested parties) will be involved in negotiating your recommendation and how could their influence be enhanced?
- Is your recommendation feasible and clearly defined?

At the end of the course, the student-ambassadors then convene a Mock ATCM
in which they formally debate and resolve their recommendations—often producing practical solutions for "real-world" issues (Box 2.2). Analogous group
decision-making forums can be modeled at all jurisdictional levels—from local
institutions (such as county commissions or state legislatures) through international conventions.

 **How can everyday observations be developed into meaningful
questions about the world we live in?**

BOX 2.2   "STUDENT-AMBASSADOR"
RECOMMENDATION FROM THE ANTARCTIC
MARINE ECOLOGY AND POLICY CAPSTONE
COURSE FOR UNDERGRADUATES AT THE
OHIO STATE UNIVERSITY[a]

Iceberg Utilization for Water and Energy

Joshua M. Ryland
Department of Zoology
Student-Ambassador from Guatemala

The Representatives:

Recalling Recommendations IX-1, X-1, Agreed Measures for the Conservation of Antarctic Fauna and Flora (AGREED MEASURES), Convention on the Conservation of Antarctic Marine Living Resources (CCAMLR), Convention on the Regulation of Antarctic Mineral Resource Activities (CRAMRA) and the Protocol on Environmental Protection to the Antarctic Treaty;

Recognizing that the Antarctic Treaty System is void of any regime which regulates the utilization of Antarctic icebergs;

Believing that the unique nature of icebergs as non-living, renewable resources warrants their distinction from all other Antarctic mineral resources:

Considering that the annual pure water yield of Antarctic icebergs will increase the world water supply by 25% and iceberg driven power plants will increase current energy output by 370%;

Recommend to their governments that:

Icebergs be considered non-mineral, thus, exempt from all mineral regimes and moratoriums on mineral usage, to enable the utilization of icebergs for the benefit of all mankind, in accordance with following provisions;

[i] The development of scientifically sounds methods of iceberg cleavage and transport which have no detrimental effect on the Antarctic marine ecosystem;

[ii] All iceberg harvests occur beyond the 200 mile Exclusive Economic Zone, and provisions for assessing liability in the event of an accident have been formulated;

[iii] All parties harvesting ice must be granted a permit in the manner established in the AGREED MEASURES and such permits will be granted yearly by the Committee for Environmental Protection (CEP) only after

each petitioning party demonstrates their activities will have no more than a minor or transitory impact on the Antarctic marine ecosystem, the transport zone ecosystems, and destination zone ecosystem;

[iv] The CEP will monitor the permits granted so that the annual amount of iceberg resources harvested will never exceed the amount calved each year.

[a] This project was completed during a 10-week quarter and was published along with other student papers in Berkman (1997a).

Continuously consulting on *matters of common interest,* as in the Antarctic Treaty system, enables individuals to share insights and build on what they already understand. Such group decision-making activities also offer valuable lessons about conceiving, designing, and implementing self-directed projects (Boxes 2.1 and 2.2). From educational institutions outward to society, group decision-making activities provide an effective formula for learning about the interdisciplinary nature of the Earth system and humankind (Fig. 2.5).

Interdisciplinary inquiry propels individuals toward understanding the complexity of our increasingly scientific and technological world. Like *Rumpelstiltskin,* the magic is turning observations into questions that illuminate answers that become new questions in an ever-growing cascade of insight.

Group Decision Making

Specific Problem or Question

+

Continuous Solution Refinement

+

Relevant Negotiating Forum

=

Effective Educational Experience

FIGURE 2.5   A group decision-making approach for integrating scientific, economic, governmental, and social perspectives into courses about our society and world. Simulating forums, such as the Antarctic Treaty Consultative Meeting, enables students to creatively explore and design strategies for resolving human impacts in the Earth system from global to local levels (Box 2.2).

PART

11

PROGRESS OF ALL MANKIND

INTERNATIONAL POLICY

Learning about the Earth as a system of interconnected events, entities, and phenomena (Fig. 2.1) is relevant to the sustainable development of our civilization. This global relevance—which extends from local communities across continents—commonly is represented by terms that connect human populations around the planet, such as global change, global economy, or global warming. Underlying these global perspectives are the technologies for viewing the entire planet at once across time with unprecedented resolution and for sharing information instantaneously around the world. We are beginning to work together as a global community—building an international society that preserves the legacy of nations while resolving global issues of common concern.

Historical perspectives on the progress of human civilization provide benchmarks for understanding our current situation and the challenges that lie ahead. As the last continent on Earth to be occupied by humans, Antarctica is unique in reflecting the succession of stages in our increasingly international society.

For all new worlds or unseen environments there are periods of speculation about riches followed by exploration of the unknown

(Chapter 3: *Terra Australis Incognita*). For Antarctica, this speculation emerged in early Greece with theories about the "unknown
southern land"—*Terra Australis Incognita*. Millennia after the Greek
philosophers—only at the end of the 18th century—James Cook
(1728–1779) ignited the era of Antarctic exploration by traveling
beyond the south polar circle. Within decades, industries began ex-
ploiting new resources. This "establishment phase" continued into
the early 20th century, with nations ultimately claiming priority so
that they could slice the continent into sovereign territories like pieces
of a giant pie.

On all other continents, concerns about territorial boundaries have
led to confrontations among nations. In Antarctica, fortunately, science gained a foothold and began demonstrating a mechanism for
cooperation among nations (Chapter 4: Awakening Science). The International Geophysical Year of 1957–1958, with its 12-nation contingent in Antarctica, became the catalyst for the Antarctic Treaty,
which was signed only a year later in 1959. With this international
framework in place—ensuring that the region south of 60° south latitude "shall be used for peaceful purposes only"—human involvement in Antarctica moved into an "international accommodation
phase" when nations continuously identify and build on their common interests (Chapter 5: International Stewardship).

Throughout the past half century, the Antarctic Treaty consultative
process (introduced in Chapter 2 as a model decision-making framework) has enabled diverse stakeholders to safeguard the only continent dedicated for *peaceful purposes*. However, like the rest of the
Earth system, Antarctica is increasingly exposed to resource and environmental impacts from human activities. In resolving these human
impacts, the Antarctic Treaty has matured into a model system for
fusing scientific insights with economic, governmental, and other societal interests to produce visionary policies for managing human activities on an international scale (CD-ROM on the Antarctic Treaty
Searchable Database: 1959–1999).

Humans are an integral part of the Earth system—depending on
it, affecting it, and responding to its variability. Geometric expansion

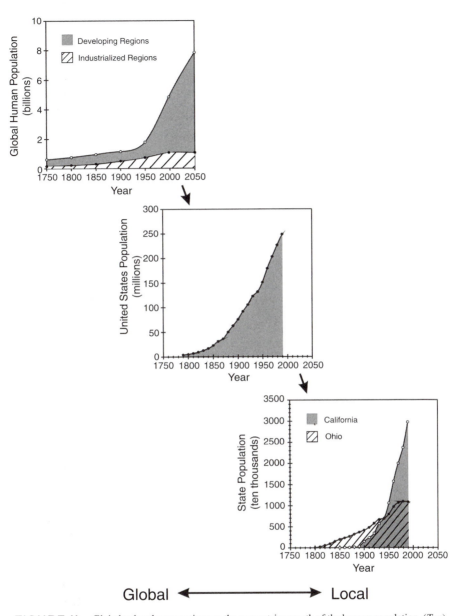

FIGURE II Global to local perspectives on the geometric growth of the human population. (*Top*) Global human population (in billions) since 1750, in industrialized and developing nations, with projected global population sizes in the 21st century reaching nearly 9 billion. Most of the global human population increase during this period has been in developing countries such as India, which alone grew from 375 million to 1 billion between 1947 and 1999. (*Middle*) United States human population (in millions) since 1790. (*Bottom*) Within the United States, state human populations (in ten thousands) for California and Ohio as representative coastal and midcontinental localities, respectively. Population statistics are from the United Nations Population Information Network (http://www.undp.org/popin) and the United States Census Bureau (http://www.census.gov/population/www).

of our global population (Fig. II), especially during the past two centuries, reflects the human dimensions of the Earth system. Whether the Antarctic Treaty System has become a precedent for a "global stewardship phase" in our evolving civilization is a matter for you to consider.

3

TERRA AUSTRALIS

INCOGNITA

To strive, to seek, to find, and not to yield.
　　　　　—Alfred, Lord Tennyson (1842), Ulysses

EXPLORING THE UNKNOWN

Antarctica had been cloaked in mythology for millennia before humans actually discovered its frozen continental features. The presence of Antarctica was first debated by Greek philosophers who propounded the need for a southern land-mass to balance the weight of the lands in the northern hemisphere. Referring to this unknown southern land, *Terra Australis Incognita,* Aristotle (384–322 B.C.) reasoned that the northern hemisphere lay under the constellation of Arktos (the bear) and that this southern land at the opposite end of the globe must be Antarktikos.

Legends of *Terra Australis Incognita* fascinated societies, particularly in Europe, and it was only a matter of time before cartographers began mapping the world. Placing the oceans and land masses on this global map, in correct orientation (Fig. I), was the real challenge. Even today with the sophistication of satellites and computer-generated images, we are still describing features on the Earth's surface. Amazingly, some of the early cartographers included a southern continent on their world maps, centuries before it was even discovered (Plate 2). These early maps of the unknown southern land, many of which were created during the 15th and 16th centuries, fanned the flames of exploration.

 Why are humans fascinated with the unknown?

TALISMAN OF PRIORITY

The quest to be the first—to discover and acquire riches for "king and country," to plant the flag for one's nation—have been primary driving forces behind exploration. In 1503, in his southern voyage of the *Espoir,* Binot Paulmier de Gonneville of France landed on a "tropical paradise" he called *Terre Australe.* Sixteen years later, Ferdinand Magellan (1480–1521) of Portugal set sail with five ships to find the "spice islands" for Spain on an expedition that became the first circumnavigation of the Earth: from Europe across the Atlantic Ocean, through the Straits of Magellan at the tip of South America, into the vast Pacific Ocean, westward to the Indian Ocean, around Africa, and back to Europe.

Magellan was followed by Sir Francis Drake (1542–1596) who, in 1577, was commissioned by the merchants and ministers of England to explore the coastline of the "continent beyond." Drake traveled to 57° south where the Pacific and Atlantic "meete in a most large and free scope," determining that Tierra del Fuego (land of fire) was not part of *Terra Australis Incognita.*

Despite Drake's observations about the frigid region south of South America, explorers could not resist the temptation to speculate wildly about the nature of the unknown southern land. Sailing southward in the *Gros Ventre* in 1772, Yves-Joseph de Kerguelen-Tremerac (1734–1797) returned to France and described a land that "holds promise of vegetable products . . . South France will provide grain crops . . . masting timber . . . salt works." Kerguelen was given a second commission to colonize La France Australe, but was soon discovered to be a fraud with ensuing court-martial and imprisonment for conduct unbecoming an officer. It is equally intriguing to ponder why someone would fantasize such stories and why a government would be willing to accept them.

It took the mettle of Captain James Cook to dispel the mystery of *Terra Australis Incognita* when, on 17 January 1773, he became the first person to travel beyond the Antarctic Circle. Overcoming nearly two millennia of speculation and surpassing the voyage of his countryman Sir Francis Drake two centuries earlier, Cook traveled into the southern land with its seasons of night and day. Remarkably, Cook sailed safely through towering icebergs and immense cresting breakers in wooden sailing ships—*Resolution* and *Adventure*—that were scarcely 34 meters in length and 11 meters wide!

With his circumnavigation of Antarctica, Cook once and for all time erased the notion that *Terra Australis Incognita* was a "tropical paradise." At his southernmost point on 30 January 1773, when he could progress southward no further, Cook wrote:

> . . . the ice extended east and west far beyond the reach of our sight. . . . It was indeed my opinion that this ice extends quite to the Pole, or perhaps joins to some land to which it has been fixed since creation.

In 1775, the *Resolution* returned to England after traveling more than 97,000 kilometers in its amazing 3-year voyage.

Why is it important to individuals and nations to establish their priority in discovering new lands or resources?

The first person to actually see the Antarctic continent was the Russian Thaddeus von Bellingshausen (1778–1852) who sailed to 69°21′ south in the *Vostok* (East) and *Mirnyi* (Peaceful) in 1820. During this voyage along the Antarctic Peninsula, which projects like a gnarled finger toward South America, Bellingshausen met Nathaniel Palmer, the 21-year-old American captain of the sealing vessel *Hero*. Three years later, the southernmost voyage of the 19th century was achieved by James Weddell (1787–1834), who sailed in the *Jane* and *Beaufoy* to 74°15′ south. During his voyage, Weddell noted that "not a particle of ice of any description was to be seen." Interestingly, as a reflection of climatic variability, it would take until 1911 before another ship could penetrate the sea ice this far south.

The first national expedition to Antarctica was conducted by Charles Wilkes (1798–1877), who led the United States South Sea Exploring Expedition between 1838 and 1842. With vivid imagery about sailing through the Southern Ocean, the expedition's surgeon wrote:

> The vessel was beset with ice, whose pale masses just came in sight through the dim haze, like tombs in some vast cemetery; and, as the hoar-frost covered the men with its sheet, they looked like specters fit for such a haunt. . . . The waves began to be stilled by the large snowflakes that fell unmelted on their surface; and, as the breeze died away into a murmur, a low crepitation, like the clicking of a death-watch, announced that the sea was freezing.

In 1841, with the goal of sailing to the South Pole in the *Erebus* and *Terror,* James Clark Ross (1800–1862) came in contact with land which he claimed as Victoria Land for the Queen of England. Ross viewed his achievement as "[the] way of restoring to England the honor of the southernmost land, which had been won by the intrepid Bellingshausen, and for more than 20 years retained by Russia."

Like a magnet, Antarctica continued to pull explorers southward, all eager to accomplish some new feat that would garner glory. The first confirmed landing on Antarctica occurred in 1895 during the Norwegian-financed voyage of the *Antarctic* when Carsten Egeberg Borchgrevink (1864–1934) and six others stepped onto the Victoria Land Coast (Fig. 3.1). Spurred by the Sixth International Geographical Congress of 1895, which identified that the "Antarctic region is the greatest piece of geographical exploration still to be undertaken," these expeditions now took on the aura of national programs:

> . . . in view of the additions to knowledge in almost every branch of science which would result from such a scientific exploration, the Congress recommends that the scientific societies throughout the world should urge, in whatever way seems to them most effective, that this work should be undertaken before the close of the century.

In 1897, the Belgian Antarctic Expedition set sail in the *Belgica* with a crew of many nationalities: Adrien Victor Joseph de Gerlache (1866–1934), the Belgian captain; Frederick Cook (1865–1940), the American surgeon; Emile Racovitza

FIGURE 3.1   (*Top*) Transantarctic Mountains, with its thick black band of coal older than 200 million years, viewed westward from McMurdo Sound in the southern Ross Sea. (*Bottom*) Sea ice across McMurdo Sound during the austral summer. Eastward view with the active Mt. Erebus volcano on Ross Island in the distance.

(1868–1947), the Rumanian zoologist; Henryk Arctowski (1871–1958), the Polish geologist; a Russian laboratory assistant; a number of Norwegians, including Roald Amundsen (1872–1928); and the complement of Belgian nationals. Beset in the pack ice in the Antarctic Peninsula region during the austral darkness, with supplies running low, Cook described the penguin meat that they were forced to consume: ". . . if it is possible to imagine a piece of beef, odiferous cod fish and a canvas-backed duck roasted together in a pot, with blood and cod-liver oil for sauce, the illustration would be complete." The following year, the British Antarctic Expedition became the first to actually winter on the Antarctic continent, in northern Victoria Land—with Carsten Borchgrevink captaining the *Southern Cross.*

Even with the many triumphs of exploration during the 19th century, the South Pole still lay beyond observation and human experience. As with the mythologies that cloaked *Terra Australis Incognita* before its discovery, there was wild speculation about what lay at the bottom of the planet. Perhaps the most intriguing suggestion came from John Cleves Symmes, Jr. (1779–1829), in 1818, when he suggested that "The earth is hollow and habitable within; containing a number of solid concentric spheres—one within the other, and that it is open at the poles 12 or 16 degrees."

The first serious attempt at the South Pole was lead by Robert Falcon Scott (1868–1912) on *Discovery* during the National Antarctic Expedition (Fig. 3.2). On 31 December 1902, after having traveled by dog sledge more than 5000 kilometers, Scott along with Ernest Shackleton (1874–1922) and Edward Wilson (1872–1912) reached 82°16′ south. Six years later, Shackleton returned to Antarctica with the express purpose of reaching the *southern geographical pole.* Through blizzards and across deep crevassed glaciers, Shackleton and his team traveled as far as 88°23′ south on 9 January 1909—just 180 kilometers from the Pole—before turning around in a life-and-death dash back to their encampment on Ross Island.

In 1910, Scott once again headed southward, this time on the British *Terra Nova* Expedition. Just prior to this departure from South Africa, Scott received a telegram from the famed Norwegian polar explorer, Roald Amundsen: "Beg leave to inform you, *Fram* proceeding Antarctica. Amundsen." The race was on (Fig. 3.3).

Scott soon was moored in McMurdo Sound and Amundsen in the Bay of Whales, 97 kilometers closer to the pole. Scott's team also was at a technical disadvantage because they used ponderous motor vehicles and ponies that eventually failed, forcing them to manhaul their sleds toward the polar plateau. Amundsen's team, in contrast, used dogs to pull their sleds through their entire journey. Although both parties had laid food depots along their polar routes, Amundsen also shot his dogs for additional food.

On 16 December 1911, Amundsen and his party of five became the first humans to reach the South Pole, as they determined from the constant altitude of the sun above the horizon as it traveled around the sky:

FIGURE 3.2 (*Top*) Scott's hut at McMurdo Station. The hut was built during the British National (*Discovery*) Expedition from 1901 to 1904. (*Bottom*) Statue in Christchurch, New Zealand, of Robert Falcon Scott, who perished with his team after arriving at the South Pole in 1912, one month after Roald Amundsen's first arrival on 14 December 1911. (*Facing page*) Inside of Scott's Hut in 1981, with mittens made from the fur of Weddell seals (foreground) along with tins of sledge-dog biscuits, skis, and other accoutrements (background).

FIGURE 3.2   (*Continued*)

It was 11 a.m. when we reached our destination. While some of us were putting up the tent, others began to get everything ready for the coming observations. A solid snow pedestal was put up, on which the artificial horizon was to be placed, and a smaller one to rest the sextant on when it was not in use. . . . It was very strange to turn in at 6 p.m., and then on turning out again at midnight to find the sun apparently still at the same altitude, and then once more at 6 a.m. to see it still no higher. The altitude had changed, of course, but so slightly that it was imperceptible with the naked eye. To us it appeared as though the sun made the circuit of the heavens at exactly the same altitude. . . . The observations soon told us that we were not on the absolute Pole, but as close to it as we could hope to get with our instruments.

One month later, on 17 January 1912, Scott and his party also reached the Pole, where they found Amundsen's tent, a welcome note, and a message for the King of Norway:

The pole. Yes, but under different circumstances from those expected. . . . Great God! this is an awful place and terrible enough for us to have labored to it without the *reward of priority*. [author's emphasis]

Laboring under the weight of defeat, Scott and his party eventually were overcome by the brutal force of the Antarctic. Eight months later, the bodies of Scott and two others in his party were found. From 29 March 1912, the last entries in Scott's journal read:

Since the 21st we have had a continuous gale from W.S.W. and S.W. We had fuel to make two cups of tea apiece and bare food for two days on the twentieth. Every day we have been ready to start for our depot 11 miles away, but outside the door of the tent it remains

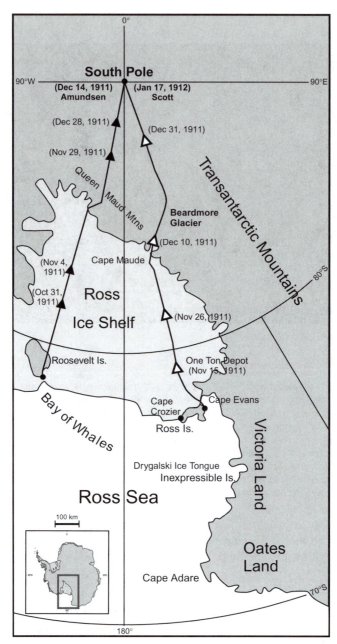

FIGURE 3.3   Race for the South Pole between Roald Amundsen of Norway (solid arrows) and Robert Falcon Scott of Great Britain (open arrows) with their crews of the *Fram* and *Terra Nova*, respectively. Scott manhauled sleds along the route established by Ernest Shackleton from McMurdo Sound in 1909, whereas Amundsen used dogs along an untested route from the Bay of Whales. On 14 December 1911, Amundsen and his team became the first humans to reach the South Pole. Scott and his team died on their return to McMurdo Sound after arriving at the South Pole on 17 January 1912. Adapted from Huntford (1979).

a scene of whirling drift. I do not think we can hope for any better things now. We shall
stick it out to the end, but we are getting weaker, of course, and the end cannot be far.

It seems a pity, but I do not think I can write more.
            R. Scott

In his last entry, freezing to death, Scott scratched:

For God's sake look after our people.

Although the South Pole had been reached and many of the geographic "firsts"
had been achieved, there still were ample opportunities for novelty in the Antarctic. Among these feats was Shackleton's expedition to undertake the "greatest
Polar journey ever attempted," with his legendary advertisement in 1913:

Men wanted for Hazardous Journey. Small wages, bitter cold, long months of complete
darkness, constant danger, safe return doubtful. Honour and recognition in case of success.

Shackleton and his crew planned to sail in the *Endurance* into the Weddell Sea
and then traverse to the South Pole, across the Beardmore Glacier, and into the
Ross Sea, where the *Aurora* would pick them up—2900 kilometers later.

As fate would have it, none of Shackleton's crew ever set foot on the continent
(Fig. 3.4). The *Endurance* was trapped in the sea ice where it lingered precariously
for more than 300 days, through the long Antarctic night, before being mercilessly
crushed. It was November 1915, the world was at war, and the 28-man crew of
Endurance was given up for dead. There was no rescue party. The only means of
survival was for Shackleton somehow to get his party back to civilization, across
freezing seas, without a ship.

The crew of the *Endurance* offloaded supplies for their survival, which were
piled into three 6-meter longboats—*Dudley Docker, Stancomb Wills,* and *James
Caird*—which they began dragging across the sea ice. For 5 months on drifting
ice floes, trudging toward the South Shetland Islands, the crew ate seal meat and
drank a concoction of seal blubber that they called "hoosh." Eventually, the sea
ice disintegrated and the castaways were forced into their longboats, which carried them all by good fortune to Elephant Island in May 1916—their first time on
land in more than 16 months. With no rescue possible, Shackleton was forced to
maroon 22 of his men on this desolate island while he and five others sailed 1300
kilometers in the *James Caird* across the godforsaken Drake Passage, where the
great oceans of the world "meete in a most large and free scope."

Soon after, with great travail along the way, Shackleton arrived in the whaling
village of Stromness on South Georgia. The effort required four attempts, but in
the end all of Shackleton's marooned crew on Elephant Island were rescued alive.
This epic tale of survival was among the final sagas in the heroic era (1901–1922)
of Antarctic exploration.

With technology entering the Antarctic, such as the airplane, which was first
brought down by Douglas Mawson (1882–1958) in 1912, it was becoming easier
to survey and map the southern continent. In 1928 and 1929, Sir Hubert Wilkins

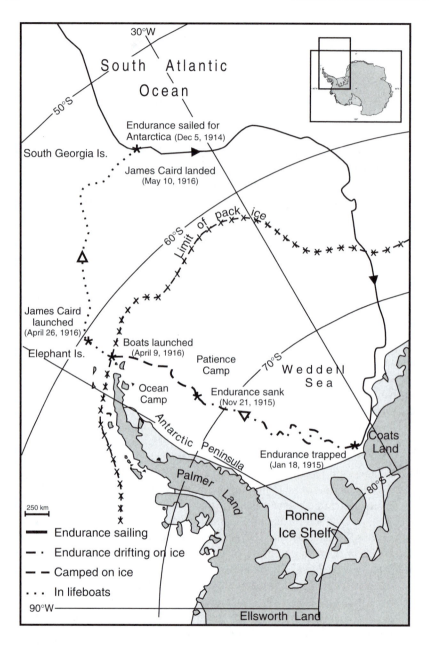

FIGURE 3.4 Amazing voyage of the *Endurance* crew lead by Ernest Shackleton after their ship was crushed in the sea ice before it even reached Antarctica to begin the *Imperial Trans-Antarctic Expedition.* All 28 members of the *Endurance* survived their 1914–1916 ordeal in the Antarctic Peninsula region. Adapted from Huntford (1985).

(1888–1958) used aerial photography to map nearly 3000 kilometers of uncharted terrain in the Antarctic Peninsula region. Still, the "reward of priority" loomed large, and it was later in 1929 that Richard Byrd (1888–1957) navigated the first flight over the South Pole—a trip in 15 hours and 51 minutes that had taken Amundsen 3 months and cost Scott's party their lives: "But you must have faith— you must have faith in the outcome, I whispered to myself. It is like a flight, a flight into another unknown." After millennia as *Terra Australis Incognita,* the continent of Antarctica was known.

CLAIMING TERRITORY

The issue of territorial jurisdiction is new nowhere on Earth. All nations have worked, contrived, and even battled over their authority. These sovereignty problems arrived in the Antarctic region along with national quests for priority and the early explorers' zeal for untapped resources.

Within a decade of Cook's voyage across the Antarctic circle, Enderby Brothers of England began sending ships toward Antarctica to harvest the vast seal populations that had been identified on islands between Terra del Fuego and the Antarctic Peninsula. Within 30 years, the fur seals (*Arctocephalus* species) on South Georgia were virtually eliminated. As the sealers moved on from South Georgia with experience and a vigorous industry, the demise of the fur seal on the South Shetland Islands took only a few years (Chapter 10: Ecosystem Conservation).

During the early 19th century, sealers also began wintering on subantarctic islands that had been recognized as strategic national outposts throughout the previous century. In 1820, the United Provinces of Buenos Aires claimed the Falkland Islands south of Cape Horn between 51° and 53° south. With the Argentine appointment of Luis Vernet (1792–1871) as governor of the Falkland Islands in 1828, territorial interests escalated into altercation as he imprisoned British and American sealers for poaching.

Angered by this high-handed action, in 1831 the United States Navy sent the corvette *U.S.S. Lexington* down to the Falkland Islands, where it destroyed the settlements, expelled the principal residents to Buenos Aires, and pronounced the islands "free of all government." The British navy followed suit and in 1833 sent down H.M.S. *Clio* and H.M.S. *Tyne* to hoist the Union Jack. Soon after, a rogue band of Argentine gauchos murdered several residents, including a British citizen who had worked with James Weddell. Curiously, it was also during this time that the H.M.S. *Beagle* arrived in the Falkland Islands with Charles Darwin (1809–1882).

Conflict and military intervention in the Falkland Islands symbolize the magnitude of national interests in Antarctica. The Falkland Islands also represent the first formal claim to Antarctic territory when, in 1908, the British Letters of Patent appointed

> . . . the Governor of the Colony of the Falkland Islands to be Governor of South Georgia, the South Orkneys, the South Shetlands, the Sandwich Islands and Graham's Land, and providing for the Government thereof as Dependencies of the Colony.

The Falkland Island Dependencies, which initially included parts of Argentina and Chile, were based on the 1765 visit by Captain John Byron (1756–1791). In 1917, however, a revision of the Letters of Patent eliminated claims in South America and expanded the British claim southward to include

> . . . all islands and territories whatsoever between the twentieth degree of West longitude and the 50th degree of West longitude which are situated south of the 50th parallel of South latitude.

This claim, shaped like a wedge converging at the South Pole, was based on the "sector theory" from the Arctic where nations extended their territorial boundaries to the North Pole. The major difference, however, was that Antarctica was a continent surrounded by ocean, unlike the Arctic, where contiguous national lands enclose an ocean.

 What are the benefits and problems with national claims to Antarctic territory?

As if slicing a pie, nations began claiming sectors of Antarctica (Fig. 3.5). Expanding its empire, the British government, by Order-in-Council gave the Ross Dependencies to New Zealand in 1923, based on the historic efforts in the region by Ross, Scott, and Shackleton. The following year, the French claimed a small sector of East Antarctica based on the voyage by Jules-Sébastien-César Dumont d'Urville (1790–1842), who had named Terre Adélie for his wife in 1840. The British then countered in 1933 with another Order-in-Council, which claimed sectors on both sides of the French claim, based in part on the British Australian New Zealand Antarctic Research Expedition (BANZARE) of 1929–1931. Despite their colonial histories, in 1938, these four nations mutually recognized each other's claims to strengthen their individual assertions of territorial sovereignty.

In 1929, from Little America near the Bay of Whales on the Ross Ice Shelf, Byrd also had unofficially claimed Antarctic territories east of 150° west and called it Marie Byrd Land in honor of his wife. Subsequently, during his aviation expedition (which included the first transantarctic flight in November 1935), Lincoln Ellsworth unofficially claimed for the United States the entire region between the British and New Zealand sectors. In 1939, coordinated under the auspices of the newly formed United States Antarctic Service, Byrd was privately instructed by President Franklin Roosevelt (1882–1945): "Take appropriate steps such as dropping written claims from airplanes, depositing such writings in cairns, et cetera, which might assist in supporting a sovereignty claim by the United States." Moreover, President Roosevelt informed Byrd about the importance of maintaining "permanent bases because of their growing value for four purposes—national defense of the Western Hemisphere, radio, meteorology and minerals." Ulti-

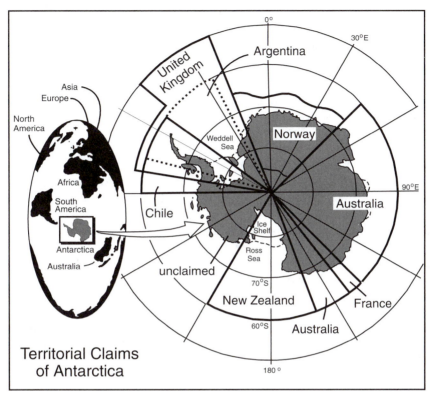

FIGURE 3.5   Sectors of Antarctica were claimed by seven nations during the 20th century: England (1908 and 1917); New Zealand (1923); France (1924); Australia (1933); Norway (1939); Chile (1940); and Argentina (1943). The only overlapping claims are between England, Chile, and Argentina in the Antarctic Peninsula region. Other nations reserved the rights to make territorial claims, including the United States, which had expressed sovereign interests in the only unclaimed area of Antarctica in Marie Byrd Land. The polar projection shows the geographic location of Antarctica relative to the other continents (Fig. I). Modified from the National Foreign Assessment Center (1978) and Berkman (1992).

mately, the United States decided to reserve the right to make its claim, creating Marie Byrd Land as the only unclaimed sector of Antarctica.

During the late 1930s, the German Reich also decided to stake claims in Antarctica. However, rather than "effective occupation," which requires territorial administration and defense, Germany decided to utilize the international laws of "constructive occupation" where "formal claim to possession" is coupled with "subsequent exploration by air or land." As a symbol of its occupation, Germany used an "aeroplane mothership" to drop 1.5-meter aluminum darts with swastikas emblazoned on the shafts to assert its territorial claim for the region between 11° west to 19° east longitude. Angered by Germany's interests in the Queen Maud

Land region, which Norway considered as her territory, King Hans van Marwijk Haakon VII (1872–1957) claimed the region between 20° west and 45° east in 1939 based on the preeminent success of Amundsen.

Overlapping territorial interests of Germany and Norway were not unique in the Antarctic. In 1940, Chilean Decree Number 1747 asserted:

> All lands, islands, islets, reefs of rocks, glaciers (pack-ice), already known or to be discovered, and their respective territorial waters, in the sector between longitudes 53° and 90° West, constitute the Chilean Antarctic or Chilean Antarctic territory.

This claim by Chile was traced to its "indisputable" title, which was proclaimed in the Treaty of Tordessillas from 1494 which gave to Spain all lands lying west of the 46th meridian. Not to be outdone by its neighbor across the Andes, Argentina made its claim in 1943 based on both the Treaty of Tordesillas and the Papal Bull (*Intera Caetera*) of 1493—as with all other claims, demonstrating the importance of priority. Despite their differences, in 1947 Argentina and Chile jointly declared their "unquestionable rights . . . over the South American Antarctic" and interests in developing a "harmonious plan of action for the better scientific knowledge of the Antarctic zone by means of explorations and technical investigations. . . ."

The biggest difficulty with the three overlapping claims in the Antarctic Peninsula sector (Fig. 3.5), however, has remained between Great Britain and Argentina. Their Falklands–Malvinas war in 1982 is an acute reminder that territorial interests remain today as the major challenge to peace in the Antarctic region.

4

AWAKENING SCIENCE

*The whole of science is nothing more than a refinement of
everyday thinking.*
—*Albert Einstein (1954),* Ideas and Opinions

DISCOVERY

Early explorers furnished the world with observations about the Antarctic: an
ocean covered by ice and teeming with life; icebergs larger than cities; bone-
piercing cold and violent winds howling off a barren ice-shrouded continent.
Their tales were more than lore—they were the seeds of science in Antarctica.

Educated sealers, such as James Weddell, focused on describing all manner of
natural phenomena. He measured the magnetic declination on South Georgia and
noted the habitats of seals and penguins throughout his voyage. Moreover, the
most southern seal species in the world is known as the Weddell seal (*Leptonychotes weddelli* Lesson 1826) even though it was inaccurately portrayed in his
drawing of the "Sea Leopard of South Orkneys." For his record southern sailing
in 1823, during an exceptionally warm summer when "not a particle of ice of any
description was to be seen," the Weddell Sea was named. This simple account,
in fact, provides an invaluable historical record for verifying past environmental
conditions around Antarctica, which modern scientific techniques can only infer.

Six years later, James Eights (a surgeon turned naturalist: 1798–1882) came to
the Antarctic on a sealing voyage with Nathaniel Palmer (1799–1877). Although
sealing was on the wane because of the ruthless overexploitation of the seal population, this trip became an important success for its science. Eights collected 13
cases of rocks, terrestrial flora, and marine animals, which he described with me-
ticulous detail between 1833 and 1852—in the earliest "professional" research
papers from Antarctica. Eights was the first to describe "tabular" icebergs, and he

became a pioneer in Antarctic marine biology with his precise reports of species such as the 10-legged spider-like pycnogonid (*Decolopoda australis* Eights 1833) and the giant trilobite-like isopod (*Glyptonotus antarctica* Eights 1833). During this period, scientific influence also began to burgeon as nations developed organizations such as the Linnaean Society (1799), Gesellschaft Deutscher Naturforscher and Ärtze (1822), the British Association for the Advancement of Science (1831), and the American Association for the Advancement of Science (1848). In 1835, for example, the British Association for Advancement of Science proposed

> That a representation be made to Government of the importance of sending an expedition into the Antarctic regions, for the purpose of making of observations and discoveries in various branches of science, as Geography, Hydrography, Natural History, and especially Magnetism. . . .

Within 3 years, Charles Wilkes had set sail for Antarctica in command of the United States South Sea Exploring Expedition, which later produced 20 volumes of scientific reports. This expedition also collected and described the type specimen of the krill (*Euphausia superba* Dana 1852), which Wilkes realized was the principal food for Antarctic penguins and seals. Similarly, the French expedition by D'Urville in 1838 produced geological reports along with well-illustrated biological atlases that included the first description of the crabeater seal (*Lobodon carcinophaga* Hombron and Jacquinot 1842), the species that accounts for nearly half of all seals on Earth.

Antarctic oceanography, glaciology, and meteorology as well as biology were all advanced by the voyages of James Ross during the first half of the 19th century. Using a hemp line fitted with swivels and weights, Ross conducted the first deep-sea soundings and determined depths of 4427 meters in a position where modern charts show 3843 meters. Ross also discovered an enormous ice shelf (now known as the Ross Ice Shelf) that he determined was floating at its seaward edge.

The Zoology of the Antarctic Voyage by H.M. Ships Erebus *and* Terror, which was edited by John Richardson (1823–1910) and John Grey between 1844 and 1875, further describes species such as the rare Ross seal (*Ommatophoca rossi* Gray 1844) and the 1.5-meter tall Emperor penguin (*Aptehodytes forsteri* Gray 1844). Joseph Hooker, in his *Flora Antarctica,* described flowering plants on subantarctic islands as well as marine algae surviving in the frigid Antarctic ocean, including abundant microscopic diatoms in melted sea-ice samples. Meteorological measurements during Ross's voyages also demonstrated that the mean barometric pressure above Antarctica was the lowest on Earth, which is why the atmosphere and ocean circulate together as giant cyclones around the continent.

During this period, Matthew Maury (1806–1873), director of the United States Naval Observatory and author of *The Physical Geography of the Sea and Its Meteorology,* began realizing that Antarctica was a giant missing piece of the puzzle in understanding the Earth system: "Within the periphery of that circle is included an area equal in extent to one sixth of the entire landed surface of our planet."

By 1860, Maury had become an outspoken advocate of ". . . all nations agreeing to unite and cooperate in carrying out one system of philosophical research with regard to the sea," especially in Antarctica:

> England through Cook and Ross; Russia through Bellingshausen; France through D'Ur-
> ville; and the United States through Wilkes; have sent expeditions to the South Sea . . . .
> The expeditions which have been sent to explore unknown seas have contributed largely
> to the stock of human knowledge, and they have added renown to nations, luster to
> diadems.

In February 1874, Antarctic science was given a huge boost when the steam-ship H.M.S. *Challenger* crossed the Antarctic circle. From 1872 through 1875, the *Challenger* had navigated more than 127,000 kilometers through the ocean on a global expedition that discovered the deepest reach of the sea in the Marianas Trench (Fig. 1.3) and nearly 5000 new species. As described by the Royal Geographical Society, the purpose of this global enterprise was to

> Investigate the physical conditions of the deep sea, in the great ocean basins—the North
> and South Pacific, and the Southern Ocean (as far as the neighborhood of the great ice-
> barrier); . . . observation and experiment of all these points being made at various ranges
> of depth from the surface to the bottom.

The outcome of this global science endeavor was the production of the *Challenger Reports,* a 50-volume opus containing the work of nearly 100 scholars that was published from 1880 through 1895. Not only did the *Challenger* expedition herald the field of oceanography, but the dredges of deep-sea sediments provided the key for Sir John Murray (1841–1914) to forcefully demonstrate that Antarctica was indeed a continent:

> These flat-topped icebergs form the most striking peculiarity of the Antarctic Ocean. Their
> form and structure seem clearly to indicate that they were formed over an extended land
> surface and have been pushed over low-lying coasts into the sea. As these bergs are floated
> to the north and broken up in warmer latitudes, they distribute over the floor of the ocean
> a large quantity of glaciated rock fragments . . . distinctively indicative of continental
> land . . . near the South Pole.

Murray's hypothetical continent became the catalyst for the era of national Antarctic expeditions that was launched by the Sixth International Geographic Congress in 1895. Within the next two decades, nine countries (Argentina, Australia, England, France, Germany, Japan, Norway, Scotland, and Sweden) had sponsored 14 expeditions to the southern continent. Knowledge that Antarctica was a continent, as opposed to a vast ice sheet, suddenly made a difference to nations. The value of Antarctic science was dawning on the world (Fig. 4.1).

SCIENCE BEYOND NATIONS

The international framework for research collaborations in Antarctica originated with the First International Polar Year (IPY) in 1882–83. The First IPY was

FIGURE 4.1   (*Top*) United States Coast Guard cutters *Polar Star* (WAGB-10) and *Polar Sea* (WAGB-11) cutting channel in the sea ice for the resupply vessel to McMurdo Station (77°50′ south, 166°40′ east) on Ross Island in the southwestern Ross Sea. (*Bottom*) New Zealand helicopter transport of equipment and personnel to Edmonson Point (74°20′ south, 165°08′ east) from the Italian Research Station in the Terra Nova Bay region in the northwestern Ross Sea. (*Facing Page*) Nansen sleds on the sea ice preparing for the Victoria Land Coast Expedition in 1994–1995 from McMurdo Sound to Terra Nova Bay.

FIGURE 4.1   (*Continued*)

organized largely by the International Meteorological Congress of 1879 under the advice of Karl Weyprecht (1838–1881), who had envisioned the benefits of co-ordinated international research:

> Decisive scientific results can only be attained through a series of synchronous expeditions, whose task it would be to distribute themselves over the Arctic regions and to obtain one year's series of observations made according to the same method.

The concept of the "same method" indicates that standardized approaches for collecting data were being developed so that the data could be analyzed efficiently and interpreted reliably. The concerted effort among nations also would expand the scope of research beyond the possible accomplishments of any individual nation. Moreover, the research coordination would promote continuity and favor the exchange of ideas among nations, both of which are inherently peaceful activities that reinforce further cooperation.

During the First IPY, 11 European nations combined expeditions to study meteorology along with magnetic and auroral phenomena in the Arctic for the welfare of the nations involved (Table 4.1). Two nations also sent research expeditions toward the south polar region. French scientists conducted research in the vicinity of Cape Horn, but only Germany succeeded in establishing a station near Antarctica. This research station at Royal Bay on South Georgia, under the leadership of K. Schrader, provided the first annual cycle of data on the weather and Earth's magnetism in the Antarctic region.

TABLE 4.1   Characteristics of the International Polar Years

	International Polar Year (IPY)		
	First IPY	Second IPY	Third IPY[a]
Dates	1882–83	1932–33	1957–58
Region	Arctic and Antarctic	Arctic	Global
Solar Activity	Maximum	Minimum	Maximum
Observations	Ground-based	10 kilometers by balloon	121,000 kilometers by rocket and satellite
Nations	11 in the Arctic, 2 in the Antarctic	40 in the Arctic	67 around the Earth (12 nations maintained 65 stations in the Antarctic)
Disciplines	Meteorology, magnetism, and aurora	Meteorology, magnetism, aurora, and radio science	World days and communications, rockets and satellites, meteorology, geomagnetism, aurora and airglow, ionosphere, solar activity, cosmic rays, longitudes and latitudes, glaciology, oceanography, seismology, gravity measurements, nuclear radiation

[a] Renamed the International Geophysical Year (IGY).

Fortuitously, 1882–83 was a year of intense sunspot activity, with two large magnetic storms that coincided with heightened auroras, providing strong evidence for an auroral connection with the Earth's magnetic field. More importantly, comparable measurements from opposite polar region demonstrated that the Arctic and Antarctic were connected by the Earth's magnetic field. It was becoming apparent that the Earth as a global systen was linked not only by the oceans, which provided planetary corridors for the early explorers, but also by the atmosphere.

After World War I (1914–18), coinciding with the close of the heroic era in Antarctic exploration (Chapter 3: *Terra Australis Incognita*), development of the airplane, aerial camera, motorized transport, and radio changed the nature of research in Antarctica. These technological advances were accelerating the pace of Earth science, making it easier to survey and communicate from remote regions of the planet (Plate 3). In many ways, Byrd's 1928–1930 expedition embodied emergence of this technological era when radio transmission of his south polar flight was picked up in New York and broadcast by loudspeaker in Times Square.

After the "Great War," interest in cooperative science activities among the victorious nations led to the development of the International Research Council (IRC). The IRC brought together prominent national science academies to sponsor international scientific unions in fields such as geodesy and geophysics, radio science, terrestrial magnetism and electricity, physical oceanography, volcanology, hydrology, biology, pure and applied physics, and pure and applied chemistry. The IRC, however, was flawed because it excluded the "defeated" nations and was not genuinely open to the international community. Because of its exclusionary character, the IRC was disbanded and eventually reestablished in 1931 as the International Council of Scientific Unions (ICSU), which remains today.

With unrestricted national participation in the scientific unions, ICSU soon began organizing the Second IPY, which would take place in 1932–33, during a sunspot minimum with reduced production of solar flares. Again, a major thrust of the polar year would be on Arctic meteorology as well as northern lights (aurora borealis), magnetism, and radio science. Participation in the Second IPY expanded to 40 nations and included observations from high-altitude balloons, generating much broader coverages than the ground-based observations of the First IPY (Table 4.1).

During this period, Antarctic expeditions also were becoming international. The British, Australian, New Zealand Antarctic Expedition (BANZARE) involved three national Antarctic programs; however, they all belonged to the British Commonwealth. The first truly international expedition to Antarctica, among nations that had no colonial relationships, was the Norwegian–British–Swedish Antarctic Expedition to Dronning Maud Land in 1949–52. This expedition not only contributed to the field of glaciology by drilling the first significant Antarctic ice core and by conducting explosive seismology through the Maudheim Ice Shelf, but it laid the logistic groundwork for international activities in Antarctic during the Third IPY, which was being planned for 1957–58 (Table 4.1).

INTERNATIONAL GEOPHYSICAL YEAR

In 1950, the concept of a Third IPY was introduced at the Maryland home of James Van Allen (discover of the Van Allen radiation belt surrounding the Earth). Technology had advanced rapidly since the Second IPY. After World War II (1939–1945), largely because of the "Cold War," there was heightened interest in the Arctic by circumpolar northern nations. Moreover, a sunspot maximum due at the end of the decade would be ideal for studying the impact of solar storms on the Earth system. These ideas were submitted to the international unions for radio science, geodesy and geophysics, and astronomy, who jointly proposed to ICSU that a Third IPY be organized.

However, in contrast to the preceding polar years (Table 4.1), it was soon recognized that the natural phenomena to be studied were global and warranted international coordination beyond the polar regions. To facilitate this study of the whole Earth, ICSU established the Comité Special de l'Année Geophysique Internationale (CSAGI) for coordinating the International Geophysical Year from 1 July 1957 through 31 December 1958.

As a nongovernmental organization (NGO), ICSU had an advantage: it could organize the International Geophysical Year (IGY) with limited political influence. Consequently, the IGY became the largest, most complex, and most comprehensive scientific undertaking ever conceived by humankind.

World Data Centers would be developed to ensure the security and accessibility of the IGY datasets. Between 20,000 and 40,000 scientists from 67 nations, involving some 4000 stations across the planet, would cooperate under the international umbrella of Earth science. Research would be integrated among 11 scientific disciplines ranging from meteorology and oceanography to ionospheric physics to geomagnetism (Table 4.1). Even though this research was supported by individual governments, the IGY provided an unprecedented foundation of international cooperation in approaching scientific questions while avoiding political problems on a global scale.

 How did the International Geophysical Year enhance the role of science in understanding the Earth system?

Part of the success of the IGY was related to observations from space that had become possible with satellite and rocket technologies. Impressions of the Earth's surface that had taken generations of mariners centuries or even millennia to acquire, could be obtained in a few quick orbits by satellites hundreds to thousands of kilometers above the Earth. Rockets launched by the United States, which were intended to orbit the Moon (but did not succeed), provided information about the Earth's magnetic field to a distance of nearly 20 Earth radii—more than 120,000 kilometers into space. Although only seven nations had rocket launching in their IGY programs (United States, Soviet Union, the United Kingdom, France, Japan, Australia, and Canada), their results were shared by all of the IGY nations.

On the Earth's surface, Antarctica became a central focus of the IGY and, in 1954, CSAGI identified that the Antarctic was

> . . . a region of almost unparalleled interest in the fields of geophysics and geography alike. In geophysics, Antarctica has many significant, unexplored aspects: for example, the influence of this huge ice mass on global weather; the influence of the ice mass on atmospheric and oceanographic dynamics; the nature and extent of Aurora Australis. . . . These and similar scientific considerations lead the CSAGI to recognize that Antarctica represents a most significant portion of the earth for intensive study during the International Geophysical Year.

In 1956, CSAGI created the Special Committee on Antarctic Research to coordinate the international science activities in the south polar region.

This Antarctic research by 12 nations led to the establishment of 65 stations in the interior and along the margins of the continent (Chapter 11: Environmental Protection). The United States established a station at the geographic south pole (90° South) while the Soviets built Vostok Station at the geomagnetic south pole (approximately 79° South). The Australians opened Davis Station in the Vestfold Hills, and the Japanese began their research at Syowa Station along the Sôya Coast of East Antarctica. Little America V on the Ross Ice Shelf continued the American presence that had begun when Byrd's first expedition in 1929 founded the first Little America. New Zealand established Scott Base with nearby McMurdo Station run by the Americans on Ross Island. The British opened Halley Station along with 10 others in the Antarctic Peninsula region. Belgian scientists opened Base Roi Baudouin in Dronning Maud Land. French and Norwegian scientists were working in Adélie Land. Chilean and Argentine nationals opened facilities in the Antarctic Peninsula. The IGY brought all of these nations together in Antarctica for the purpose of cooperative scientific discovery.

From Little America V, a team of glaciologists began a 1000-kilometer Sno-cat traverse across the continental ice toward the Antarctic Peninsula to Byrd Station. At the time, the ice mass of West Antarctica was considered to be relatively thin, merely a residue of earlier glaciations, compared to the massive ice sheet on East Antarctica. With new seismic, magnetic, and gravity technologies in hand, these scientists determined that the ice sheet covering West Antarctica in fact had thicknesses exceeding 3000 meters. Determining the thickness of the Antarctic ice sheets was an amazing feat for a group of scientists, particularly young researchers (all were graduate students except for their 28-year-old leader, Charles Bentley, who had just completed his doctorate). In 5 weeks they had unlocked a major mystery of Antarctic physiography—a mystery that had eluded more experienced scientists for the previous five decades.

Seismology had made important technological advances during the IGY, and it was soon discovered that the Ross Ice Shelf, the "great barrier" of the early explorers, covered an area of nearly 600,000 square kilometers with thicknesses exceeding 330 meters overlying seawater hundreds of meters deep. The relationship between this floating ice shelf and its contact with grounded ice was established, representing the extrusion of the ice sheet into the ocean. Complementary geophysical surveys on the polar plateau by Russian scientists also showed that the East Antarctic Ice Sheet had an average thickness of around 2000 meters and a volume of more than 30 million cubic kilometers. The ice sheet contained enough frozen water that if it all melted into the ocean, it would raise sea level nearly 60 meters around the Earth.

The West Antarctic Ice Sheet near Byrd Station also was drilled, producing an ice core more than 1500 meters in length with a detailed record of the Earth's history. As Roger Revelle, a member of the United States IGY committee, had said to the United States House of Representatives at IGY budget hearings in 1957:

> Now here in the glaciers you have a kind of library of what has happened in the past, locked up and frozen. It is a big icebox in which all of the geophysical events of the last million years are preserved. . . . Here you have a layer of volcanic ash that will settle and form a distinct layer in the ice, and you can pick it up all beautifully preserved . . . such things as changes in the ratio of gases in the atmosphere. . . . Here again you have this wonderful uncontaminated layer of snow and ice which is just a series of pages turning over. In them has been kept a continuous record of the amount of meteoric dust coming into the atmosphere.

Ice coring also was conducted in Greenland, at Camp Century, for comparison with the Byrd core for the purpose of revealing historical environmental variations that extended across the Earth.

With most of Antarctica covered by kilometers of ice, it was difficult to analyze many geological formations. Nonetheless, IGY scientists climbed mountains extending above the ice and found new clues that the Antarctic had once been warm. As stated by Laurence Gould (1896–1995), who was the chairman of the United States IGY committee:

> As a geologist, I must single out one exciting discovery of the Byrd Station Traverse during the past summer season . . . to their amazement and delight, they found a tremendous store of fossils: a petrified tree trunk 12 feet long, leaf fossils, fossil bivalve shells and coal beds.

Similar fossil deposits had been found by the early explorers, but these recent discoveries heightened the search to explain how Antarctica could have supported species that only live in warm environments today. Had the entire Earth, including the polar regions, been warmer in the past (Fig 3.1, *top*)? If so, how could forests have flourished in a polar environment that is dark for 6 months each year? If Antarctica had been in a warmer latitude, how could it have moved to its present polar position? (See Chapter 6: Spreading Planet.)

Exposed coastal areas, such as the McMurdo Dry Valleys in southern Victoria Land, contained deposits of rocks and stones piled by past glaciers—moraines revealing the glacial advances and retreats that had occurred during the past million years. The presence of raised beaches emerging out of the ocean around Antarctica further indicated that the last deglaciation was relatively recent, as these coastal areas were still rebounding because of the diminished burden of overlying ice. In all, these geological formations provided independent and complementary evidence to the ice-core records about the glacial history of Antarctica and the Earth (Chapter 7: Flowing Planet).

Oceanography around Antarctica during the IGY was mostly opportunistic and not well coordinated. Only the *Ob* from the Soviet Union, in its cruises during 1956–1958, provided any oceanographic focus. In contrast, 23 stations around the continent focused on aurora and airglow as well as ionospheric studies, contributing to 19 of the 48 volumes in the *Annals of the International Geophysical Year.*

 How does science extend beyond national boundaries and contribute to international cooperation?

The IGY was generating important questions about the dynamics of the Earth as a system of integrated natural phenomena. However, before the IGY had even begun in July 1957, it was apparent that the 18-month IGY period would generate only superficial insights into the natural phenomena in the Antarctic region. For this reason, recommendations were made to ICSU to establish a permanent organization to continue the scientific cooperation in Antarctica after the conclusion of the IGY. In January 1958, ICSU created the Scientific Committee on Antarctic Research (SCAR) for "furthering the coordination of scientific activity in Antarctica with a view to framing a scientific program of circumpolar scope and significance." The IGY focused scientific attention on Antarctica and provided a concrete example of how scientific collaboration can lead to international cooperation. This international scientific framework became the catalyst and basis for the 12 IGY nations in Antarctica to craft and sign the Antarctic Treaty less than a year later, in December 1959.

5

INTERNATIONAL

STEWARDSHIP

To boldly go where no one has gone before.

—*Star Trek*

ANTARCTIC TREATY SYSTEM

The significance of scientific cooperation in Antarctica during the International Geophysical Year (IGY) reverberated through the participating nations. Recognizing their historic opportunity, in 1959 the seven claimant nations (Fig. 3.5) and five nonclaimant nations (Belgium, Japan, South Africa, Soviet Union, and the United States) crafted the Antarctic Treaty and became the initial signatories "with the interests of science and the progress of all mankind" (Box 5.1). The Antarctic Treaty came into force on 23 June 1961, having been ratified by the 12 IGY nations, with the goal of managing Antarctica for the benefit of humanity—an entire continent governed by international cooperation "forever to be used exclusively for peaceful purposes only."

 How does the Antarctic Treaty promote international cooperation and peaceful use of the region south of 60° south latitude?

The Antarctic Treaty is elegant in its simplicity and profound in its capacity to accommodate the "interests of all humankind." The Antarctic Treaty also establishes a precedent for managing regions or resources that exist beyond national jurisdiction. [To facilitate your understanding of the Antarctic Treaty and its ensuing legal framework, texts of the documents that have been signed by the Antarctic Treaty nations from 1959 to 1999 are incorporated into a searchable for-

BOX 5.1   1959 ANTARCTIC TREATY[a]

PREAMBLE

The Governments of Argentina, Australia, Belgium, Chile, the French Republic, Japan, New Zealand, Norway, the Union of South Africa, the Union of Soviet Socialist Republics, the United Kingdom of Great Britain and Northern Ireland, and the United States of America,

Recognizing that it is in the interest of all mankind that Antarctica shall continue forever to be used exclusively for peaceful purposes and shall not become the scene or object of international discord;

Acknowledging the substantial contributions to scientific knowledge resulting from international cooperation in scientific investigation in Antarctica;

Convinced that the establishment of a firm foundation for the continuation and development of such cooperation on the basis of freedom of scientific investigation in Antarctica as applied during the International Geophysical Year accords with the interests of science and the progress of all mankind;

Convinced also that a treaty ensuring the use of Antarctica for peaceful purposes only and the continuance of international harmony in Antarctica will further the purposes and principles embodied in the Charter of the United Nations;

Have agreed as follows:

[a] From the *Antarctic Treaty Searchable Database: 1959–1999.*

mat for interpreting the historical and topical contexts based on your choice of key words or phrases on the Antarctic Treaty Searchable Database: 1959–1999 CD-ROM]. The Preamble and 14 articles of the Antarctic Treaty (Box 5.2) will be used to illustrate this process of analyzing the language and intent of these documents.

 How do the articles of the Antarctic Treaty reflect the history of nations in the region?

Like any good book, the Antarctic Treaty opens in the preamble by introducing the principal characters and their story. The 12 initial signatories were convinced that

```
         BOX 5.2   OUTLINE OF THE
             ANTARCTIC TREATY

Preamble          Interest of all Mankind
Article I         Peaceful Purposes Only
Article II        Freedom of Scientific Investigation
Article III       International Cooperation in Scientific
                    Investigation
Article IV        No Basis for Asserting, Supporting or
                    Denying Claims
Article V         No Nuclear Explosions or Radioactive
                    Waste Disposal
Article VI        Area of Application South of 60°
                    South Latitude
Article VII       Complete Freedom of Access and In-
                    spection by Designated Observers
Article VIII      Jurisdiction by the Contracting Parties
                    over their own Nationals
Article IX        Consulting and Recommending Mea-
                    sures of Common Interest
Article X         Consistent with Charter of the United
                    Nations
Article XI        Resolve Disputes by Peaceful Means
Article XII       Antarctic Treaty Modifications and
                    Amendment
Article XIII      Accession and Ratification
Article XIV       Official Languages and Depository
                    Government
```

. . . a treaty ensuring the use of Antarctica for peaceful purposes only and the continuance of international harmony in Antarctica will further the purposes and principles embodied in the Charter of the United Nations.

This central premise of using Antarctica for "peaceful purposes only" was reinforced in Article I, which expressly prohibited "any measures of a military nature." Moreover, these peaceful activities precluded the establishment of "military bases and fortifications" as well as "carrying out of military maneuvers" or "testing of any type of weapons." "Military personnel or equipment," however, could be used for "scientific research or any other peaceful purpose."

Similarly, Article II fosters the "freedom of scientific investigation" that was originally identified in the Preamble. Article III further promotes "international cooperation in scientific investigation" through information and personnel exchanges "to permit the maximum economy and efficiency of operations." In implementing this article, every encouragement would be given to the "establishment of cooperative working relations with those specialized agencies of the United Nations and other international organizations having a scientific or technical interest in Antarctica." Although the role of the Scientific Committee on Antarctic Research (SCAR) was contemplated in Article III, it was not until the first Antarctic Treaty Consultative Meeting (ATCM) in 1961 that the advisory role of SCAR was specifically identified. This marriage between the policy-making framework of the Antarctic Treaty and the advisory role of SCAR effectively established an open international system for managing human activities in the Antarctic region (Fig. 5.1).

Conversely, it also was necessary to prevent Antarctica from becoming the "scene or object of international discord." In this light, Article IV created an innovative strategy for holding all of the claimant issues in abeyance "while the present Treaty is in force." Nothing in the treaty would be interpreted as a renunciation of "previously asserted rights of or claims to territorial sovereignty." Moreover, the position of nations would not be prejudiced by their "recognition

Antarctic Treaty System

Antarctic Treaty Nations

(International Policy Formulation)

International Organizations

(Scientific or Technical Advice)

FIGURE 5.1   The Antarctic Treaty System was initiated by integrating policy formulation with international "scientific or technical advice" through the Antarctic Treaty and "specialized agencies of the United Nations and other international organizations" (Fig. 2.4b). The Scientific Committee on Antarctic Research, which preceded the 1959 Antarctic Treaty, was formally identified as a relevant international organization along with the International Council of Scientific Unions at the first Antarctic Treaty Consultative Meeting in 1961 (Recommendation I-I). Subsequent Antarctic institutions, committees, and annexes are described in Table 5.2. (See also Antarctic Treaty Searchable Database: 1959–1999 CD-ROM).

or non-recognition of any State's claim," and "no acts or activities shall constitute a basis for asserting, supporting or denying a claim to territorial sovereignty in Antarctica or create any rights of sovereignty in Antarctica."

The Antarctic Treaty was crafted during a period of increasing international tension between the United States and the Soviet Union, with the erection of the Berlin Wall and the precarious fence of the Cold War. Antarctica could have become a nuclear testing or dumping ground because it was a remote, ice-covered environment without permanent human occupation. However, such activities would have involved military personnel and created an "object of discord" among nations. For these reasons, Antarctica was established as the first nuclear-free zone on the Earth (Article V): "Any nuclear explosions in Antarctica and the disposal there of radioactive waste material shall be prohibited."

This Antarctic zone was specified in Article VI as "the area south of 60° South Latitude, including all ice shelves." However, there was a potential conflict with the 1958 United Nations Conventions on the High Seas, which also applied to this region beyond the sovereignty of nations, where "the term 'high seas' means all parts of the sea that are not included in the territorial sea or in the internal waters of a State." For this reason, Article VI of the Antarctic Treaty further clarified that nothing "shall prejudice or in any way affect the rights or exercise of the rights, of any State under international law with regard to the high seas within that area." These "rights" of the high seas include the freedoms of navigation, fishing, laying submarine cables and pipelines, overflight, and scientific research (Chapter 12: The Science Keystone).

"In order to promote the objectives and ensure the observance of the provisions" of the Antarctic Treaty, Article VII provides for the designation of observers who "shall have complete freedom of access at any time to any or all areas of Antarctica." Moreover, this provision means that

> . . . all stations, installations and equipment within those areas, and all ships and aircraft at points of discharging or embarking cargoes or personnel in Antarctica shall be open at all times to inspection. . . .

This provision for unilateral inspections in the Antarctic Treaty area is exceptional among international agreements, especially among other disarmament treaties. In addition, Article VII requires all Antarctic Treaty nations to inform each other about any expeditions and stations as well as any military personnel or equipment that are being used for peaceful purposes.

As with any legal system, laws are only as good as the level of enforcement behind them. However, in Antarctica, enforcement by the international community becomes problematic, especially when military personnel are specifically prohibited for any purpose other than those which are peaceful. To solve this dilemma, Article VIII indicates that all personnel "shall be subject only to the jurisdiction of the Contracting Party of which they are nationals in respect of all acts or omissions." Essentially, each nation has the responsibility and obligation of enforcing the legal principles of the Antarctic Treaty over its own nationals.

Article VIII further requires that all nations "shall immediately consult together with a view to reaching a mutually acceptable solution" if there is a dispute. This "gentlemen's agreement" for enforcing legal principles in Antarctica is unique among nations in cooperatively managing an international region and its resources "for peaceful purposes only."

Article IX.1 of the Antarctic Treaty (Box 5.3) describes the consultative process that is the foundation for the ATCM and the evolution of legal principles in the Antarctic Treaty System (ATS) since 1961. To become a consultative nation, however, a Contracting Party also must demonstrate (Article IX.2)

> . . . its interest in Antarctica by conducting substantial scientific research activity there, such as the establishment of a scientific station or the dispatch of a scientific expedition.

Those nations that have signed the Antarctic Treaty, but have not conducted "substantial scientific research," are referred to as acceding nations, as opposed to consultative nations (Table 5.1). At the turn of the 21st century, there are 27 consultative and 17 acceding nations in the ATS.

 What is the importance of continuous consultation in environmental and resource management?

BOX 5.3   1959 ANTARCTIC TREATY[a]

ARTICLE IX.1: CONSULTING ON MATTERS OF COMMON INTEREST

Representatives of the Contracting Parties named in the preamble to the present Treaty shall meet at the City of Canberra within two months after the date of entry into force of the Treaty, and thereafter at suitable intervals and places, for the purpose of exchanging information, consulting together on the matters of common interest pertaining to Antarctica, and formulating and considering and recommending to their Governments, measures in furtherance of the principles and objectives of the Treaty, including measures regarding:

   a. use of Antarctica for peaceful purposes only;
   b. facilitation of scientific research in Antarctica;
   c. facilitation of international scientific cooperation in Antarctica.
   d. facilitation of the exercise of the rights of inspection provided for in Article VII of the Treaty;
   e. questions relating to the exercise of jurisdiction in Antarctica.
   f. preservation and conservation of living resources in Antarctica.

[a]From the Antarctic Treaty Searchable Database: 1959–1999.

TABLE 5.1   Antarctic Treaty Nations[a]

Nation	Year of accession	Consultative status
Argentina	1961	Yes[b]
Australia	1961	Yes[b]
Austria	1987	No
Belgium	1960	Yes[b]
Brazil	1975	Yes (1983)
Bulgaria	1978	Yes (1998)
Canada	1988	No
Chile	1961	Yes[b]
Columbia	1989	No
Cuba	1984	No
Czech Republic[d]	1993	No
Democratic Peoples Republic of Korea	1987	No
Denmark	1965	No
Ecuador	1987	Yes (1990)
Finland	1984	Yes (1989)
France	1960	Yes[b]
Germany[d]	1979	Yes (1979)
Greece	1987	No
Guatemala	1991	No
Hungary	1984	No
India	1983	Yes (1983)
Italy	1981	Yes (1987)
Japan	1960	Yes[b]
Netherlands[e]	1967	Yes (1990)
New Zealand	1960	Yes[b]
Norway	1960	Yes[b]
Papua New Guinea	1981	No
Peoples Republic of China	1983	Yes (1985)
Peru	1981	Yes (1989)
Poland	1961	Yes (1977)
Republic of Korea	1986	Yes (1989)
Republic of South Africa	1960	Yes[b]
Romania	1971	No
Russian Federation[f]	1960	Yes[b]
Slovak Republic[d]	1993	No
Spain	1982	Yes (1988)
Sweden	1984	Yes (1988)
Switzerland	1990	No
Turkey	1996	No
Ukraine	1992	No
United Kingdom of Great Britain	1960	Yes[b]
United States of America	1960	Yes[b]
Uruguay	1980	Yes (1985)
Venezuela	1999	No

[a] Based on information from the United States Department of State (Ocean Affairs).

[b] Original signatory nation.

[d] Czechoslovakia acceded in 1962 and ceased to exist in 1992. The Czech Republic and Slovak Republic acceded separately in 1993.

[d] German Democratic Republic and the Federal Republic of Germany acceded in 1974 and 1979, respectively, and became one nation after their reunification on 2 October 1990.

[e] Accession for Kingdom in Europe, Suriname, and the Netherlands Antilles.

[f] Original signatory was the Union of Social Socialist Republics in 1960.

Measures that are recommended by these consultative nations "shall become effective when approved by all of the Contracting Parties whose representatives were entitled to participate" in the ATCM, meaning that a measure will not become effective if there is opposition from any single nation. This unanimous consensus rule is an essential feature of the "gentlemen's agreement" (Article VIII) that requires nations to enforce the legal principles which they themselves approved. Moreover, each nation that has contracted with the Antarctic Treaty is obligated under Article X to "exert appropriate efforts, consistent with the Charter of the United Nations," in conducting activities that are not contrary to the "principles or purposes" of the Antarctic Treaty.

 Why is the Antarctic Treaty called a "gentlemen's agreement"?

If a dispute occurs among nations that extends beyond an immediate "mutually acceptable solution," then those Contracting Parties (Article XII)

> . . . shall consult among themselves with a view to having the dispute resolved by negotiation, inquiry, mediation, conciliation, arbitration, judicial settlement or other peaceful means of their own choice.

Any disputes that are not resolved by these approaches shall be referred to the International Court of Justice in The Hague, the Netherlands. However, in all cases, nations will not be absolved from their responsibility to continue seeking dispute resolution "by any of the various peaceful means."

The Antarctic Treaty was designed to accommodate changing international perspectives, and Article XII indicates that the Antarctic Treaty "may be modified or amended at any time by unanimous agreement of the consultative parties." However, it is this article more than any other that has created confusion among the general public because of the statement:

> If *after the expiration of thirty years* [author's emphasis] from the date of entry into force of the present Treaty, any of the Contracting Parties . . . so requests . . . a Conference of all the Contracting Parties shall be held as soon as possible to review the operation of the Treaty.

This statement does not indicate that the treaty "expires" after 30 years from its "date of entry into force," only that a conference may be convened after this 30-year period, which ended in 1991. If this conference ever is convened, however, then any modifications or amendments to the treaty could be approved by a "majority of the Contracting Parties whose representatives are entitled to participate in the meetings provided for under Article IX" (i.e., consultative nations). This majority decision would be far less rigorous than the current unanimous requirement for amending the Antarctic Treaty at all other times. Article XII further specifies the conditions in which nations may withdraw from the ATS and further reflects the nature of the "gentlemen's agreement" through which nations have successfully cooperated in Antarctica during the last half century.

Article XIII discusses the ratification process and identifies the United States of America as the Depository Government because the initial signing of the Antarctic Treaty occurred in Washington, D.C., on 1 December 1959:

> Upon the deposits of ratification by all the signatory States, the present Treaty shall enter into force. . . . Thereafter, the Treaty shall enter into force for any acceding State upon the deposit of its instrument of accession.

In 1961, after all of the deposits of the instruments of accession were received, the Antarctic Treaty was formally "registered by the depository Government pursuant to Article 102 of the Charter of the United Nations." Article XIV concludes that "equally authentic" versions of the Antarctic Treaty "shall be done in English, French, Russian and Spanish languages."

Together, the 14 articles of the Antarctic Treaty, which were signed in 1959 and ratified by all 12 of the original signatories by 1961, have established a unique international system for managing nearly 10% of the Earth "for peaceful purpose only." Throughout its five-decade history, the marriage between science and policy in Antarctica has enabled the ATS (Fig. 5.1) to evolve and accommodate the interests of diverse stakeholders in the world community (Chapter 12: The Science Keystone).

DIVERSE STAKEHOLDERS

Stakeholders, groups that have a demonstrated interest in an activity or region, define the dimensions of the relevant policy framework. In turn, the policy framework identifies the relative roles of the stakeholders in designing and implementing management strategies for that activity or region. In Antarctica, as with most other situations, the variety of stakeholders has expanded over time along with the operation and utility of the policies that govern their activities (Fig. 5.2).

The first stakeholders in the Antarctic were the early explorers and hunters as well as the industries and nations that supported them. Nations such as France and England supported the 18th-century quests of Kerguelen and Cook while Antarctica was still hidden as the unknown continent (*Terra Australis Incognita*). Commercial enterprises, as with the Enderby brothers of England, financed large sealing fleets to Antarctica during the early 19th century. These commercial expeditions mapped large regions of the Antarctic and stimulated further national interests, such as the United States South Sea Exploring Expedition by Wilkes. Technological advances such as the harpoon gun, which was invented for whaling by Svend Foyn (1809–1894) of Norway around 1870, brought new industries to Antarctica—particularly whaling, which was introduced by C. A. Larsen (1860–1924) on South Georgia in 1904.

Soon after, national clamor for priority in the geographical exploration of Antarctica had erupted with a host of government-sponsored expeditions (Chapter 4: Awakening Science). Along with the luminaries who worked in the Antarctic—people such as Bellingshausen, Palmer, Ross, D'Urville, Mawson, Scott, and

FIGURE 5.2   (*Top*) McMurdo Station (77°51′ south, 166°40′ east), operated year-round by the
National Science Foundation, Office of Polar Programs, as part of the United States Antarctic Program. McMurdo Station was established in 1955 for the International Geophysical Year (IGY), which
ran from July 1957 through December 1958. McMurdo Station is the largest national research facility
on Antarctica with over 1500 persons during the austral summer, and several hundred during the
winter. (*Bottom*) Scott Base (77°51′ south, 166°46′ east), operated year-round since the IGY as part
of the New Zealand Antarctic Research Program on Ross Island south of McMurdo Station. Scott
Base currently supports up to 70 persons during the summer and 10 during the winter. (*Facing page*)
Stazione Baia Terranova (74°41′ south, 64°6′ east), operated during the summer since 1985 by the
Italian Programma Nazionale di Ricerche in Antartide along the coast of northern Victoria Land.
Stazione Baia Terranova currently supports more than 70 persons during the summer.

FIGURE 5.2   (*Continued*)

Amundsen—these government and commercial groups represented the initial stakeholders in Antarctica.

Governments soon began to solidify their interests by claiming territories and becoming sovereign authorities. From 1908 through 1943, seven nations identified sectors of Antarctica that they called their own (Fig. 3.5). In each of these sectors, the claimant nation defined itself as the sole stakeholder and authority for managing its region.

Some claimant nations (Australia, France, New Zealand, Norway, and the United Kingdom) recognized each other's sovereignty. Conversely, some claimant nations disagreed with each other's designation as sole authority for a sector— particularly in the Antarctic Peninsula, where the United Kingdom, Chile, and Argentina had overlapping claims. There also were nations, such as the United States, that had expressed territorial interests in Antarctica but had never formalized a specific claim. This diverse assortment of national stakeholders was engaged in Antarctica as the world entered the IGY in 1957–58.

The IGY introduced a new stakeholder into Antarctica, namely the international scientific community. Scientists had been part of various national and commercial expeditions to Antarctica during the previous two centuries, but never before with the mandate of international cooperation on a continental scale. In 1958, the role of science in Antarctica was institutionally strengthened with the establishment of SCAR as the first nongovernmental organization with influence over Antarctic activities. Practically, the international scientific community had become the proprietor of information about Antarctic natural phenomena.

When the Antarctic Treaty came into force in 1961, the original signatories were identified as consultative nations with the collective authority for "formulating, and considering and recommending" all management strategies for the Antarctic region (Box 5.3). This consultative arrangement involved an internal accommodation among the claimant and nonclaimant nations that precluded any "basis for asserting, supporting or denying a claim to territorial sovereignty." The Antarctic Treaty also created a second management tier for nations to accede without the prerogatives of consultative status until they demonstrated "substantial scientific research." By holding all claims in abeyance and by fostering the participation of all nations, the ATS became the unified international stakeholder for the region (Fig. 5.1).

Given the history of Antarctic sealing and whaling (Chapter 10: Ecosystem Conservation), the ATS immediately began resolving issues associated with species' conservation (Table 5.2). In 1963, the Agreed Measures on the Conservation of Antarctic Fauna and Flora became an initial benchmark for protecting Antarctic species and areas. Strategies for dealing with the age-old problem of Antarctic sealing were introduced through the Convention on the Conservation of Antarctic Seals in 1972. During this period, there also was an expanding fishery for a small shrimplike organism called krill (*Euphausia superba*)—which is the central food source of whale, bird, seal, and fish species in the Antarctic marine ecosystem. Recognizing the value of managing ecosystems rather than individual species, the ATS then crafted the 1980 Convention on the Conservation of Antarctic Marine Living Resources.

Living resource issues clearly drew the attention of stakeholders inside and outside of the ATS, but not nearly as much as concerns about nonliving resources (Chapter 11: Environmental Protection). In 1973–1974, the world was faced with the "oil embargo." Coincidentally, while drilling in the seafloor of the Ross Sea to interpret the sedimentary history of Antarctic glaciation, the *Glomar Challenger* also uncovered petroleum residues. Within months, results of this scientific investigation were being reported in the *Wall Street Journal* with implications about significant petroleum deposits on the Antarctic continental shelf. This public speculation about the mineral resource potential of Antarctica, dramatically shifted international attention southward.

During the "establishment phase" of the ATS, from 1961 through 1976, less than one new nation acceded to the Antarctic Treaty every 2 years (Fig. 5.3). With speculation about mineral resources, the entrance rate of nations into the ATS skyrocketed, rising more than 500%! In response, the ATS set out to draft a mineral resources convention, which only further antagonized stakeholders because of perceptions about Antarctica being opened to mineral exploitation.

During the ensuing "international accommodation phase," the ATS stakeholders also began changing qualitatively (Fig. 5.3). In 1977, Poland became the first new consultative nation after being an acceding nation for 16 years. In contrast, the Federal Republic of Germany became the second new consultative nation in 1979 only 2 years after acceding to the Antarctic Treaty. In 1983, India was ad-

TABLE 5.2 Antarctic Resource Management Regimes

Antarctic document	Year signed	Year ratified	Depository government	Associated institutions	Area of jurisdiction
Antarctic Treaty	1959	1961	United States	Specialized agencies of the United Nations and other international organizations having a scientific or technical interest in Antarctica	South of 60°S
Agreed Measures[a]	1964	1964	United States	Scientific Committee on Antarctic Research (SCAR)	South of 60°S
Seals Convention[b]	1972	1978	United Kingdom	SCAR	South of 60°S + sea ice
Living Resources Convention[d]	1980	1984	Australia	CCAMLR Commission, Scientific Committee, Secretariat and Arbitral Tribunal	South of 60°S + Antarctic Convergence
Mineral Resources Convention[d]	1988	Not ratified	New Zealand	CRAMRA Commission, Advisory Committee, Regulatory Committees, Secretariat and Arbitral Tribunal	South of 60°S
Environmental Protocol[e]	1991	1998	United States	PROTOCOL Committee on Environmental Protection and Arbitral Tribunal along with: Annex I: Environmental Impact Assessment Annex II: Conservation of Antarctic Fauna and Flora Annex III: Waste Disposal and Management Annex IV: Prevention of Marine Pollution Annex V: Area Protection and Management	South of 60°S

[a] Agreed Measures for the Conservation of Antarctic Fauna and Flora (AGREED MEASURES).
[b] Convention on the Conservation of Antarctic Seals (CCAS).
[d] Convention on the Conservation of Antarctic Marine Living Resources (CCAMLR).
[d] Convention on the Regulation of Antarctic Mineral Resource Activities (CRAMRA).
[e] Protocol on Environmental Protection to the Antarctic Treaty (PROTOCOL).

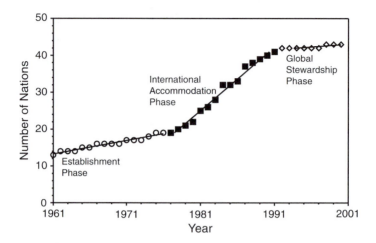

FIGURE 5.3   Stages of international involvement in the Antarctic Treaty System. (Fig. 5.1), based on the combined number of consultative and acceding nations over time (Table 5.1). On average, less than one nation entered the Antarctic Treaty System (ATS) every two years during its "establishment phase" from 1961 to 1976. With heightened concerns about Antarctic resources (Table 5.2), particularly minerals, the entrance rate of nations into the ATS jumped more than 500% during its "international accommodation phase" from 1976 to 1991. After the Protocol on Environmental Protection to the Antarctic Treaty was signed in 1991, with a provision (Article VII) for prohibiting mineral resources activities, the entrance rate of new nations into the ATS leveled as the Antarctic Treaty System progressed into a "global stewardship phase." Modified from Berkman (1992).

mitted directly to consultative status. Along with India as a leader among the "Group of 77" developing nations, Brazil also gained consultative status in 1983 after having been an acceding nation since 1975. During this period, the Antarctic Treaty Consultative Parties also crafted the 1988 Convention on the Regulation of Antarctic Mineral Resource Activities. These changes reflected the external accommodation developed by the ATS to expand its international composition "in the interest of all mankind."

Continuation of the ATS was not taken for granted. As early as 1972, the Second World Conference on National Parks in Grand Teton National Park had recommended that

> . . . the nations party to the Antarctic Treaty should negotiate to establish the Antarctic Continent and the surrounding seas as the first world park, under the auspices of the United Nations.

This conference, which was cosponsored by the International Union for the Conservation of Nature and Natural Resources (IUCN), represented the growing interest and influence of NGOs with regard to Antarctica. IUCN alone had a membership of more than 300 NGOs from more than 100 countries. Creation of the Antarctic Southern Ocean Coalition (ASOC) in 1977, with its membership of more than 80 NGOs, brought additional focus on protecting the Antarctic wilderness.

IUCN along with the World Wildlife Fund and United Nations Environmental Programme continued to develop the concept of a "World Park Antarctica." In 1980, they crafted the World Conservation Strategy, which identified "Antarctica and the Southern Ocean as a priority for international action." It was during this period that the ASOC, representing "citizens from all over the world," began pressing for involvement in the resource negotiations under the ATS.

Developing nations, particularly Malaysia, also began pushing for Antarctica to be internationalized as a "common heritage of mankind" under the authority of the United Nations (Chapter 12: The Science Keystone). As stated by the Malaysian delegate in the First Committee of the United Nations in 1985:

> We wish to see that the system for the management of that continent is one which would be accountable to the international community, which would make it possible for the relevant international agencies to be more directly involved and which would ensure that the *fruits of the exploitation* [author's emphasis] of its resources could be more equitably shared as the common heritage of mankind. . . .

Based on previous on United Nations resolutions on the "Question of Antarctica" in 1983 and 1984, Resolution 40/156 was produced and ultimately approved at the 40th General Assembly in 1985 with large majorities. This resolution called for an expanded United Nations study on the "significance of the United Nations Convention on the Law of the Sea in the southern ocean." In particular, the intent of Resolution 40/156 was reflected in the preamble of the 1982 United Nations Convention on the Law of the Sea (UNCLOS), which states that

> . . . the area of the sea-bed and ocean floor and the subsoil thereof, beyond the limits of national jurisdiction, as well as its resources, are the common heritage of mankind, the exploration and exploitation of which shall be carried out for the benefit of mankind as a whole, irrespective of the geographical location of States.

Did Antarctica fall under the international designation of a "common heritage of mankind" region? Was the United Nations' role in managing Antarctica the same as in the UNCLOS? More pointedly, Resolution 40/156 raised the question of whether the ATS was capable of managing the Antarctic region for the "benefit of all mankind."

Resolution 40/156 also reflected concerns by the developing nations about the closed ATS negotiations on the development of an Antarctic mineral resource regime. Consequently, the Antarctic Treaty Consultative Parties were invited by the United Nations "to inform the Secretary-General of their negotiations to establish a regime regarding Antarctic minerals." In addition, Resolution 40/156, urged the "Antarctic Treaty Consultative Parties to exclude the racist apartheid regime of South Africa." Together, these United Nations resolutions and subsequent responses by the ATS represents the emergence of the developing nations of the world as stakeholders in Antarctica.

"Fruits of the exploitation" have been a preoccupation of nations and all commercial enterprises since humans first arrived in the Antarctic region more than two centuries earlier. In simply stating that "Any activity relating to mineral resources, other than scientific research, shall be prohibited," the 1991 Protocol on Environmental Protection to the Antarctic Treaty removed a potential source of confrontation that had been hanging over the ATS since its inception (Table 5.2).

Consequently, entrance of new nations into the ATS suddenly leveled in 1991 as though the ATS was shifting into a "global stewardship phase" (Fig. 5.3). This transition in the entrance rate of nations in 1991 also coincided with the "expiration of thirty years" from the signing of the Antarctic Treaty in 1961. From the original 12 signatories in 1961, there now are 27 consultative nations and an additional 17 acceding nations in the ATS—which together represent greater than two-thirds of the human population.

Sustainable management of any resource or region requires the effective integration of government, public-policy, economic, and scientific perspectives demonstrated by relevant stakeholders. In Antarctica, the governmental stakeholders are represented by consultative and acceding nations in the ATS as well as developing nations who are participating through the United Nations. The public policy stakeholders are the NGOs and citizenries they represent along with the tourists who are visiting Antarctica in exponentially expanding numbers (Chapter 11: Environmental Protection). The scientific stakeholders are the scientists themselves and the national and international scientific organizations that they compose. The economic stakeholders are the actual or potential private commercial corporations who seek profit through the exploitation of Antarctic resources. Together, these diverse stakeholders will continue to redefine management strategies for Antarctica along with their relative roles and responsibilities.

INTERNATIONAL COOPERATION

All of the stakeholders have an interest in Antarctic resources and jurisdiction, but with disparate agendas and perspectives. Considering their diversity, it is even reasonable to wonder if there is any common ground among them. The solution for building a common focus is at the heart of the ATS and its process of continuous consultation (Chapter 2: Conceptual Integration).

The history of human involvement in Antarctica is analogous to that of civilization, except that Antarctica's trajectory has been accelerated by the relatively uncomplicated dimensions of its remote location and absence of indigenous societies (Fig. 5.3). First there was speculation about the resources and region. When humans finally arrived in the Antarctic region during the late 18th century, they began the process of uncontrolled resource exploitation. Eventually, governments began defining territorial boundaries and asserting sovereignty. This last stage embodies the current status of our civilization—mired in wars and rhetoric as nations continually contest their control over territories and resources.

In Antarctica, however, nations have begun transcending the next level into "global stewardship," where they work together under a realm of common authority without "asserting, supporting or denying" their sovereign claims. At this fundamental level, which is prerequisite for sustainable development in the international arena, the central common interest of all stakeholders is that "Antarctica shall continue forever to be used exclusively for peaceful purposes."

Beyond this starting point, questions of "use" compel the stakeholders to exchange and consider information with a view toward formulating mutually acceptable strategies (Box 5.3). However, this information must first be collected, and thus another common interest of the stakeholders is science. Because of the vastness of Antarctica, which is beyond the logistic capacity of any stakeholder to study alone, there also is common interest in "facilitating international scientific cooperation." These common interests explain why "conducting substantial scientific research" is required for consultative status in the ATS.

Emanating from the "freedom of scientific investigation in Antarctica as applied during the International Geophysical Year," science legitimized international control over Antarctica by creating a mechanism for its management and a goal for its continued rational use. As an evolving foundation of information, science also has linked the past with the future, providing continuity and common ground among stakeholders over time. In essence, international scientific cooperation has become the keystone for using Antarctica for "peaceful purposes only . . . in the interest of all mankind," (Chapter 12: The Science Keystone).

OUR DYNAMIC PLANET

INTERDISCIPLINARY SCIENCE

Connections among geological, physical, chemical, and biological phenomena influence Earth system variability across myriad time and space scales (Fig. III). Parts I and II of this book highlighted Antarctica to introduce the relevance of Earth system science and the spirit of exploration in our evolving global society. Moreover, integrative approaches were identified for individuals to personally assess the interdisciplinary context of the Earth as a system with natural and human dimensions (Chapter 2: Conceptual Integration). This book section will employ these inquiry and relational strategies to foster insights about the fusion of events, entities, and phenomena that shape the world around us.

Over the longest time scales, geological processes create the underlying platforms for subsequent environments (Chapter 6: Spreading Planet). For example, before life could survive on Earth, molten rocks on the surface had to cool and water had to condense into the oceans billions of years ago (Fig. 1.6). As continents subsequently collided and separated, mountain ranges and new ocean basins were produced. What caused this continental movement? What happened in the Earth system as the continents moved across the planet sur-

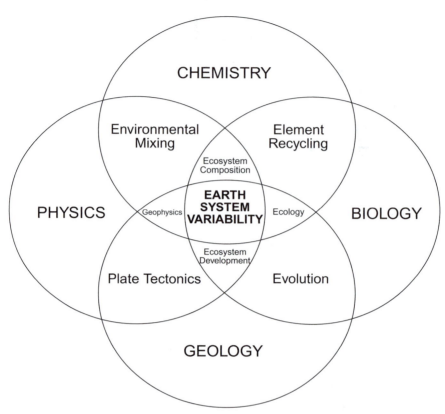

FIGURE III   Rosette of interdisciplinary phenomena that influence Earth system variability over diverse time and space scales. Modified from Berkman (1997b).

face? As a keystone continent, Antarctica illustrates how geological processes have transformed the global environment over millions of years.

Water is a predominant feature of Earth's climate (Chapter 7: Flowing Planet)—whether in the atmosphere as a vapor, in the ocean as a liquid, or in the ice sheets as a solid. During interglacial (warm) and glacial (cold) climate periods, water volumes fluctuate in these different reservoirs (Figs. 1.4 and 1.5)—causing sea level to rise and fall in rhythm with the retreat and advance of the Earth's ice sheets.

Climate also influences the temperature and salinity of water masses that circulate through the sea, redistributing heat and atmospheric gases around the planet like an elaborate conveyor belt. As the coldest region on Earth, where surface seawater sinks into the deep sea because of its low temperature and high density, Antarctica has become the principal source of bottom water in the ocean. Moreover, the frozen isolation of Antarctica forces the persistent atmospheric vortex that spirals westward around the continent, propelling the largest current system in the sea.

Isolated over the South Pole and surrounded by the Southern Ocean, Antarctica further reveals a circumpolar environmental system that expands and contracts in synchrony with the Earth's seasons (Chapter 8: Breathing Planet). Following the polar cycle of night and day, the sea surface around Antarctica freezes and melts annually across more than 14 million square-kilometers—an area that is larger than Europe. In a climate context, this sea-ice oscillation underscores the global variability in evaporation, precipitation, and other factors that regulate ocean-atmosphere dynamics around the planet.

As the Earth's heat sink, with the oldest ice sheets, Antarctica is key to understanding climate changes that are relevant to humankind. Cores of Antarctic ice reveal that greenhouse gases associated with global warming (Chapter 8: Breathing Planet), particularly carbon dioxide from burning fossil fuels, today have the highest atmospheric concentrations in the past half-million years. Ice-core records also provide detailed insights about decadal and century climate changes over the past several millennia—complementing written chronicles about Earth's environment and providing objective insights into the development of our civilization.

Environmental features of the Earth system influence species' adaptations and survival as well as their own biological interactions (Chapter 9: Living Planet). Within the Southern Ocean, even though seawater temperatures hover below 0°C and the environment is dark for nearly half of the year, there are well-adapted and diverse assemblages of species that are among the most productive in the sea—from the single-celled plants consumed by shrimp-like krill up to the fish, bird, seal, and whale predators.

In contrast to the marine ecosystem, the frozen and barren landscapes on Antarctica shelter the most impoverished terrestrial biota of any continent. Eking out a living in permanently ice-covered lakes or even within the interstices of sandstone, these terrestrial species provide analogs for life elsewhere in our solar system. Together, Antarctic marine and terrestrial ecosystems illustrate general ecological principles that govern the dynamics of biological assemblages.

Earth system variability is influenced by geological, chemical, physical, and biological phenomena (Fig. III). With a view toward the future, Antarctica provides a well-constrained framework for learning about the interdisciplinary nature and dynamics of the Earth system over time and space.

6

SPREADING PLANET

To one who thoughtfully ponders the centuries
and surveys the whole in the clear light of the spring,
oceans and continents alone are of account.
                    —Johann von Goethe (1808), Faust

GEOLOGIC TIME

Time and space (Fig. 2.3) provide the conceptual framework for interpreting events, entities, and phenomena that influence the Earth system (Fig. 6.1). Most of Earth's history is written in the rocks and sediments over geological time scales involving the transformation of oceanic and continental environments during millions and billions of years. Moreover, geologic phenomena influence the evolution and extinction of species, creating wholesale changes in the ecosystems that characterize different eras of the Earth system (Fig. 1.6).

Geologic time, however, is only a relative term. For example, within a geologic era climate conditions can shift with the advance and retreat of ice masses on Earth. Such glacial–interglacial cycles can extend across tens of millennia with ice-volume changes that alter sea level, ocean circulation, atmospheric connections, and habitat characteristics across the planet.

Within a given climatic period, populations persist along with their aquatic or terrestrial habitats over ecological time scales. Based on the species' adaptations, populations may even survive in a single location for millennia as exemplified by stands of bristlecone pines (*Pinus longaeva*) in the White Mountains of California or banks of moss (*Polytrichum alpestre* and *Chorisodontium aciphylum*) in the Antarctic Peninsula region that are 5000 to 6000 years old.

Along with their spatial dimensions, geological and ecological periods reveal

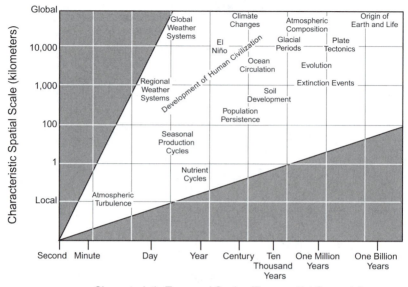

FIGURE 6.1   The envelope of Earth system phenomena represented across exponential scales of time and space (Fig. 2.3). Geological processes transform oceanic and terrestrial environments over millions and billions of years (Fig. 1.6). Ecological processes operate, on the opposite end of the spectrum, in relation to the persistence of populations and their habitats over periods that may be shorter than seasons. Modified from Earth System Science Committee (1988).

the spectrum of dynamic processes that activate the Earth system (Fig. 6.1). Just as the Earth can be portrayed over space in relation to density layers through the atmosphere and planetary interior (Figs. 1.1 and 1.2), time intervals are represented by depositional layers in rocks, sediments, ice, and various biota.

> **How can sediment cores and other stratigraphic records be used for interpreting environmental variability?**

Over geological periods, from top to bottom, the Transantarctic Mountains contain strata that increase in age from several million to greater than 1 billion years (Fig. 3.1). In the East Antarctic Ice Sheet, there are superimposed layers of snow that have accumulated over several glacial–interglacial cycles during the past half-million years. Over ecological time scales, growth rings in trees and other living organisms reveal seasonal to millennial periods. In general, such stratigraphic sequences are progressively formed by relatively recent deposits overlaying older materials.

Beyond their chronological features, stratigraphic sequences also contain compositional information about the environmental conditions that existed when and where the strata were deposited. For example, extensive coal seams along the Transantarctic Mountains indicate that the environment was wet and warm enough to support the luxuriant growth of temperate forests more than 200 million years ago. Compiled in a global context—from ocean and land areas, lakes and ice, trees and other organisms—such proxy records provide clues for reconstructing the history of the Earth system and its varying environmental conditions over geological and ecological periods (Fig. 6.1).

 Why would the Antarctic environment have been wet and warm in the geologic past?

CONTINENTAL SEPARATION

Viewed from outer space, the Earth is a blue planet covered mostly by oceans with a scattering of various land masses (Plate 1), which primarily occur in the northern hemisphere (Fig. 1.4). The largest land masses are continents, of which there are seven today: Africa, Antarctica, Asia, Australia, Europe, North America, and South America. Development of these continents and the oceans that separate them is a fundamental feature of the Earth system.

Two hundred million years ago, lush floras with large glossopterid ferns covered the Earth while dinosaurs roamed the land. By 65 million year ago, *Glossopteris* and the dinosaurs had gone extinct. Nonetheless, fossils of these species can be found on all continents, including Antarctica. The vast seams of coal running through the Transantarctic Mountains (Fig. 3.1, *top*) also overlay the Beacon sandstone formation, which exists in Australia, Africa, and South America.

 What does the distribution of extinct species and geological formations—across land masses that are now separated by oceans—suggest about past continental configurations and the dynamics of the Earth system?

To interpret the past configuration of the Earth's land masses, take a look at a world map that outlines the opposing continents across the Atlantic Ocean in the northern and southern hemispheres. This view of the planet, along with fossils and distinctive geological features that crossed continental boundaries, motivated Alfred Wegener (1880–1930) to speculate in 1912 that the continents had actually drifted apart from a supercontinent which he called Pangaea (all land).

Wegener argued that if the Earth could move vertically in relation to vertical forces, as with mountains, then it also could move laterally. However, largely because there was no known geophysical process that could laterally transport continents of rock through solid sea floor in a rigid Earth, Wegener's hypothesis of "continental drift" was rejected for the next half century.

84

In 1937, Alexander Du Toit (1878–1948) began to revive the "continental drift" hypothesis with geological and paleontological data from the Southern Hemisphere. However, it was not until 1962, when Harry Hess (1906–1969) developed arguments about sea-floor spreading, that the underlying mechanisms for "continental drift" began emerging. Rather than having the continents move actively through the ocean, as suggested by Wegener, Hess reasoned that the continents are being transported by giant convection cells within the Earth's interior that create and destroy crustal material (Fig. 6.2).

Support for the sea-floor spreading mechanism also came in the early 1960s with the discovery of mirror-image patterns of magnetic stripes on opposite sides of the 40,000 kilometer volcanic ridge that runs through the middle of the entire ocean. Locked into molten magma as it cooled and spread away from this mid-ocean ridge, these magnetic stripes represent reversals in the Earth's magnetic field as it switched between the north and south polar regions. Today, for example, the north geomagnetic pole is located around the latitude of 79° north (in the vicinity of northwest Greenland), which is more than 1000 kilometers away from the north geographic pole at 90° north. Additional evidence about sea-floor spreading was revealed by the increasing thickness and age of sedimentary deposits from the mid-ocean ridge toward the continental margins.

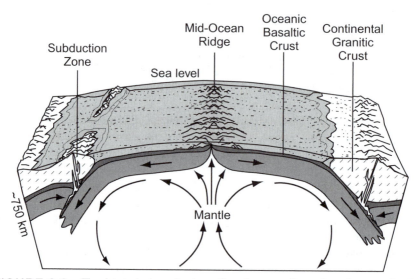

FIGURE 6.2   The plate tectonic mechanisms of sea-floor spreading and mantle convection that have been used to explain how oceans are created as continents drift apart. Crust and mantle of the Earth form the lithosphere, which varies in density and thickness between the oceans and continents (Fig. 1.2). Rigid lithospheric plates float on the molten mantle, which extends through the core of the Earth. Convection cells in the mantle, associated with upwelling magma at mid-ocean ridges and downwelling crust at subduction zones, push and pull the continents apart to account for their changing geometry through geologic time (Fig. 6.3). Modified from Wylie (1976).

During the 1960s, seismic measurements through the Earth further revealed that the crusts of the continents and oceans were different. Continents have a relatively light granitic crust that is 30 to 40 kilometers thick. In contrast, the ocean basins have a relatively dense basaltic crust that is only 6 to 10 kilometers thick—which is why the continents are above sea level and the sea-floor is an average of 4 kilometers below (Fig. 1.3). Together, these oceanic and continental crusts compose the upper part of the lithosphere, which has a total thickness of 100 to 150 kilometers (Fig. 1.2).

In turn, the lithosphere is broken into seven major "plates" (along with several minor plates) around the Earth that are separated by ridges and fracture zones. These lithospheric plates are internally rigid and are floating on the underlying molten asthenosphere (Fig. 1.2) in continuous motion relative to each other and the Earth's rotational axis. In 1965, T. J. Wilson unified this global framework of lithospheric plate motion with observations of continental drift and sea-floor spreading into the theory of plate tectonics.

As hypothesized by Hess, plate tectonics works like giant convection cells: cool, rigid slabs of lithosphere flow downward through the asthenosphere, where they are melted and recirculated in the mantle up through the crust at the mid-ocean ridge (Fig. 6.2). Regions on the Earth where the lithosphere is subducting into the mantle occur at plate boundaries and are characterized by earthquakes and volcanism, such as along the "ring of fire" surrounding the Pacific Ocean. Subduction zones also create the deepest trenches in the ocean, such as the Marianas Trench, which exceeds 11,000 meters below the sea surface and is deeper than the height of Mt. Everest (Fig. 1.3).

To illustrate plate tectonics, consider a simple experiment the next time you take a bath. Place several pieces of paper (which correspond to rigid lithospheric plates) on the water surface. Then circle your left hand counterclockwise and your right hand clockwise (top to bottom) underneath the pieces of paper to mimic mantle convection cells upwelling toward the surface of the Earth at the mid-ocean ridge. Subsequent motion of the overlying paper pieces is analogous to the global geometry of lithospheric plates over geologic time.

Oceans with subduction zones spread faster than those without because they are being pulled apart as well as being pushed apart at the mid-ocean ridge. For example, the north Pacific Ocean is spreading 6 centimeters per year, in contrast to the Atlantic Ocean, which is spreading less than 2 centimeters per year in the absence of substantial subduction. Considering that the Pacific Ocean has an average width of 13,000 kilometers, at its current spreading rate it would take around 200 million years for this ocean basin to achieve its modern dimensions. In contrast, formation of the 5000-kilometer-wide Atlantic Ocean of today would have taken around 250 million years. These back-of-the-envelope estimates (Chapter 1: Global Dimensions) indicate that oceans are created over hundreds of millions of years.

Based on the various datasets associated with plate movements, it is now recognized that around 180 million years ago Pangaea fractured into two smaller

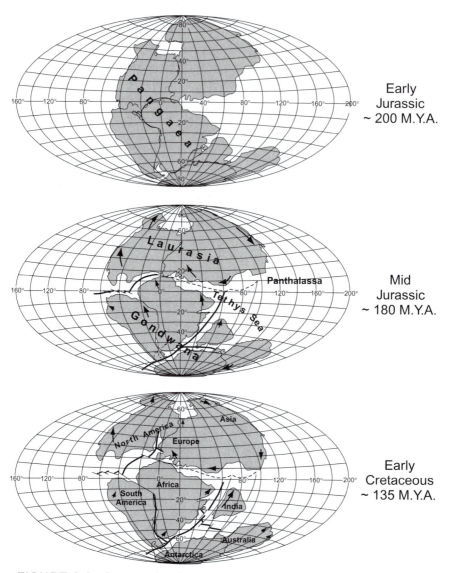

Early
Jurassic
~ 200 M.Y.A.

Mid
Jurassic
~ 180 M.Y.A.

Early
Cretaceous
~ 135 M.Y.A.

FIGURE 6.3   Reconstruction of Pangaea (all land) during the early Jurassic surrounded by the ancestral Pacific (Panthalassa) and Mediterranean (Tethys) oceans. Pangaea separated into the Laurasia and Gondwana supercontinents around 180 million years ago (mya). By the early Cretaceous, the North Atlantic and Indian oceans had begun opening along with the separation of the West Gondwana continents (South America and Africa). India and Madagascar separated from the Antarctica–Australia complex of East Gondwana, which had become positioned over the South Pole by the late Cretaceous. Australia and South America subsequently separated from Antarctica by 55 and 25 mya, respectively. Global configurations of continents today and predicted 50 million years into the future are shown. Arrows indicate plate motion directions. Solid lines in the ocean are spreading ridges and dashed lines are trenches (Fig. 6.2). Modified from Dietz and Holden (1976).

Glacier Bay Eagles Nest Lodge
915 North State
Orem, Utah 84057
801-426-8217
www.Glacierbayfishing.com

Salmon, Halibut, Lingcod
Yelloweye, Rockfish
Save hundreds over comparable trips.
All inclusive $2,500.00
We accept Visa and Mastercard.
Ask about group discounts.

T19 P1 DAVID A DIRLAM
21013 HICKORY BND
GARDEN RIDGE TX 78266-2541

Worlds Best
Halibut Fishing

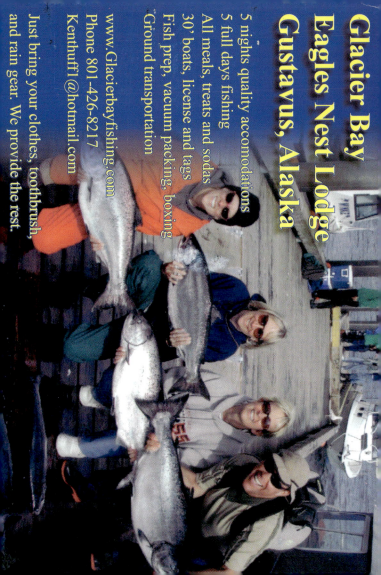

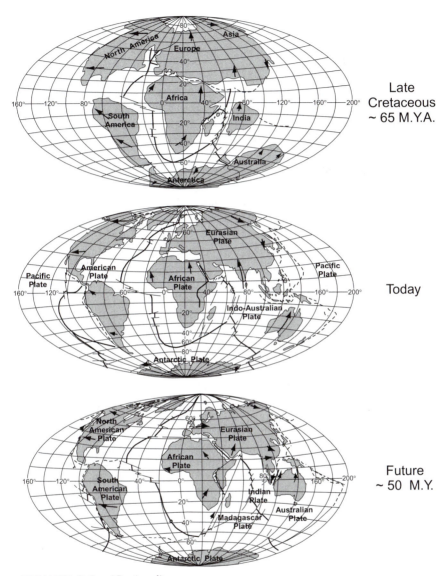

FIGURE 6.3   (*Continued*)

supercontinents: Laurasia in the northern hemisphere and Gondwana in the southern hemisphere (Fig. 6.3). Twenty million years later, Gondwana itself began
fracturing into two smaller continental masses: East Gondwana (Antarctica, Australia, India, Madagascar) and West Gondwana (South America and Africa).
    Detachment of South America and Africa followed with the formation of the

South Atlantic Ocean during the late Jurassic (Fig. 6.3). By 135 million years ago, Madagascar and India began moving northward from Australia and Antarctica. Eventually, India slammed into Asia and created the Himalayas. Like a giant jigsaw puzzle being pulled apart, the individual continental pieces of the modern Earth system began to appear.

At the end of the "age of dinosaurs," 65 million years ago, Antarctica already was located over the South Pole where—as Captain Cook remarked—it had been "fixed since creation." This polar position of Antarctica was like a key that finally unlocked the remaining sub-continents of the Gondwana complex during the Cenozoic (Table 6.1).

Around 55 million years ago, as the South Tasman Rise and Australia separated from the Gondwana Province of East Antarctica (30° west to 160° east longitude), a shallow-water connection between the southern Indian and Pacific Oceans was created. By the start of the Oligocene, around 38 million years ago, an ocean

TABLE 6.1   Antarctic Environmental Changes and Events during the Cenozoic Epochs[a]

Age (million years)	Cenozoic epoch	Antarctic environmental change or climatic event
55	Paleocene	Australia began to separate from Antarctica; complete circumpolar current blocked by South Tasman Rise
39	Eocene	South Tasman Rise separated and allowed circumpolar current; shallow water connection between Southern Indian and Pacific Oceans
38	Oligocene	Climate–glacial threshold at the Eocene–Oligocene boundary; sea ice began to form; rapid temperature decrease to nearly 5°C; crisis in deep sea faunas; increased bottom water formation and thermohaline circulation initiated; major deepening of the calcium carbonate compensation depth
38–25	Oligocene	Antarctic glaciation, but no ice cap; cool temperate vegetation disappearing from Antarctica
30–25	Oligocene	Opening of the Drake Passage; deeper and unrestricted circumpolar flow; change in deep-sea sediment distribution patterns
14–11	Miocene	Antarctic ice cap formed; closure of Australian–Indonesian deep sea passage; calcareous biogenic sediments displaced northward and replaced by siliceous sediments from diatoms with higher sedimentation rates; development of Antarctic Polar Front at the Antarctic Convergence
5	Pliocene	Ice volume increased beyond present; global climate cooling
3	Pliocene	Closure of the Isthmus of Panama and Northern Hemisphere ice-sheet development
1.8	Pleistocene	Increased upwelling at the Antarctic Divergence and increased biogenic productivity around Antarctica; glacial–interglacial cycles

[a] See Figure 6.5.

already had formed southward of Australia that enabled the development of an incomplete circumpolar current system around Antarctica.

The Andean Province of West Antarctica, in the Antarctic Peninsula and Ross Sea regions, began separating from South America around 30 million years ago. With the full opening of the Drake Passage between South America and the Antarctic Peninsula, around 25 million years ago, Antarctica finally was surrounded completely be a circumpolar ocean—geographically and thermally isolating the entire continent from the other land masses on Earth.

Another major oceanographic event occurred around 3 million years ago, when the Isthmus of Panama between North and South America closed, altering oceanographic and atmospheric exchanges between the equatorial Pacific and Atlantic Oceans—coincident with glacial development of the Arctic. Driven by plate tectonics over geologic time scales (Figs. 6.2 and 6.3), such changes in the configurations of the continents and ocean basins effectively establish boundary conditions that constrain the environmental dynamics of the Earth system.

ANTARCTIC GLACIATION

With its progressive isolation during the Cenozoic (Fig. 6.3), Antarctica became the coldest region on Earth. Moreover, Antarctic cooling has persisted and intensified over millions of years with temperature decreases propagating across the planet. This impact of Antarctica—as the global heat sink—is recorded over geological time scales in the sediments of the surrounding Southern Ocean.

 How did plate tectonics influence the progressive glaciation of Antarctica?

Profiles of sedimentary deposits commonly are generated remotely, across hundreds of square kilometers, by the reflection of sound waves traveling through the sea floor. This acoustic technique is based on the principle that sound velocities vary with the density of the medium (i.e., sound propagates fastest through solids, slower through liquids, and slowest through gases), such that different density or compositional layers can be contrasted. One of the most powerful acoustic techniques in marine research—multichannel seismic reflection—utilizes streamers of hydrophones (often extending several kilometers behind a vessel) that record the two-way travel time of sound waves emitted from the ship through the sediments and reflected back to the ship.

Based on the velocity of the sound waves from the multichannel seismic surveys (around 2 kilometers per second), two-way travel times indicate that the underlying sediments in the Ross Sea are thousands of meters thick (Fig. 6.4). The acoustic profiles also reveal well-stratified sedimentary deposits as well as erosional surfaces. Aside from the spatial features of the sediments, however, the acoustic profiles lack information on sediment compositions and ages.

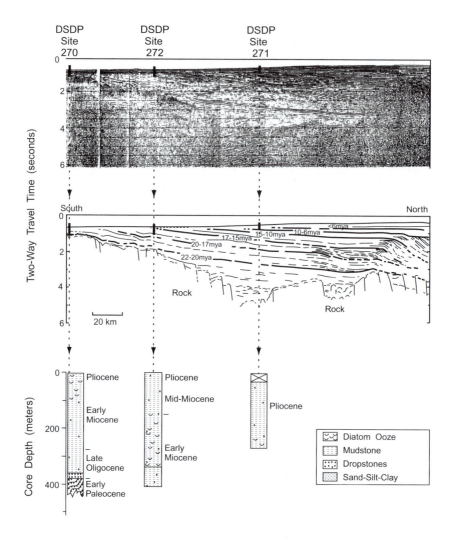

FIGURE 6.4 (*Upper panel*) Multichannel seismic profile collected in north-westward direction from the Ross Ice Shelf (around 77° south and 175° west) showing acoustically well-stratified sediments. Two-way travel times of the multichannel seismic data (based on sound-wave velocities around 2 kilometers per second) indicate that the sediments are thousands of meters thick in the Ross Sea. Locations of the Deep Sea Drilling Project (DSDP) Leg 28 core sites 270, 271, and 272 are identified. (*Middle panel*) Interpretation of the multichannel seismic data with ages (in millions of years ago, mya) for the major sedimentary horizons. (*Lower panel*) Information about the composition and origin of the different sediment layers that were cored and collected during DSDP Leg 28 (see text). Based on multichannel seismic data from Cooper *et al.* (1991) and sediment stratigraphy interpretations from Anderson and Bartek (1992).

To groundtruth these acoustic profiles with compositional data on the sedimentary deposits, sophisticated coring technologies from the Deep Sea Drilling Program (DSDP) and its Ocean Drilling Program successor have been required. For example, cores from DSDP Leg 28, which were collected from the Ross Sea by the *Glomar Challenger* in 1972–73, recovered sediments from the early Cenozoic when Antarctica was separating from Australia (Table 6.1). These Ross Sea sediment cores contained deposits of planktonic algae (diatoms) and single-celled animals (foraminifera) that were distributed by currents and water masses in the ocean (Chapter 7: Flowing Planet). In particular, the diatom oozes reflect high concentrations of nutrients upwelling from the deep sea that enhanced their productivity (Chapter 9: Living Planet). In addition, sediment cores from DSDP Leg 28 contained ethane and methane which subsequently roused international interest in potential Antarctic mineral resources (Chapter 11: Environmental Protection).

Together, the combination of sediment acoustic and core profiles (Fig. 6.4) indicate that there was extensive ice-sheet scouring in the Ross Sea region by 24 million years ago. During the next 15 million years, there were episodes of glacial erosion followed by prolonged periods of marine deposition when the ice sheet was not grounded on the sea floor. Since the beginning of the Pleistocene epoch, nearly 2 million years ago, the frequency of ice-sheet grounding events has increased along with the pronounced occurrence of glacial–interglacial cycles in the Earth system (Table 6.1).

Sediments from other deep-sea cores around Antarctica indicate that diatom deposition has shifted toward the lower latitudes along with the northern boundary of the Southern Ocean since the early Oligocene. Throughout this period, there also was a northward shift in the deposition of ice-rafted debris (stones dropped onto the seafloor) from melting icebergs around Antarctica. Similarly, there was a northward displacement of planktonic foraminifera, which have calcium carbonate shells that increasingly dissolve as seawater temperatures become colder. Together, these sedimentary deposits paint a rough picture of intensifying Antarctic glaciation and climate cooling during the last 38 million years.

Within individual foraminifera, however, there are higher resolution geochemical signatures of the ambient environmental conditions that existed when their calcareous shells were precipitated. Specifically, shells of these microscopic animals contain both heavy and light isotopes of oxygen (^{18}O and ^{16}O, respectively) that can be related directly to global temperatures and ice volumes. During periods of seawater cooling, marine carbonates increasingly incorporate ^{18}O relative to ^{16}O. In addition, because ^{18}O evaporates more slowly than ^{16}O, seawater concentrations of the heavy isotope increase as the light isotope is transported by water vapor from the ocean onto the ice caps. Therefore, during glacial periods when the seawater is relatively cold and enriched in the heavy oxygen isotope, calcareous marine species precipitate more ^{18}O than ^{16}O.

The ratios (R) of $^{18}O/^{16}O$ in samples and standards, after being multiplied by

1000 to magnify the small differences, conventionally are expressed by delta notation (δ) in units of parts per thousand (per mil, ‰):

$$\delta = \left(\frac{R_{sample}}{R_{standard}} - 1 \right) \times 1000 \qquad (6.1)$$

Given the fractionation of oxygen isotopes, $\delta^{18}O$ values become more positive in
marine carbonates and more negative in glacial ice during climate cooling conditions. Conversely, under climate warming conditions, $\delta^{18}O$ values become more
negative in marine carbonates and more positive in glacial ice. For marine carbonates, a 1‰ increase in $\delta^{18}O$ equates with a temperature decrease of nearly 4°C in
the ambient seawater.

Cenozoic sedimentary deposits from around Antarctica contain calcareous foraminifera that had been living in the water (plankton) near the sea surface as well
as on the sediment (benthos) in the deep sea. Even though these planktonic and
benthic foraminifera lived in widely separated habitats, the $\delta^{18}O$ values in their
calcium carbonate shells had increased overall from around -1‰ to 4‰ during
the past 55 million years. This 5‰ change in the oxygen isotope composition
of the foraminifera equates with a temperature drop of more than 15°C—reflecting the long-term cooling trend of the Earth system throughout the Cenozoic
(Fig. 6.5).

Within the Cenozoic epochs (Table 6.1), seawater temperatures dropped suddenly at the Eocene–Oligocene boundary, to approximately 5°C. During the Oligocene it appears that Antarctic glaciation became widespread and that there was
extensive sea-ice production. As a consequence of Antarctic cooling, surface waters became denser and began sinking into the deep sea, where they subsequently
form the bottom waters of the ocean.

The next major climate cooling threshold was achieved during the middle
Miocene, around 14 million years ago, when foraminifera $\delta^{18}O$ values from the
Southern Ocean dramatically increased by more than 2‰ as seawater temperatures decreased to nearly 0°C (Fig. 6.5). This temperature decrease was associated
with enlargement of the East Antarctic Ice Sheet and a circumpolar temperature
drop in the coastal zone around the continent. As a consequence of this middle
Miocene cooling event around Antarctica, the slope of the temperature gradient
between high and low latitudes markedly steepened in the ocean and atmosphere.

The most recent climatic cooling transition was reached during the Pliocene,
around 3 million years ago, when seawater temperatures dipped below 0°C around
Antarctica and ice sheets began developing in the Northern Hemisphere. Decreasing temperatures associated with expanding ice sheets in West Antarctica and circumpolar sea-ice extent during the Pliocene intensified the circulation, upwelling,
and ensuing productivity of the Southern Ocean. During this period, coastal marine species' extinctions occurred in the Arctic and Antarctic along with the emergence of deep-sea faunas into shallow polar oceans. At lower latitudes, in areas
such as New Zealand, there also were the first appearances of cold-water marine
fauna during the late Pliocene.

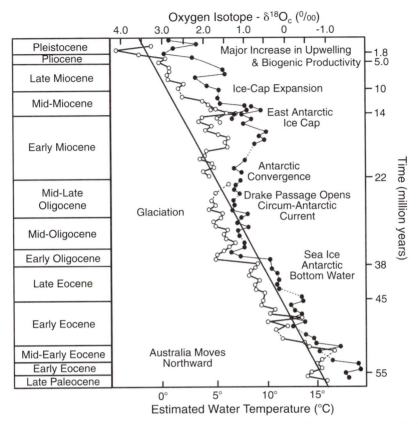

FIGURE 6.5 Estimated seawater temperature changes during different Cenozoic eras (Table 6.1) based on the oxygen isotope ratios in the calcium carbonate shells of planktonic (closed circles) and benthic (open circles) foraminifera from marine sediment cores around Antarctica. A 1‰ shift in the $\delta^{18}O$ value equates with a temperature change of nearly 4°C. Note the major cooling events at the Eocene–Oligocene and Pliocene–Pleistocene boundaries. The long-term cooling trend has been ongoing throughout the past 55 million years (solid line) with relatively short-term fluctuations that presumably will continue into the future. Modified from Kennett (1977).

Northern Hemisphere glaciation during the Pliocene, which occurred nearly 10 million years after the middle Miocene climate threshold, was influenced by the closure of the Isthmus of Panama between North and South America. With the Middle American Seaway shut down, changes in the oceanic current systems and atmospheric precipitation patterns allowed more moisture to be transported into the Arctic region (Chapter 8: Breathing Planet). Subsequent shifts in the $\delta^{18}O$ values in the ocean, by more than 1‰, reflect the glacial–interglacial cycles that have dominated Earth's climate ever since (Chapter 7: Flowing Planet).

PLATE 1   Apollo 17 view of the Earth system (December 1972) showing clouds, oceans, continents, and the Antarctic ice sheets at the bottom of the planet (National Aeronautics and Space Administration).

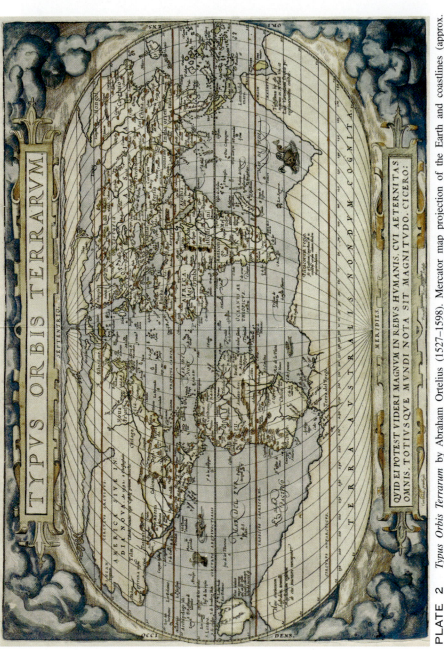

PLATE 2 *Typus Orbis Terrarum* by Abraham Ortelius (1527–1598). Mercator map projection of the Earth and coastlines (approx. 1:80,000,000 scale) produced in Antwerp circa 1570 showing the results of Ferdinand Magellan's circumnavigation of the globe 1519–1522. Reproduced with permission from the Nan Kivell Map Collection, National Library of Australia.

PLATE 3 **(Top)** Remote sensing of Earth longitude, latitude, and elevation above sea level measured with global positioning system (GPS) antennas receiving satellite signals in Taylor Valley, on the west side of McMurdo Sound along the coast of Victoria Land. **(Bottom)** Remotely operated vehicle (ROV) with 100-meter umbilical cord attached to the joystick controls, generator, monitor, and video recorder after making a dive under the sea ice at Edmonson Point.

PLATE 4   (**Top**) Moon moving around the horizon (as opposed to overhead at low latitudes) taken with a 30-second film exposure during the austral winter in 1981 across McMurdo Sound. (**Bottom**) Cold, dense air masses falling from 3000-meter elevations on the polar plateau along the Priestly Glacier, forming the katabatic winds with speeds exceeding 100 knots blowing snow dozens of kilometers off the coast. Viewed over Inexpressible Island (74°54′ south, 163°39′ east), with emerged beaches seen as parallel bands of snow near the coastline that reflect changes in sea level during the past 10,000 years.

PLATE 5   (Top) Adélie penguin, *Pygoscelis adeliae,* rookery at Adélie Cove (74°32′ south, 164°50′ east) with guano deposits that have been radiocarbon-dated as being 6000 years old. (Bottom) Paired shells of 5000-year-old radiocarbon-dated fossil scallops in life position from emerged-beach terraces near South Stream (77°27′ south, 163°44′ east) in west McMurdo Sound.

PLATE 6   (Top) Giant helmet jellyfish, *Periphylla periphylla,* which can exceed 35 centimeters in diameter (showing a human hand for scale), floating in the plankton in front of Stazione Baia Terranova. (Middle) Diverse benthic species on the sea floor in Explorers Cove (77º34′ south, 163º35′ east) in west McMurdo Sound, including coralline algae, polychaete worms, feather stars, brittle stars, sponges, scallops, and a giant sea squirt. (Bottom) Tagged Antarctic scallops, *Adamussium colbecki,* in Explorers Cove in 1986. Some of these 80-millimeter scallops were recovered in the late 1990s. After more than a decade, they had grown only a few millimeters, indicating that this benthic species has a century-long lifespan.

PLATE 7 **(Top)** Emperor penguin, *Aptenodytes forsteri,* colony, with chicks in gray down, on the sea ice at Cape Washington (74°39′ south, 165°25′ east) in December 1998. **(Bottom)** Weddell seal, *Leptonychotes weddelli*, with cub on the sea ice at Hutton Cliffs (77°44′ south, 166°51′ east) along Ross Island in east McMurdo Sound. The tidal crack, where the sea ice contacts the coast, is shown under the icefalls.

PLATE 8   (Top) View from a C-130 Hercules. Antarctica is the continent of extremes with the largest ice sheets, highest average elevation, greatest volume of freshwater, coldest temperatures, lowest average humidity, simplest terrestrial ecosystems, largest annual variation in sea-ice coverage, deepest continental shelves, largest production of marine biomass, and longest history of international stewardship. (Bottom) "Recognizing that it is in the best interest of all mankind that Antarctica shall continue forever to be used exclusively for peaceful purposes . . . ."

7

FLOWING PLANET

*Since the measuring device has been constructed by the ob-
server . . . we have to remember that what we observe is not
nature in itself but nature exposed to our method of questioning.*
—*Werner Karl Heisenberg (1958),* Physics and Philosophy

FLUCTUATING ICE SHEETS

The geological framework imposed by the tectonic movement and ultimate positioning of the continents has exerted a major influence on Earth's climate. Not only have vast oceans been created as continents drifted apart, but pathways for air and sea currents to circulate heat and moisture around the planet have been produced.

Along with the progressive isolation of Antarctica in its polar position during the Cenozoic (Table 6.1), the Earth system has been cooling. However, superimposed on this long-term cooling trend are short-term climate fluctuations (Fig. 6.5). These climate shifts, particularly since the Pliocene, underscore the ocean–atmosphere coupling that connects environments across the Earth.

 How is Antarctica related to the global climate?

Atmospheric and oceanic engines of the climate system are fueled by incoming solar radiation. The average flux of solar energy that reaches the top of the Earth's atmosphere—called the "solar constant"—is taken to be 1367 watts per square meter. The "solar constant," however, is a misnomer because it varies in relation to solar activity with changes that may range several watts per square meter during the 11-year sunspot cycle or other periods.

For scale, a 1-watt increase in the solar constant would be equivalent to adding a single small Christmas tree light every square meter across the surface of the Earth. Even such tiny changes in solar output have a measurable effect on global temperatures, as suggested by the co-occurrence of the Maunder Minimum in sunspot activity and the most intense cold period of the "Little Ice Age" between 1640 and 1710, which is well chronicled in paintings from Europe.

At all latitudes, the annual solar radiation budget is influenced by the tilt of the Earth's axis during its 365-day orbit around the Sun. Incoming radiation and heating from the Sun is least variable in the zone along the equator (Fig. 7.1). Daily, in these low-latitude regions, there are 12-hour periods of sunlight and darkness as the Earth completes a revolution around its axis. Toward higher latitudes, solar radiation variability increases, ultimately to the poles, which have 24-hour periods of continuous summer sunlight and winter darkness (Plate 4).

The general profile of solar radiation across the Earth also varies over millennial time scales with changes in the tilt of the Earth's rotational axis and shape of its elliptical orbit around the Sun (Fig. 7.2). Every 23,000 years, precession of the equinoxes changes the month when the Earth is closest to the Sun (perihelion) from December to June. On a 41,000-year cycle, the obliquity or tilt of the Earth's axis wobbles between 22.1° and 24.5° away from the plane of the Earth's orbit. Approximately every 100,000 years, there is a slight change in the eccentricity of the Earth's elliptical orbit around the Sun.

These long-term shifts in the orbital geometry between the Earth and the Sun were first calculated in 1941 by the Yugoslavian astronomer Milutin Milankovitch (1879–1958), who recognized that solar radiation cycles could be a dominant

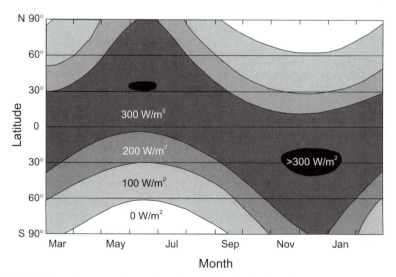

FIGURE 7.1   Contours of incoming solar radiation (with units of watts per square meter) on the Earth's surface each month across all latitudes today. Modified from Pickard and Emery (1982).

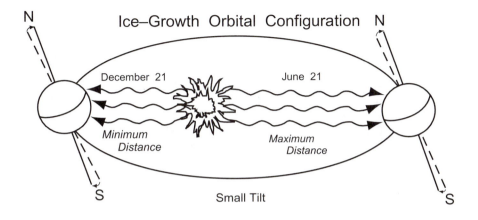

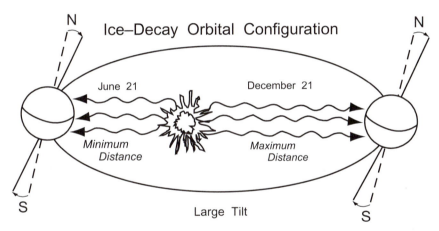

FIGURE 7.2   Variations in the Earth's orbit around the Sun that influence glacial–interglacial climate cycles over millennial time scales (Fig. 7.3). As hypothesized first by Milankovitch (1938), changes in Earth's insolation are influenced by precession of the equinoxes every 23,000 years as the period when the Earth is closest to the Sun moves between December and June. Every 41,000 years, the obliquity or tilt of the Earth's axis wobbles between 22.1° and 24.5° away from the plane of its orbit. Every 100,000 years, the eccentricity of the Earth's elliptical orbit around the Sun reaches its maximum. Together, these orbital changes influence the growth and decay of the Earth's ice sheets during glacial and interglacial climate phases as identified during the past half-million years (Fig. 7.4). Modified from Kennett (1982).

force behind glacial–interglacial oscillations in the Earth system. The combined effect of changing precession, obliquity, and eccentricity is illustrated by Fig. 7.3 in relation to summer solar radiation at 30° latitude in both hemispheres during the past 500,000 years. Although the average annual solar radiation in the Earth system has been nearly uniform throughout this period (reflecting the general na-

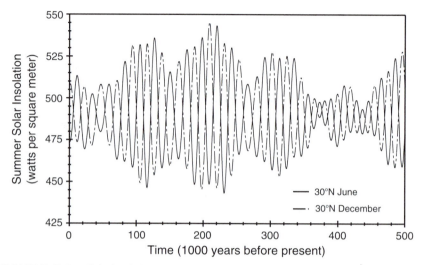

FIGURE 7.3   Solar insolation (in watts per square meter) at the top of the Earth's atmosphere during the summer at 30° latitude in the Northern Hemisphere (June) and Southern Hemisphere (December) during the past 500,000 years, based on orbital variations between the Earth and Sun (Fig. 7.2). In both hemispheres, 30° latitude is close to the region where the highest levels of solar insolation occur today (Fig. 7.1). Note that the global average insolation is nearly constant despite marked changes between hemispheres over time. Based on calculations from Berger and Loutre (1991).

ture of the "solar constant"), the seasonal and latitudinal distribution of solar energy across both hemispheres has been altogether variable.

As we all know, daily and seasonal warming are related to periods when sunlight is maximal. Assuming that *the present is the key to the past*—as suggested in the 18th century by James Hutton with his concept of "uniformitarianism"— it is reasonable that orbital relationships between the Earth and Sun (Figs. 7.2 and 7.3) also affected global temperatures in the past. To assess the Earth's paleoclimate record, in an experimental manner with controlled boundary conditions, it is appropriate to consider the post-Pliocene period when continental and ocean configurations have been most similar to the present (Chapter 6: Spreading Planet).

One of the most powerful innovations in paleoclimate research has been the analysis of atmospheric gases and particles trapped in ice masses around the Earth. These ice-core records, which come from both polar regions as well as high mountains at lower latitudes, contain information for interpreting temperature and precipitation variability in relation to atmospheric composition, moisture sources, and prevailing winds.

 How does the chemistry of the atmosphere and ocean reflect the Earth's climate conditions?

The longest and oldest ice core collected thus far comes from the East Antarctic Ice Sheet at the Russian research station (Vostok) near the geomagnetic south pole (78° south, 106° east) at an elevation of 3488 meters above sea level. The Vostok ice core extends more than 3600 meters through the ice sheet, profiling changes in the composition of Earth's climate over the past 420,000 years at a resolution of century increments (Fig. 7.4).

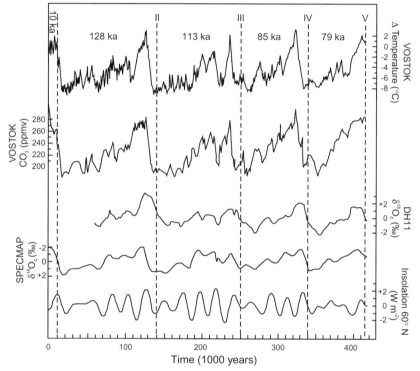

FIGURE 7.4 Earth's climate history during the previous 500,000 years based on atmospheric, marine, and terrestrial records that continuously cover the last five glacial–interglacial transitions (identified by dashed vertical lines with Roman numerals and the duration of the period in thousands of years, ka). Temperature profile from the Vostok ice core from Antarctica has been calculated in relation to the oxygen and hydrogen isotope content of the snow. Close correlation between atmospheric temperatures and greenhouse gases is further revealed by the carbon dioxide (CO_2) concentrations in the Vostok ice core, which are higher today than at any previous period during the last four climate cycles. The calcium carbonate vein from Devils Hole (DH11) in North America and the SPECMAP composite of calcareous planktonic foraminifera in 17 sediment cores from the Atlantic Ocean reveal coupled climate shifts and interacting dynamics of air–sea–land reservoirs in the Earth system. All of these profiles are compared to variability of the Earth's insolation, which is forced by the orbital relationship with the Sun (Figs. 7.2 and 7.3). Units are ppmv (parts per million by volume), ‰ (parts per thousand), W m^{-2} (watts per square meter), and °C (degrees Celsius). Modified from published information on the Vostok ice core (Petit *et al.*, 1999), Devils Hole core (Winograd *et al.*, 1992) and SPECMAP composite core (Imbrie *et al.*, 1989).

Atmospheric gases trapped within the Vostok ice core reflect changes in global ice volumes and the overall hydrological cycle (Fig. 1.5). In addition, hydrogen and oxgyen isotopes in water (H_2O) vapor and snow can be calibrated directly to atmospheric temperatures. When global temperatures cool and there are expanding volumes of ice on Earth (Fig. 6.5), the ocean becomes relatively enriched in ^{18}O while atmospheric precipitation becomes relatively enriched in ^{16}O (which is easier to evaporate). Consequently, based on the notation for $^{18}O/^{16}O$ ratios (Eq. 6.1) glacial $\delta^{18}O$ values are relatively negative in ice sheets and terrestrial carbonates and relatively positive in marine carbonates during glacial periods. Conversely, during interglacial periods, when global temperatures are warm and there is more seawater from melting ice sheets, $\delta^{18}O$ values become more negative in marine carbonates while becoming more positive in terrestrial carbonates and ice masses (Chapter 6: Spreading Planet).

As the longest high-resolution record of Earth's climate, the Vostok ice core indicates over the last four climate cycles that the amplitude of glacial–interglacial temperature change is around 8°C (Fig. 7.4). In addition, the 10,000-year duration of the current interglacial climate (Holocene) is the longest stable warm period recorded in Antarctica during the past 420,000 years. The sawtooth temperature profile from the Vostok ice core also shows the dominance of the 100,000-year cycle along with strong imprints of the 41,000-year and 23,000-year periodicities associated with Milankovitch changes in Earth's insolation (Figs. 7.2 and 7.3).

To evaluate the global synchrony of changes in the hydrological cycle during the past half million years, $\delta^{18}O$ climate records also have been compiled from marine and terrestrial reservoirs (Fig. 7.4). Like marine sedimentary strata through the Cenozoic (Fig. 6.5), $\delta^{18}O$ shifts in the calcium carbonate of planktonic foraminifera from the SPECMAP composite of marine sediment cores in the Atlantic Ocean reflect the same climate cycles as in the Vostok ice core. These climate shifts are reproduced again by the $\delta^{18}O$ in a calcium carbonate vein that precipitated continuously in the Devils Hole groundwater discharge area in Nevada, North America.

Together, these independent and synchronous records of $\delta^{18}O$ variability during the last four glacial–interglacial climate periods (Fig. 7.4) demonstrate global cycling of water between air, sea, land, and ice reservoirs in the Earth system. Moreover, these climate records indicate that the Earth system has tended to be in a glacial condition most of the time during past half-million years, with only punctuated periods of interglacial warmth.

The Vostok ice core also reveals shifts in the carbon dioxide (CO_2) concentrations in the atmosphere (Fig. 7.4). In contrast to the external forcing of the Earth system by the sun, CO_2 changes indicate that global climate also is influenced internally by life on our planet [Eq. (1.1), Fig. 2.2]. During every glacial–interglacial transition, the atmospheric CO_2 increased from about 180 to 300 parts per million, respectively. Methane (CH_4) concentrations, which also were measured in the Vostok ice core, increased in phase with CO_2 from about 320 to 770 parts per billion by volume during each climate transition.

With a view toward understanding future climate changes, stratigraphic records of terrestrial, marine, and atmospheric variability (Fig. 7.4) reveal a strong linkage between the pace of glacial–interglacial cycles and the predictable orbital dynamics between the Earth and the Sun (Figs. 7.2 and 7.3). However, the underlying relevance to human civilization is related to more immediate changes in the weather patterns that ultimately are integrated over time in the global climate (Fig. 6.1).

 What is the difference between weather and climate?

SEA-LEVEL SEESAW

Over geological time scales, sea-level rise and fall are related directly to the temperature history of the Earth system (Fig. 1.6). During cold periods, as evaporated water from the sea is locked into glaciers and ice sheets, sea level drops. Conversely, when climate warms and glacial meltwater flows back into the ocean, sea level goes up. Interpreting this coupling between ice sheets and sea level is fundamental to understanding impacts associated with global climate change that are relevant to the world we live in.

At present, nearly 90% of the ice on the planet is locked in the Antarctic ice sheets. The vast majority of the ice occurs in the land-based East Antarctic Ice Sheet, which if it melted entirely would raise sea level more than 50 meters. In contrast, ice is in contact with the ocean in the marine-based West Antarctic Ice Sheet, which has about the same ice volume as the Greenland Ice Sheet and could raise sea level around 5 meters if it entirely melted.

Because of its connection to the ocean, the West Antarctic Ice Sheet is considered to be particularly responsive to climate warming that elevates seawater temperatures and sea level. Melting or floating basal areas of the ice sheet that are grounded on the sea floor may remove critical "pinning points" that anchor the West Antarctic Ice Sheet. In the absence of these terminal restraints, relatively fast-flowing streams of ice in the interior of the West Antarctic Ice Sheet would be free to discharge into the sea. Although the future dynamics of this marine-based ice sheet and its "ice streams" are still largely unknown, there are marine sedimentary records that suggest the West Antarctic Ice Sheet has collapsed at least once during the past million years.

At the end of the Last Glacial Maximum, which ended around 17,000 years ago, the Earth's ice sheets were more extensive than they are today (Fig. 7.5a)—particularly since the Laurentide Ice Sheet in the Arctic has completely vanished. Regions in the middle of North America, for example, were covered by more than a kilometer of ice. As these ice sheets retreated, meltwater began gushing down streams and rivers back into the ocean, causing sea level to rise (Fig. 7.5b). Even-

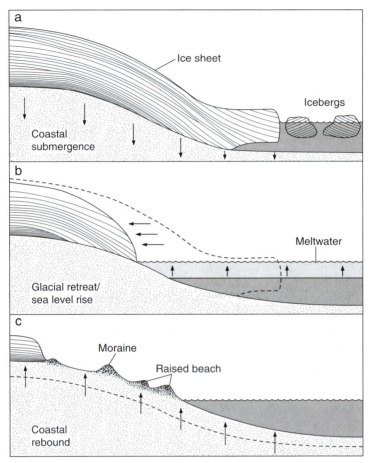

FIGURE 7.5   Illustration of a generalized ice-sheet retreat sequence. (a) Ice sheets extend through ice shelves into the ocean, covering and submerging coastal areas. (b) Retreating ice sheets add meltwater to the ocean, which raises sea level and alters seawater chemistry. (c) Afterward, moraines (piles of rocks and boulders) remain that represent changes in the margin of the ice sheets over time. With the diminished weight of the ice sheets, coastal areas begin rebounding and producing raised beaches that have emerged with marine fossils above sea level (Plate 4). Modified from Berkman *et al.* (1992).

tually, as the massive weight of the overlying ice sheets disappeared, coastal areas began rebounding above sea level to produce raised beaches with fossils that constrain the timing and magnitude of ice-sheet retreat (Fig. 7.5c).

In the Arctic, raised beaches have elevations that exceed 100 meters above sea level with fossils that have radiocarbon ages older than 14,000 years before present. Around Antarctica, however, raised beaches have elevations less than 35 meters above sea level with marine fossils with radiocarbon ages younger than

9000 years before present (Plate 8). These data alone demonstrate that climate impacts are asymmetric around the Earth with ice sheets retreating earlier and more massively in the northern hemisphere than around Antarctica after the Last Glacial Maximum.

The combined effect of this last deglaciation across the Earth is reflected by sea-level records extracted from coral reefs (Fig. 7.6), in tropical seas far from any direct ice-sheet impacts or tectonic movements. This paleoenvironmental record shows that global sea level has risen more than 120 meters since the Last Glacial Maximum.

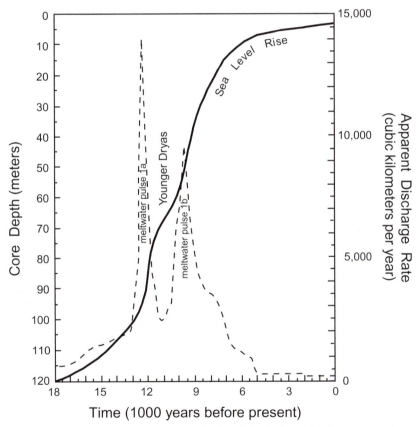

FIGURE 7.6   Record of sea-level rise (solid line–left axis) from 18,000 years ago to the present that was obtained from the calcium carbonate of reef corals, *Acropora palmata,* in the Caribbean Sea near Barbados. Based on oxygen isotope changes in seawater composition, two principal pulses of meltwater into the ocean (dashed line–right axis) occurred around 13,000 years ago (meltwater pulse 1a) and 10,000 years ago (meltwater pulse 1b) with an intervening climatic cooling period called the Younger Dryas. As the Younger Dryas was ending, starting 10,000 years ago, the Earth system entered the current climatic regime, which is called the Holocene. Modified from Fairbanks (1989).

Between 13,000 and 9000 years ago, when sea level was rising most rapidly (Fig. 7.6), there also were two major pulses of glacial meltwater into the North Atlantic. At their peaks, these two meltwater pulses discharged 14,000 and 9500 cubic kilometers of water per year—far greater than the Amazon (the largest river system on Earth today), which discharges around 6300 cubic kilometers per year.

At least 90 meters of the sea-level rise since the Last Glacial Maximum was associated with the northern hemisphere ice sheets, indicating that the past ice volume over the Arctic was nearly 50% larger than across all of Antarctica today. Moreover, the Arctic ice sheets melted in less than 20,000 years, signifying that glacial–interglacial climate shifts can occur over relatively short periods. In fact, transitions in the climate system can be downright abrupt, as illustrated by the termination of the Younger Dryas (named after a tundra flower that was living in northern Europe at the time) when Arctic temperatures warmed nearly 7°C within a couple of decades 11,640 years ago. The timing of this climatic event is well constrained by annual layers of snow accumulation that were counted in ice cores from Greenland. The Younger Dryas also is exhibited by the interval between the two major meltwater pulses into the ocean after the Last Glacial Maximum (Fig. 7.6).

In addition, the Younger Dryas suggests that there are ocean–atmosphere feedbacks in the Earth system that affect global climate dynamics. After the Last Glacial Maximum, with massive volumes of meltwater flowing from North America through the Gulf of St. Lawrence, a buoyant lid of freshwater floating on the denser seawater in the North Atlantic would have been produced. It has been hypothesized that such a meltwater lid would have changed oceanic and atmospheric circulation patterns—reversing the warming trend of the Earth system that began after the Last Glacial Maximum.

At the end of the Younger Dryas, climate warming and ice-sheet melting abruptly switched on again—shifting the Earth system into the current interglacial period. This current climate regime, which began 10,000 years ago, is known as the Holocene.

It is speculated that the second pulse of meltwater was initiated from Antarctica, possibly from the marine-based West Antarctic Ice Sheet in response to the earlier sea-level rise from the retreating ice sheets in the Arctic. Nonetheless, subsequent sea-level rise during the Holocene must have been influenced by Antarctic melting because the northern hemisphere ice sheets had already vanished. Following the "climate optimum" around 6000 years ago, when temperatures were warmer than today by 1 or 2°C, sea level effectively stabilized in concert with reduced variability of the interglacial climate.

During this period, as reflected by calendars that have been updated continuously for nearly 6000 years, diverse human cultures also began emerging. Apparently, along with bristlecone pines and other biotic assemblages (mentioned in Chapter 6: Spreading Planet), our civilization has been flourishing under relatively stable climate warmth since the mid-Holocene (Plate 5).

OCEANIC CONVEYOR

Heating from the Sun drives the cycling of water through the Earth system. On a global scale, over millennia and longer time spans, climate cooling causes water to accumulate in polar ice sheets and lower-latitude glaciers. Conversely, during periods of climate warming, the ice sheets and glaciers will release water back into the ocean—potentially much more quickly than it accumulated, as exhibited at the end of the Younger Dryas (Fig. 7.6). Water also flows through land, air, and sea reservoirs in response to daily and seasonal weather processes (Fig. 1.5). Since nearly 98% of the water on Earth is in the ocean, internal dynamics of the sea are fundamental to understanding the Earth system.

Water is special because of its unique properties for transferring heat and moderating environmental changes as well as for sustaining life in the Earth system (Table 7.1). Unlike other molecules, water exists in all three phases (liquid, solid,

TABLE 7.1   Properties of Water in the Earth System

Properties	Characteristics	Ecosystem impacts
Boiling point	High (100°C) for molecular size	Water exists as a liquid at Earth surface temperatures and pressures
Freezing point	High (0°C) for molecular size	Water exists as a liquid at Earth surface temperatures and pressures
Latent heat of vaporization	High (540 calories/gram)	Liquid–gas interaction moderates temperatures of oceans and other large water bodies by transferring heat to the atmosphere through evaporation
Latent heat of fusion	High (80 calories/gram)	Solid–liquid thermal interactions inhibit large-scale freezing of the oceans and other water bodies
Heat capacity	High (1 calorie/gram/°C)	Moderate daily and seasonal temperature changes, stabilize body temperatures of organisms
Density	Unique	Causes ice to float and inhibits large-scale freezing of the oceans and other water bodies
Solvent power	Dissolves more substances in greater amounts than any other liquid	Maintains large variety of substances in solution which enhances chemical reactions because of the polar nature of bonding between the oxygen and hydrogen atoms
Sound transmission	1500 meters/second	Travels farther and faster than in air (334 meters/second)
Light transmission	Proportional to water clarity	Varies with scattering of different wavelengths, with blue-green wavelengths deepest transmission and red shallowest attenuation
Surface tension	High	Critical to maintaining position of organisms in aquatic habitats

and gas) at standard atmospheric pressures and temperatures on the Earth's surface. These three phases of matter are distinguished by the degree of bonding between adjacent molecules—generally with solids having the strongest and closest bonding between molecules while gases have the weakest bonding with molecules furthest apart.

An important feature of water is its unusually high latent heats, where phase transitions occur without continuous temperature changes. For example, while being heated, liquid water will increase in temperature continuously, whereas ice remains at the freezing point (0°C for freshwater) until after it has completely melted. Actually, an extra 80 calories of heat are required to melt each gram of ice before it becomes a liquid and can continue warming.

Similarly, liquid water will warm until the vaporization point (100°C for freshwater) and stay at this temperature until 540 calories of heat have been absorbed by each gram of liquid water. Afterward, the water vapor can continue warming (if the gas is confined) until the water molecules finally disassociate into hydrogen and oxygen atoms. There also is a latent heat of sublimation, involving a direct transition between the solid and gas phases, which is why ice cubes get smaller over time in your freezer. Together, these latent heats for water represent the energy that is either absorbed when molecular bonds are broken or liberated when molecular bonds are formed.

On a global scale, the latent heat of vaporization causes the ocean to cool as liquid water evaporates (because the evaporating water absorbs heat) and the atmosphere to warm as water vapor condenses (because the condensing water liberates heat). As an analogy, consider why your skin cools after getting out of the shower. Similarly, the latent heat of fusion causes heating and cooling of the atmosphere as ice forms and melts seasonally. Together, these latent heats limit the temperature variability in the Earth system as water shifts among its solid, liquid, and gas phases.

Without the salt, the ocean would act like freshwater, with its maximum density 3.98°C above its freezing point (Fig. 7.7a). This unusual density behavior of freshwater (Table 7.1) occurs because the lattice of an ice crystal contains fewer molecules than liquid water (Fig. 7.7b). Seawater, however, has an average content of 34.7 grams of dissolved salts per thousand grams of water (Table 7.2)—about 96.5% water and 3.5% salt, most of which is common table salt (sodium chloride). Dissolved elements alter the basic properties of freshwater such that seawater, with salinities above 24.7 parts per thousand (‰), has its maximum density at the freezing point (Fig. 7.7a). Fortunately, in both freshwater and seawater, ice floats because it is less dense than the underlying water (Table 7.1). Otherwise, aquatic systems across the planet would have frozen from the bottom upward and the evolution of life on Earth would have been vastly different.

Together, the thermohaline (temperature and salinity) properties of seawater influence the vertical distribution of water masses in the ocean. Unlike currents at the sea surface, which are driven by winds (Chapter 8: Breathing Planet), the deep water masses are driven by their relative densities—where cold saline waters sink

a

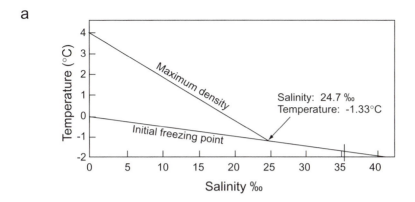

b

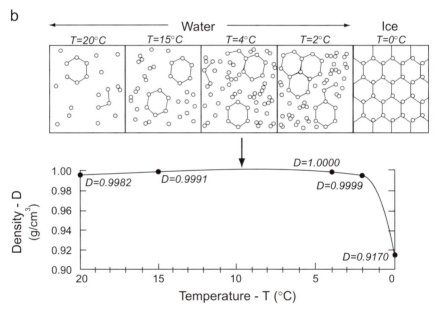

FIGURE 7.7   **(a)** Effect of salinity on the freezing point and maximum density temperatures of seawater (Table 7.2). Note that with salinities above 24.7‰ (parts per thousand), the freezing points and maximum densities of seawater occur at the same temperatures. **(b)** Freshwater with the density of water molecules (D), in grams per cubic centimeter, increases to a maximum at 3.98°C before freezing into the regular-spaced lattice of an ice crystal at 0°C. Modified from Thurman (1978).

under less dense warm and fresh waters. These water masses, which are characterized by their distinct properties (i.e., temperatures, salinities, trace elements, gases, organic compounds, nutrients, and even species), underscore the mixing processes in the ocean.

TABLE 7.2   Major Ionic Constitutents in Seawater with a Salinity of 35 Parts per
Thousand (‰)[a]

Element	Chemical symbol	Concentration (‰)	Percentage
Chloride	Cl^-	19.27	55.04
Sodium	Na^+	10.71	30.61
Sulfate	SO_4^{2-}	2.69	7.68
Magnesium	Mg^+	1.29	3.69
Calcium	Ca^+	0.41	1.16
Potassium	K^+	0.39	1.10
Bicarbonate	HCO_3^-	0.14	0.40

[a] Salinity (in parts per thousand, ‰) is defined as 1.80655 times the chlorinity (in
parts per thousand, ‰), where chlorinity represents the concentration of chloride and
other halogen ions (i.e., bromine, iodine, and fluorine). Adapted from Thurman (1978).

 How does Antarctica influence global climate conditions through the oceans and atmosphere?

Around Antarctica, surface water masses are the coldest in the ocean, with temperatures approaching $-2°C$. Antarctica also has a relatively narrow and deep continental shelf, which further facilitates the exchange of water masses between the sea surface and deep sea (Fig. 7.8). Together these oceanographic features enable extremely cold dense water masses to sink into the deep sea from the Weddell and Ross Sea basins—forming Antarctic Bottom Water as the primary source of the abyssal circulation in the ocean.

As we move northward between 60° and 50° south latitude, sea surface temperatures sharply warm 2 to 3°C. In this region, Antarctic Surface Waters downwell with warmer Sub-Antarctic Surface Water to form the Antarctic Convergence (Fig. 7.8). These surface water masses produce Antarctic Intermediate Water, which can be recognized throughout much of the ocean as a tongue of relatively low salinity and high oxygen content at around 1500 meters depth. This Antarctic Polar Front Zone is the northern boundary of the Antarctic marine ecosystem (Chapter 9: Living Planet).

Sea-surface temperatures suddenly increase an additional 4°C around 40° south latitude, with consequent downwelling at the Subtropical Convergence. This Sub-Antarctic Front Zone is the northern boundary of the Southern Ocean.

Between the Antarctic Intermediate Water and Antarctic Bottom Water, there is a relatively warm and salty water mass that originates in the North Atlantic. Sinking of this dense North Atlantic Deep Water, primarily in the Norwegian Sea region, is influenced by cooling and evaporation of warm Gulf Stream surface waters flowing northward from the tropics. Arriving in the Antarctic region—long after

a

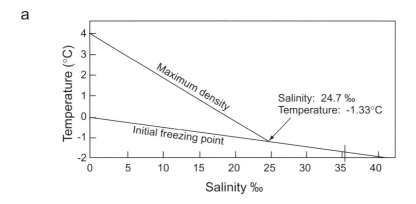

b

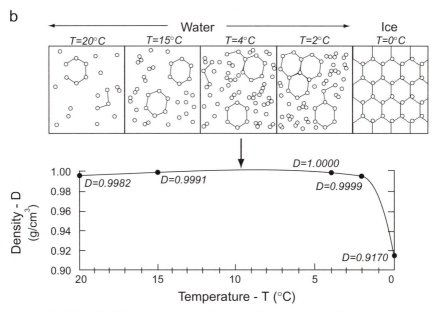

FIGURE 7.7   **(a)** Effect of salinity on the freezing point and maximum density temperatures of seawater (Table 7.2). Note that with salinities above 24.7‰ (parts per thousand), the freezing points and maximum densities of seawater occur at the same temperatures. **(b)** Freshwater with the density of water molecules (D), in grams per cubic centimeter, increases to a maximum at 3.98°C before freezing into the regular-spaced lattice of an ice crystal at 0°C. Modified from Thurman (1978).

under less dense warm and fresh waters. These water masses, which are characterized by their distinct properties (i.e., temperatures, salinities, trace elements, gases, organic compounds, nutrients, and even species), underscore the mixing processes in the ocean.

TABLE 7.2   Major Ionic Constitutents in Seawater with a Salinity of 35 Parts per
Thousand (‰) [a]

Element	Chemical symbol	Concentration (‰)	Percentage
Chloride	Cl^-	19.27	55.04
Sodium	Na^+	10.71	30.61
Sulfate	SO_4^{2-}	2.69	7.68
Magnesium	Mg^+	1.29	3.69
Calcium	Ca^+	0.41	1.16
Potassium	K^+	0.39	1.10
Bicarbonate	HCO_3^-	0.14	0.40

[a] Salinity (in parts per thousand, ‰) is defined as 1.80655 times the chlorinity (in parts per thousand, ‰), where chlorinity represents the concentration of chloride and other halogen ions (i.e., bromine, iodine, and fluorine). Adapted from Thurman (1978).

 How does Antarctica influence global climate conditions through the oceans and atmosphere?

Around Antarctica, surface water masses are the coldest in the ocean, with temperatures approaching $-2°C$. Antarctica also has a relatively narrow and deep continental shelf, which further facilitates the exchange of water masses between the sea surface and deep sea (Fig. 7.8). Together these oceanographic features enable extremely cold dense water masses to sink into the deep sea from the Weddell and Ross Sea basins—forming Antarctic Bottom Water as the primary source of the abyssal circulation in the ocean.

As we move northward between 60° and 50° south latitude, sea surface temperatures sharply warm 2 to 3°C. In this region, Antarctic Surface Waters downwell with warmer Sub-Antarctic Surface Water to form the Antarctic Convergence (Fig. 7.8). These surface water masses produce Antarctic Intermediate Water, which can be recognized throughout much of the ocean as a tongue of relatively low salinity and high oxygen content at around 1500 meters depth. This Antarctic Polar Front Zone is the northern boundary of the Antarctic marine ecosystem (Chapter 9: Living Planet).

Sea-surface temperatures suddenly increase an additional 4°C around 40° south latitude, with consequent downwelling at the Subtropical Convergence. This Sub-Antarctic Front Zone is the northern boundary of the Southern Ocean.

Between the Antarctic Intermediate Water and Antarctic Bottom Water, there is a relatively warm and salty water mass that originates in the North Atlantic. Sinking of this dense North Atlantic Deep Water, primarily in the Norwegian Sea region, is influenced by cooling and evaporation of warm Gulf Stream surface waters flowing northward from the tropics. Arriving in the Antarctic region—long after

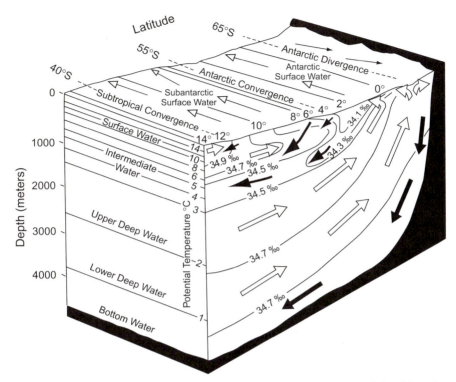

FIGURE 7.8 Vertical profile of the temperature, salinity, and depth characteristics of the major water masses in the Southern Ocean (Fig. 8.3). From bottom to top, the major water masses include the northward-flowing Antarctic Bottom Water (solid arrows), southward-flowing North Atlantic Deep Water (open arrows), and northward-flowing Antarctic Intermediate Water (solid arrows) which are predominant features in the world's ocean (see text). Modified from Knox (1970) and Berkman (1992).

its last breath from the atmosphere—North Atlantic Deep Water has extremely low oxygen concentrations and radiocarbon ages that exceed 1000 years.

As it upwells at the Antarctic Divergence (Fig. 7.8), North Atlantic Deep Water also carries carbon, nitrogen, phosphorus, silicon, and other nutrients from plants and animals that had dissolved in the deep sea. This divergence is like a giant fountain pumping nearly 50 million cubic meters of nutrient-rich water per second from the deep sea into the Antarctic marine ecosystem (Chapter 9: Living Planet).

These water masses generate the density-driven conveyor that circulates heat, salt, nutrients, and gases throughout the ocean (Fig. 7.9). In this global circulation system, there is a cold and salty deep-water branch that is driven by dense water-mass formation in the North Atlantic and Antarctic (Fig. 7.8). There also is a relatively warm and fresh surface-water branch from the Pacific and Indian Oceans that flows back into the North Atlantic and renews the conveyor. Connec-

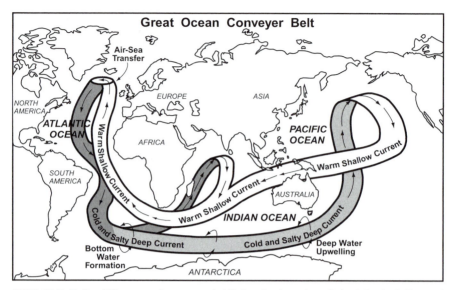

FIGURE 7.9 "Great oceanic conveyor belt" that circulates through the Atlantic, Indian, and Pacific Oceans (with ocean volumes around 340, 280, and 710 million cubic kilometers, respectively). Cold and salty water masses in the deep sea originate in the North Atlantic and Antarctic (Fig. 7.8). Relatively warm and fresh water masses at the sea surface flow from the Indian and Pacific Oceans into the Gulf Stream and back to the North Atlantic, where this density-driven thermohaline (temperature and salinity) circulation is renewed. This oceanic conveyor influences weather patterns, particularly in the North Atlantic region and across Europe (see text). After Stommel (1958) and Broecker (1987).

tions between the deep and shallow branches of the oceanic conveyor occur in regions where water masses downwell (in the North Atlantic and Antarctic) and upwell (around Antarctica as well as in the northern Indian and Pacific Oceans).

An amazing feature of this thermohaline conveyor is its role in weather patterns, particularly in the North Atlantic region. In fact, one of the most striking anomalies on the Earth is in Europe, where temperatures today are 10 to 20°C warmer than at comparable latitudes in North America or Asia. Underpinning the exceptionally warm temperatures of Europe is the 10^{15} watts of heat—nearly one-third of the total solar heating over the entire North Atlantic—that are transported poleward with the Gulf Stream.

In addition to heating Europe, warm Gulf Stream waters evaporate when they come in contact with cold air from the Canadian Arctic. This evaporation raises seawater salinities to the point that surface waters become dense enough to sink into the deep sea. As this North Atlantic Deep Water moves southward toward Antarctica, it is replaced on the surface by the northward-flowing Gulf Stream. This connection between surface and deep-water flows—like a conveyor belt—suggests that the Gulf Stream heating of Europe could be diminished by reducing deep-water formation in the North Atlantic.

The Younger Dryas is a notable example of a shutdown in the thermohaline circulation that was triggered by a meltwater lid over the North Atlantic following the deglaciation phase after the Last Glacial Maximum (Fig. 7.6). The ensuing cooling period, around 11,000 years ago, returned northern Europe into a glacial condition for nearly 700 years. There also are indications that the impact of the Younger Dryas was global with concurrent cooling in many other regions on Earth.

Apparently, such climatic flip-flops in the North Atlantic region have been an ongoing phenomenon since the Last Interglacial period, nearly 110,000 years ago (Fig. 7.4). In ice cores from Greenland, more than 20 climate warming intervals (Dansgaard–Oeschger events) have been inferred from elevated concentrations of carbon dioxide [Eq. (1.1)], which is a well-mixed gas in the atmosphere that reflects global climate changes. Ice-rafted debris in the sediments (Chapter 6: Spreading Planet) indicate that there also have been periodic iceberg discharges (Heinrich events), with accompanying meltwater pulses and subsequent cooling intervals in the North Atlantic every few millennia. The overall implication of these offset warming and cooling records is that climate oscillations are driven internally within the Earth system by ocean–atmosphere dynamics as well as externally by orbital relationships with the Sun (Figs. 2.2, 7.2–7.4).

8

BREATHING PLANET

With thee conversing I forget all time,
All seasons, and their change; all please alike.
Sweet is the breath of morn. . . .
            —*John Milton (1867),* Paradise Lost, Book IV

CIRCUMPOLAR CYCLONE

Solar radiation is the principal heat engine powering the Earth system. Across the planet, there are air–sea interactions that are forced by seasonal sunlight, most notably in the high latitudes where the winter–summer contrasts are most extreme. For example, around Antarctica, the absence of solar radiation during the winter cools sea-surface temperatures and causes sea-ice coverage to expand from a summer minimum of 3 million square kilometers to nearly 20 million square kilometers (Fig. 8.1)—across an area nearly equal to that of North America. Eighty-five percent of this sea ice in the unbounded Southern Ocean is formed annually, as opposed to the enclosed Arctic Basin where only 15% of the sea ice is new each year (Fig. 3.1).

 Why does Antarctica have circumpolar environmental systems?

As seen already, variable warming or cooling of different regions on the planet influences climate cycles (Figs. 7.2–7.4) as well as the density-driven dynamics of the ocean (Figs. 7.8 and 7.9). Differential heating across the Earth also influences atmospheric circulation patterns and winds which, in turn, drive the surface

Summer   Winter

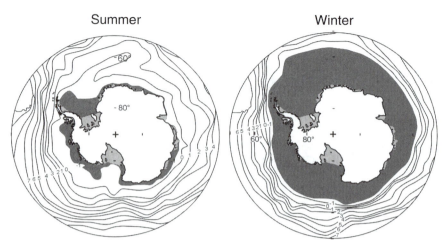

FIGURE 8.1   Latitudinal profile of the average Antarctic Surface Water temperatures (from 0 to 10 meters depth) during the austral summer (December through February) and winter (June through August) in the Southern Ocean (Figs. 7.8 and 8.3). Sea ice minimum and maximum coverages are shown as shaded areas during the summer (February 1974) and winter (August 1974), respectively—extending from around 3 million to 20 million square-kilometers each year (Fig. 3.1). Modified from Schwerdtfeger (1970).

currents of the ocean. This coupled movement of the ocean and atmosphere is further regulated by the motion of the planet itself.

On a non-rotating Earth, air would rise where it is warm and sink where is it is cold. These thermodynamic features of the atmosphere basically involve temperature and pressure as defined by Robert Boyle for an "ideal" gas (Equation 8.1). For example, in a container with a constant volume, a heated gas will cause pressures to rise—as in a pressure cooker. Higher pressures, which are associated with enhanced molecular motion at higher temperatures, also explain why a balloon (which has a flexible volume) inflates as it is warmed and deflates as it is cooled. Similarly, when a heated gas occupies a larger volume it will have a lower density of molecules—which is why hot air rises over cold air. In relation to the Earth's atmosphere, Eq. (8.1) (the "ideal gas law") shows generally that temperatures and pressures proportionally increase and decrease together:

$$P \, V = n \, R \, T \tag{8.1}$$

where P is gas pressure; V, gas volume; n the amount of gas; R, a constant; and T, gas temperature. An "ideal gas" involves molecular collisions with negligible cohesive forces between the molecules.

As opposed to a stationary body, however, the Earth is spinning around its axis (Figs. I and 7.2) at approximately 1670 kilometers per hour at the equator, completing one rotation every 24 hours (Chapter 1: Global Dimensions). This daily rotational period is the same at all latitudes. However, given that distances around the Earth decrease north and south of the equator, the apparent speeds of rotation decrease toward higher latitudes, such that the Earth is only moving half as fast at 60° latitude.

This spinning of the Earth not only influences day and night periods throughout the year, but also influences the trajectory of air and water masses around the planet. As a simple experiment: draw a line across a piece of paper. Now draw the same line while somebody rotates the piece of paper. The curvature of your line is analogous to the directional changes imposed on all air and water masses that are in motion across the planet. Similarly, from the perspective of outer space, moving fluids are deflected in opposite directions in the two hemispheres—curving to the right of their original path in the Northern Hemisphere and to the left in the Southern Hemisphere. This impact of a rotating Earth, which causes the apparent trajectory of a moving fluid to be deflected at right angles to its original path, is known as the "Coriolis effect" after the Frenchman Gaspard Gustav de Coriolis (1792–1843), who proposed the concept in the early 19th century.

Like a marble rolling down an incline, air masses will move from high to low pressures—gaining velocity in proportion to the slope of the pressure gradient. Greater than 1000 meters above the Earth, atmospheric motion also will be unimpeded by surface frictional forces—resulting in winds that flow eastward in the direction of the Earth's rotation.

Around low-pressure regions, air masses will converge and spiral inward to form cyclones that gyrate counterclockwise in the Northern Hemisphere and clockwise in the Southern Hemisphere. Conversely, air masses will diverge and spiral outward from high-pressure regions to form anticyclones that circulate in reverse directions.

As the coldest region on the planet, Antarctica has the lowest regional atmospheric pressures on Earth [see Eq. (8.1) about the temperature–pressure relationship]. Moreover, around 5000 meters altitude (which is well above Antarctic surface elevations), atmospheric pressures decrease continuously toward the high southern latitudes—producing a latitudinal pressure gradient (Fig. 8.2) that mirrors the temperature gradient at the sea surface (Fig. 8.1). This barometric gradient persists throughout the year, during both winter and summer seasons, because of the enormous thermal inertia generated by Antarctica and its vast ice reservoir. Moreover, this zonal pressure gradient has been maintained over millions of years—as long as Antarctica has been a global heat sink surrounded by warmer regions (Fig. 6.3, Table 6.1).

Because fluids move from high to low pressures, the atmospheric pressure gradient toward Antarctica creates winds that are acted upon by the Earth's rotation, generating an enormous cyclonic circulation that exists across half of the Southern Hemisphere. Clockwise movement of this polar vortex generates the West Wind Drift (Fig. 8.3).

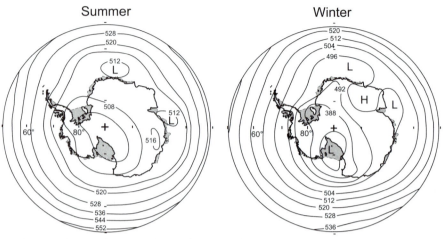

FIGURE 8.2   Circumpolar bands of atmospheric pressures at the 500 millibar height (about 5000 meters above sea level), which includes the atmosphere over the entire continent, during the summer (January) and winter (July). Note that atmospheric pressures are lower during the cooler winter months [as described in Eq. (8.1)]. Progressive increase in atmospheric pressures with decreasing latitude establishes the zonal pressure gradient that generates the giant cyclonic circulation of the West Wind Drift across half of the southern hemisphere (Fig. 8.3). Parallel patterns of atmospheric pressures, seasonal sea surface temperatures, and sea ice extent (Fig. 8.1) are influenced by the annual solar radiation cycle (Fig. 7.1). Modified from Schwerdtfeger (1970).

Like the oceanic density gradients that drive water-mass circulations (Chapter 7: Flowing Planet), atmospheric pressure gradients generate wind-driven currents. Because of its persistent frictional drag on the sea surface, the West Wind Drift produces a clockwise circulation in the underlying Southern Ocean. This coupling between the atmosphere and ocean has produced the largest current system on Earth—the Antarctic Circumpolar Current—which flows around the continent at an average rate of 120 million cubic meters every second. This volume transport of the ocean around Antarctica is two to three times that of the Gulf Stream in the North Atlantic.

The high volume transport of the Antarctic Circumpolar Current is not due to its velocities—only a tenth of those for the Gulf Stream, which travels around 200 centimeters per second. Rather, the massive transport of the Antarctic Circumpolar Current is due to its immense breadth (up to 1000 kilometers wide), depth (over 2000 meters deep), and circumpolar trajectory, which is virtually unobstructed by continental land masses.

Between the Antarctic Circumpolar Current and the continent is the counterclockwise East Wind Drift (Fig. 8.3). The East Wind Drift creates the Antarctic Coastal Current, which flows around the continent from the Antarctic Peninsula along a narrow band near the continent before being incorporated into the northward-flowing Weddell Sea Drift.

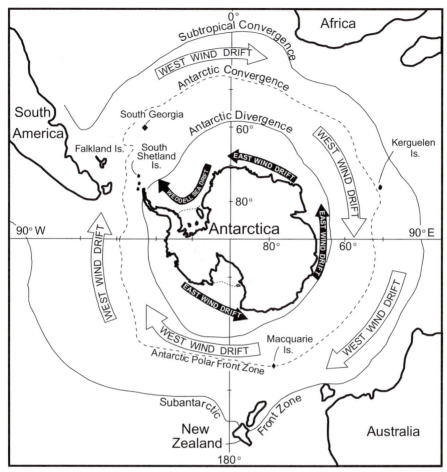

FIGURE 8.3   Currents of the *Southern Ocean,* which is bounded by the Antarctic Continent and the sea floor south of the Subtropical Convergence (Subantarctic Front Zone). The predominant clockwise trajectory of the West Wind Drift in the atmosphere drives the Antarctic Circumpolar Current. The Antarctic Convergence (Antarctic Polar Front Zone) is the northern boundary of the Antarctic marine ecosystem. South of the West Wind Drift is the counter-clockwise East Wind Drift, which drives the Antarctic Coastal Current. Between the East and West Wind Drifts is the circumpolar upwelling zone at the Antarctic Divergence (Fig. 7.8). Modified from Knox (1970) and Berkman (1992).

    Wind-driven currents around Antarctica (Fig. 8.3) are coupled with the atmosphere, as are thermohaline circulations propagating through the ocean (Figs. 7.8 and 7.9). In both cases, the principal connections involve solar radiation and transferring water between its solid, liquid, and gas phases (Chapter 7: Flowing Planet).

WATER IN, WATER OUT

Because of differential heating across the planet (Fig. 7.1) and the "Coriolis effect," there are six wind belts around the Earth. These wind zones are formed by three convection cells of converging (flowing together) and diverging (flowing apart) air masses in each hemisphere (Fig. 8.4).

Regions where air masses converge at the surface and diverge aloft produce zones of ascending air. In these regions, warm air rises and then cools at higher altitudes as atmospheric pressures decrease. Owing to the general pressure–temperature relationship of gases [Eq. (8.1)], temperatures of rising air masses will decrease by around 10°C every 1000 meters. In addition, because warm air can retain more moisture than cold air, the moisture in the rising air masses will condense at higher altitudes. For these reason, zones of ascending air—which occur at the equator and at 60° latitude in both hemispheres—are characterized by high levels of precipitation (Fig. 8.5).

Conversely, regions where air masses converge aloft and diverge at the surface represent zones of descending air. At higher altitudes, cold air retains small volumes of moisture. As it descends, atmospheric pressures increase and the cold, dry air warms [Eq. (8.1)]. This warmed dry air then contacts the Earth's sur-

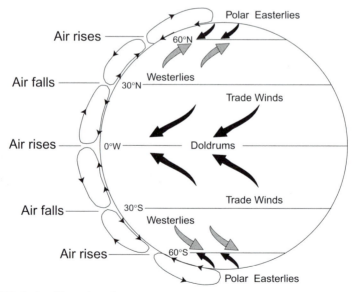

FIGURE 8.4 Illustration of the convection cells in the atmosphere showing the latitudinal zones where warm, wet air masses rise and cold, dry air masses fall across the Earth. Wind directions, which are mirror images in both hemispheres, are influenced by this relative heating of the atmosphere and the "Coriolis effect" associated with the Earth's rotation (see text).

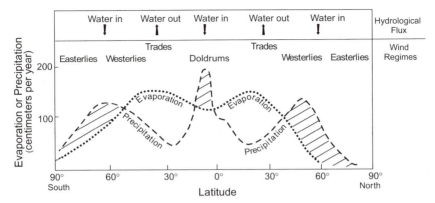

FIGURE 8.5   Evaporation and precipitation zones across latitudes on the Earth, which are influenced by solar radiation (Fig. 7.1) and wind regimes from the doldrums near the equator to the trade winds at mid-latitudes to the cyclonic gyres at high latitudes (Fig. 8.4). Ocean salinities (Table 7.2) are highest in the evaporative mid-latitude regions. Modified from Garrels *et al.* (1975) and Pickard and Emery (1982).

face and promotes evaporation, primarily around 30° latitude in both hemispheres (Fig. 8.5).

Consequently, the mid-latitude zone of high evaporation accounts for high salinities in the ocean and many of the great deserts on Earth, such as the Sahara in Africa. Descending dry air over the polar regions also causes evaporation, which contributes to Antarctica being the largest desert on Earth. The nature of the Antarctic desert is enhanced by the persistently cold temperatures over the continent. Together, these Antarctic conditions produce minimal levels of snow accumulation that progressively decrease away from the oceanic moisture source—from the circumpolar coastline toward the center of the ice sheet (Fig. 8.6).

Moreover, high elevations of the Antarctic ice sheets (Fig. 8.6) also establish a highly coupled system with direct connections between the stratosphere (Fig. 1.5) and the depths of the ocean (Fig. 7.8) over relatively short time scales compared to all other continents. This ocean-atmosphere coupling is facilitated by the katabatic winds (Plate 4), which are dense cold-air masses falling from the polar plateau and warming as they travel at high velocities (sometimes exceeding 40 meters per second) toward sea level. In turn, these katabatic winds often create huge open-water areas in the middle of the sea ice called polynyas—covering tens to hundreds of thousands of square kilometers and generating dense shelf water masses that sink into the deep sea.

In each hemisphere, wind belts correspond with the zones of ascending and descending air masses. These winds are named for the directions they come from, as opposed to currents, which conventionally are named for the directions they move toward. For example, the East Wind Drift and West Wind Drift around Ant-

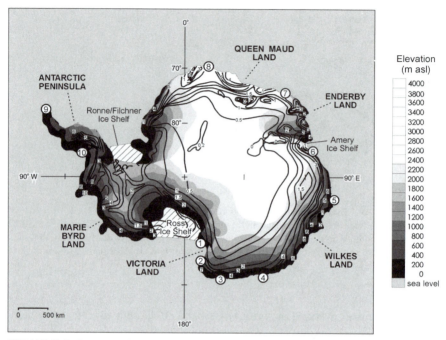

FIGURE 8.6   Approximate snow accumulation rates at different elevations around Antarctica decreasing from 20–80 grams per square centimeter per year in the circum-Antarctic coastal zone to less than a gram per square centimeter per year at elevations above 2000 meters on the polar plateau. Atmospheric moisture transport is maximal in the circum-Antarctic coastal zone and decreases with increasing distance from the ocean and elevation onto the polar plateau (Jacobs, 1992). Circumpolar distribution of ice-free coastal oases occur along the Antarctic ice-sheet margin (Berkman et al. 1998): 1, McMurdo Dry Valleys; 2, Terra Nova Bay; 3, Cape Adare and Cape Hallett; 4, Cape Denison; 5, Bunger Hills; 6, Larsemann Hills and Vestfold Hills; 7, Sôya Coast; 8, Untersee Oasis; 9, Hope Bay; and 10, Marguerite Bay. The three-dimensional view of Antarctica, with elevation contours in meters above sea level, was derived from Drewry (1983).

arctica (Fig. 8.3) are coming from the east and west, respectively. Moreover, these two wind regimes represent the general character of the polar easterlies and westerlies, which are blowing in both hemispheres (Figs. 8.4 and 8.5). Between the polar easterlies and the westerlies is the polar front zone, as shown around Antarctica (Fig. 8.3).

Equatorward of the westerlies are the northeast and southeast trade winds, which were named by the early mariners who recognized their commercial importance (Figs. 8.4 and 8.5). Between the two trade wind zones is a band of cloudy, rainy weather at the equator, which is called the doldrums by mariners or the Intertropical Convergence Zone by meteorologists.

Seasonally, the global wind belts shift poleward during the spring and equatorward during the fall—causing distinct wet and dry seasons. Within a given latitudinal zone, however, environments vary between hemispheres, with more land north and ocean south of the equator (Fig. 1.4). These land–sea contrasts influence weather and climate patterns because rock warms and cools faster than water, which has an unusually high heat capacity and ability to moderate temperature changes (Table 7.1).

This differential heating between the land and sea causes winds to blow onshore and offshore depending on solar radiation. On a daily or seasonal basis, relatively moist air over the sea is sucked onshore as the sun heats the land and causes the overlying air to rise rapidly. These warm, moist air masses then condense at higher altitudes, often causing high levels of rainfall. Conversely, more arid winds blow offshore from the land as night or winter cooling causes overlying air masses to fall faster than those over the sea. These onshore–offshore processes are associated with the shifting winds and currents of the monsoons (from the Arabic word mausim, "a season"), which seasonally deluge areas in India, Asia, and even North America.

Today, the most pronounced oscillation in the global weather system is associated with a weakening of the southeast trade winds every 2 to 7 years. Normally, high pressure over South America and low pressure over Indonesia causes the south equatorial current to flow westward across the Pacific Ocean. To replace the westward flowing surface waters, cold nutrient-rich bottom waters upwell along the coast of South America. Conversely, surface seawater in the west Pacific is nearly 8°C warmer and a half meter higher than in the east Pacific. This ocean–atmosphere coupling leads to dry coastal areas in Peru and lush rainforests in Indonesia.

When the sea surface becomes abnormally warm in the east Pacific, however, the normal pressure gradient across the ocean is reduced—causing the southeast trade winds to weaken. The accompanying shift in the low pressure regions from west to east also causes a reversal of the south equatorial current across the Pacific Ocean. As warm water piles up in the eastern Pacific, upwelling nutrient-rich waters are shut down along with the rich marine ecosystems which they support. Commonly referred to as El Niño (the boy or Christ child), because of its occurrence during the Christmas season, this southern oscillation also leads to droughts in Indonesia and fires in Australia while the Americas are blanketed in torrential rains.

In 1997–98, the El Niño Southern Oscillation (ENSO) caused the sea surface to rise by nearly 40 centimeters near the Americas—creating a warm pool of water with temperatures above 20°C and a volume that was 30 times greater than all of the water in the United States, including the Great Lakes. Additional estimates from the National Oceanic and Atmospheric Administration indicate that the abnormal amount of heat in this warm pool was nearly 100 times greater than the heat produced from all of the fossil fuel energy consumed in the United States in 1995.

ENSO impacts propagate across the Earth today, and there are hints that this ocean–atmosphere phenomenon is coupled with global climate conditions. Distinct appearance of warm water mollusks in beaches along the Pacific coast of South America signal that ENSO events turned on around 6000 years ago (Plate 5), during the mid-Holocene when the Earth's climate began stabilizing into its present mode (Chapter 7: Flowing Planet). Cores from corals that have been growing continuously in the Pacific suggest that ENSO events occurred around every 15 years during the 17th century and that their frequency has increased toward the present—coincidentally as the Earth system has been warming.

GREENHOUSE RESPIRATION

Heating from the Sun (Fig. 7.1) circulates around the Earth because of ocean currents (Fig. 7.9), winds (Fig. 8.4) and latent heat exchanges associated with the hydrological cycle (Fig. 8.5). Over millennia, changes in insolation also will influence the Earth's climate (Figs. 7.2–7.4). Ultimately, however, the blanket of mixed gases in the lower atmosphere (primarily the troposphere—Figs. 1a and 1b) is why the Earth system retains the solar heating and remains relatively warm.

To understand the average surface temperature of Earth (nearly 150,000,000 kilometers from the Sun), it is helpful to consider sister planets in the solar system. Venus is almost twice as far from the Sun (nearly 110,000,000 kilometers) as Mercury (nearly 58,000,000 kilometers). Nonetheless, Venus has a stable average temperature around 480°C, whereas the surface of Mercury fluctuates broadly from around −180°C to only 430°C. Relative to Mercury, the tremendous warmth of Venus (which is hot enough to melt lead) clearly is influenced by factors other than its distance from the Sun. The answer lies in the composition of the planets' atmospheres.

 How do atmospheres influence the surface temperatures of planets in our solar system?

Mercury is without an atmosphere. In contrast, Venus is enshrouded in a dense cloud of carbon dioxide (nearly 96% of the atmosphere), which produces surface pressures that only occur on Earth at ocean depths below 1000 meters. Venus's carbon-dioxide-rich atmosphere allows incoming solar radiation to pass through but absorbs outgoing radiation, trapping it within. Absorption of outgoing radiation—like the daytime heating of an indoor plant nursery—is called the "greenhouse effect."

To understand the greenhouse effect, it is necessary to start with the Sun, which has a surface temperature around 6000°C. This solar energy radiates through space in particles (photons) as well as in waves—embracing the "duality of light." Waves are further represented by their wavelengths (distances from crest to crest or trough to trough), like the different colors in the humanly visible region of the electromagnetic spectrum (Fig. 8.7).

The maximum wavelength emitted by the Sun or any other radiating body is

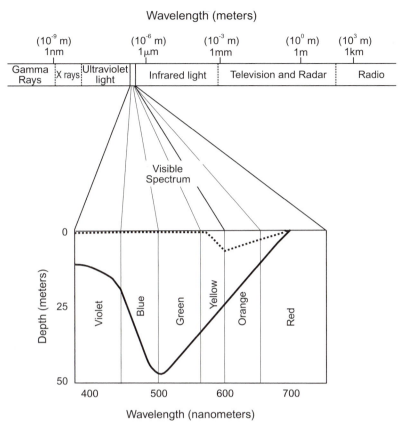

FIGURE 8.7   The electromagnetic spectrum, from gamma rays that have wavelengths less than a trillionth (10^{-12} or 0.000000000001) of a meter to radio wavelengths that can exceed 10 kilometers. The visible part of the spectrum occurs between the ultraviolet and infrared regions, with wavelengths between approximately 380 and 750 nanometers (10^{-9} meters). The distribution of visible colors in clear oceanic waters (solid line) and turbid coastal waters (dotted line) is shown, with blue and green being the deepest penetrating. Modified from Sumich (1996).

inversely proportional to its absolute temperature (Box 8.1: Wien's law). Radiating bodies also emit energy in proportion to the fourth power of their temperatures (Box 8.1: Stefan–Boltzmann law).

Incoming solar radiation has a maximum wavelength around 0.5 microns (0.0000005 meters) with 44% in the visible, 48% in the infrared, and the remainder in the ultraviolet regions of the electromagnetic spectrum (Figs. 8.7 and 8.8a). When this solar radiation reaches the Earth system, around 26% is immediately reflected by clouds and scattered through the blue sky back into space. Another 4% of the solar radiation is reflected at the Earth's surface, primarily from white ice-covered regions, which have high albedo or reflectance. Incoming solar ra-

BOX 8.1   TEMPERATURE–RADIATION
RELATIONSHIPS

WIEN'S LAW

Maximum wavelength (λ_{max}) = constant #1/Absolute temperature (°K)

STEFAN–BOLTZMANN LAW

Radiation emission = constant #2 $\times$ (Absolute temperature)^4

where:
absolute temperature (°K, degrees Kelvin) = °C (degrees celsius) + 273.15;
constant #1 = 2898 λm °K;
constant #2 = 5.67 $\times$ 10^{-8} Watts m^{-2} °K^4.

diation also is absorbed—19% by the atmosphere and 51% by Earth's surfaces (largely in the oceans). This solar energy budget warms the Earth system to around −18°C.

Although much colder than the Sun, the Earth also emits radiation (Box 8.1), but at a much lower wattage and with a maximum wavelength in the infrared region around 10 microns (Fig. 8.8a). This outgoing radiation, which has longer wavelengths than red light (Fig. 8.7), acts much like an infrared lamp that warms food in a restaurant. Rather than escaping into space, however, more than 70% of this infrared radiation is absorbed in the troposphere by "greenhouse" gases (Fig. 1.1b, Table 8.1). In the Earth system, it is estimated that the surface temperature is warmed by more than 30°C because of this atmospheric trapping of outgoing radiation—without which the oceans would freeze and life as we know it would not exist.

The most important greenhouse gas—in terms of both total volume and capacity to absorb infrared radiation—is water vapor (Table 8.1). The breadth of infrared wavelengths absorbed by water vapor exceeds all of the other greenhouse gases (Fig. 8.8b). Water vapor can even close the "atmospheric window" (infrared wavelengths between 8 and 12 microns that are least absorbed in the atmosphere), which is why it is warmer during calm winter nights with clouds rather than with stars above. Because liquid water evaporates and precipitates regionally (Figs. 8.4 and 8.5), over hours to weeks, it is difficult to estimate the geographic distribution and "greenhouse effect" of water vapor on a global scale. This regional effect is compounded by the asymmetric areas of the ocean north and south of the equator (Fig. 1.4)—potentially magnifying climate warming when insolation is greater in the Southern Hemisphere (Fig. 7.3) because of increased water-vapor production.

In contrast, greenhouse gases with longer atmospheric lifetimes become well mixed and uniformly distributed on a global scale. Next to water vapor, carbon

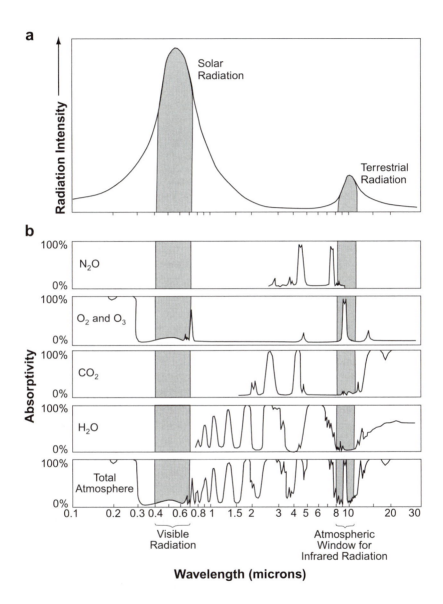

FIGURE 8.8   (a) Relative intensities of radiating wavelengths emitted from the Sun (5780°K) and Earth (255°K) based on their absolute temperatures (Box 8.1). (b) Absorptivity of different wavelengths across the electromagnetic spectrum (Fig. 8.7) by major greenhouse gases in the troposphere (Fig. 1.1b), showing the "windows" for incoming solar shortwave radiation and outgoing terrestrial infrared radiation. Modified from Lutgens and Tarbuck (1998).

TABLE 8.1   Principal Greenhouse Gases in the Earth Systems[a]

Gas	Atmospheric percentage 1850	Atmospheric percentage 1999	Atmospheric lifetime	Global warming potential[b]
Water vapor (H_2O)	0.4	0.4	Hours to weeks	NA[c]
Carbon dioxide (CO_2)	0.0280	0.0365	120 years	1
Methane (CH_4)	0.000079	0.000172	12 years	21
Nitrous oxide (N_2O)	0.0000275	0.0000314	120 years	310
Surface ozone (O_3)	0.0000025	0.0000026	Hours	NA[c]
Chlorofluorocarbon-11 (CCl_3F)	0	260 ppt[d]	50 years	12,400
Chlorofluorocarbon-12 (CF_2Cl_2)	0	530 ppt[d]	102 years	15,800

[a] Within the troposphere (Fig. 1.1b) estimated on a global scale.

[b] Relative capacity of a "greenhouse gas" to absorb outgoing infrared radiation within the next century, as determined by the Intergovernmental Panel on Climate Change (Houghton *et al.*, 1996).

[c] Not applicable to gases and aerosols that have nonuniform distributions in the global atmosphere.

[d] ppt (parts per trillion: 0.000000000000001).

Data Sources: Intergovernmental Panel on Climate Change (Houghton *et al.*, 1996) and NASA Goddard Institute for Space Studies (http://www.giss.nasa.gov/data/si99/ghgases).

dioxide contributes most to the greenhouse effect because of its relatively high concentrations, long atmospheric lifetime, and broad absorption of infrared radiation (Table 8.1 and Fig. 8.8b).

Like other greenhouse gases that are naturally produced (as opposed to chlorofluorocarbons, which are human engineered), carbon dioxide is coupled directly with biological processes [Eq. (1.1)]. For carbon dioxide, this biological connection is well illustrated by the seasonal photosynthesis of leaves on deciduous trees that blossom in spring and drop onto the ground in autumn, tangibly converting carbon dioxide into biomass. This seasonal cycle of photosynthesis has been recorded continuously from both hemispheres—inhaling and exhaling throughout the Earth system—since the mid-20th century (Fig. 8.9).

Atmospheric measurements from Mauna Loa, Hawaii, also reveal that the global concentration of carbon dioxide has been increasing during the past five decades (Fig. 8.9). Telescoping backward in time, ice-core records from Antarctica further indicate that global carbon dioxide concentrations have been increasing exponentially (Fig. 8.10) along with the human population since the mid-19th century (Fig. II). Moreover, the current concentrations of carbon dioxide (around 365 parts per million by volume) are the highest at any time during the past 420,000 years (Fig. 7.4).

These recent atmospheric changes in carbon dioxide are largely related to the industrial burning of fossil fuels, which has added previously buried carbon dioxide to the atmosphere. Carbon dioxide increases have been further compounded by the removal of forests, grasslands, and other plant communities that

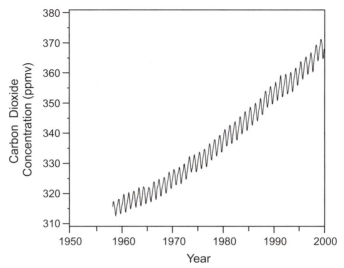

FIGURE 8.9 Atmospheric carbon-dioxide measurements that have been collected continuously since 1958 at the Mauna Loa Observatory, Hawaii. The seasonal oscillation of carbon dioxide (CO_2) reflects the relative photosynthesis [Eq. (1.1)] in the Northern and Southern Hemispheres associated with the breathing of the Earth system. During this half-century period, the global concentration of atmospheric carbon dioxide has been continuously increasing. Modified from Keeling and Whorf (2000).

would have extracted carbon dioxide from the atmosphere through photosynthesis [Eq. (1.1)].

After remaining relatively constant for almost 10,000 years, global carbon dioxide concentrations have increased nearly 30% (from 280 to 365 parts per million) just since 1850 (Fig. 8.10), along with the geometric growth of the human population (Fig. II). Given the close historical relationship between global temperature and carbon dioxide concentrations throughout the past half-million years (Fig. 7.4), it appears that the dramatic increase in the volume of carbon dioxide in the atmosphere has contributed significantly to the 20th century being the warmest period in the past millennium.

 What forces influence environmental variability over various space and time dimensions in the Earth system?

Despite these apparent relationships between global carbon dioxide concentrations and temperatures, it is important to recognize that there are other factors that contribute to global warming and that *correlation does not mean causation*. The role of water vapor through time, in particular, remains an enigma in understanding the dynamics of greenhouse gases that contribute to the Earth's heat budget.

In many ways, the relatively pristine nature of Antarctica acts as a sentinel of

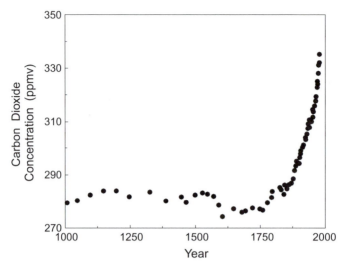

FIGURE 8.10   Ice-core measurements of trapped atmospheric gases from Law Dome Station, Antarctica, which indicate that global carbon dioxide concentrations (in parts per million) during the past millennium have been increasing geometrically since the mid-19th century concurrent with the ongoing expansion of our civilization (Fig. II). Modified from Ethridge *et al.* (1998).

global changes not only in the past but for the present and future. Perhaps the most compelling example of Antarctica as an human impact indicator is the "ozone hole" that forms in the stratosphere (Fig. 1.1b) above Antarctica each spring. In 2000, the area of the ozone hole (where ozone concentrations are depleted by more than 50%) extended across nearly 30 million square kilometers—which is larger than the entire continent of North America.

The ozone layer in the stratosphere (Fig. 1.1a)—which is distinct from ozone in the troposphere that contributes to ground-level smog and air pollution— absorbs incoming high-energy ultraviolet radiation from the Sun. The concern is that decreased stratospheric ozone concentrations will allow more ultraviolet radiation, especially ultraviolet-B (240 to 320 nanometers; Fig. 8.7), to reach the Earth's surface and dramatically increase genetic mutations among living organisms.

Since the early 20th century, millions of tons of chlorofluorocarbons from aerosols, solvents, and various coolant systems have been introduced into the atmosphere. Over time, these anthropogenic chemicals mixed upward into the overlying stratosphere where they began persisting (Table 8.1). Equation (8.2) shows the stratospheric chemistry of ozone depletion. In the presence of sunlight, ultraviolet radiation causes the constant regeneration of ozone from diatomic oxygen molecules and individual oxygen atoms [Eqs. (8.2a–8.2c)]. With chlorofluorocarbons in the stratosphere, however, these oxygen atoms will bind with chlorine

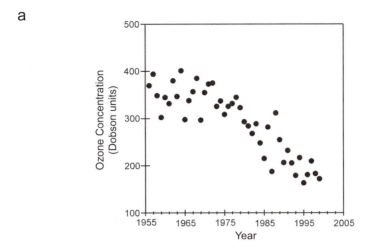

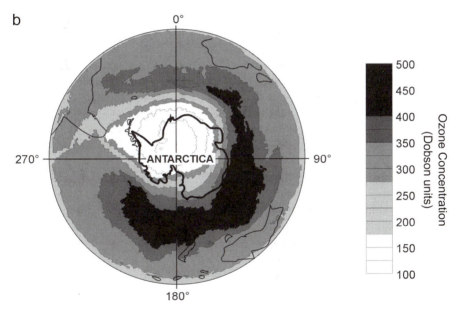

FIGURE 8.11   (a) Antarctic measurements of ozone at Halley Station (75° south, 26° west) showing average concentrations in October, when ozone levels generally are lowest each year. Ozone concentrations are measured in Dobson units, in parts per billion, which represent the amount of ozone in a square-centimeter column through the atmosphere. Based on data from the British Antarctic Survey (http://www.nerc-bas.ac.uk/public/icd/jds/ozone/data/zoz5699.dat). (b) The "ozone hole" over Antarctica on 7 October 2000, showing the circumpolar concentrations of stratospheric ozone, which were minimal over the continent and lower part of South America and increasing toward the lower latitudes (continental perimeters are outlined). Based on "Earth Probe" satellite data collected with the total ozone mapping spectrometer (TOMS) from the Goddard Space Flight Center, National Aeronautics and Space Administration (http://toms.gsfc.nasa.gov/ozone/ozone01.html).

atoms [Eq. (8.2d)], each of which robs oxygen atoms and effectively destroys around 100,000 ozone molecules:

$$O_2 + UV \rightarrow O + O \tag{8.2a}$$

$$O_2 + O + M \rightarrow O_3 + M \tag{8.2b}$$

$$O_3 + UV \rightarrow O_2 + O \tag{8.2c}$$

$$Cl + O \rightarrow ClO \tag{8.2d}$$

where UV is ultraviolet radiation; M, catalyst; O, oxygen atom; O_2, molecular oxygen gas; and O_3, ozone.

Baseline observations from the British Antarctic Survey indicate that levels of ozone centered around 300 Dobson units from 1957 to 1975 and then decreased precipitously to levels less than 100 Dobson units today (Figs. 8.11a). The shape and location of the ozone "hole" (Fig. 8.11b) are another reflection of the circumpolar nature of the Antarctic environmental system (Figs. 8.1–8.3 and 8.6). These observations from Antarctica, which confirmed earlier hypotheses about stratospheric ozone depletion, were the harbingers that motivated the international community to eliminate chlorofluorocarbon production by the end of the 20th century (Chapter 11: Environmental Protection).

The mere fact that ozone depletion was detected most severely over Antarctica, far removed from the populated regions of the planet where chlorofluorocarbons were introduced into the atmosphere, alone is a strong demonstration of the global dynamics of the Earth's atmosphere. In addition, stratospheric ozone and carbon dioxide both demonstrate the overall value of long-term measurements, over decades and centuries, for assessing environmental trends and events that can affect society.

The essence of global climate variability is that long-term climate trends (Fig. 6.5) are influenced by shorter-term climate cycles (Fig. 7.4), which are further superimposed on even shorter-term climatic events (Figs. 7.6, 8.9, and 8.10). Distinguishing the underlying forces that influence the dynamics of the Earth system over different time and space scales (Figs. 2.3 and 6.1)—from the movement of continents to the combustion of fossil fuels—is essential to understanding relationships between environmental variability and humankind.

9

LIVING PLANET

The chess board is the world,
the pieces are the phenomena of the universe,
the rules of the game are what we call the laws of Nature.
  —*Thomas Henry Huxley (1868),* A Liberal Education
                          and Where to Find It

BIOCOMPLEXITY

Life is the ultimate expression of natural variability. Through the course of the Earth system, organisms have evolved within kingdoms of differing biological complexity from bacteria to the plants and animals. Within each kingdom, organisms are further distinguished across hierarchies of taxonomic complexity (e.g., Table 2.1). Even within unique species—which are defined by their ability to interbreed and produce viable offspring—there are biochemical, physiological, or morphological variations that influence the fitness of individuals to propagate their genes into future generations.

Adaptations also enable species to interact with other organisms within habitats that are constrained by physical, chemical, and geological phenomena (Fig. III). These ecological interactions exist at the population level where individuals of the same species utilize resources within a defined area to increase their density and biomass. Additionally, within habitats, interacting populations of different species form communities that are characterized by their diversities. Different communities subsequently interact within the natural boundaries of a region—forming ecosystems that are further characterized by the flow of organic production. At the pinnacle of species' interactions (Table 9.1), all biological systems unite into the biosphere, which embodies the dynamics of life on Earth.

TABLE 9.1   Levels of Ecological Organization for Interpreting Interactions Between Species and Their Habitats

Ecological level	Ecological characteristics
Individual	Energetics of an organism that are influenced by available resources, environmental variability, and its inherent adaptations (Figs. 9.8–9.10)
Population	Density, biomass, and size frequency of individuals from the same species interacting within a specific habitat (Figs. 9.3 and 9.5)
Community	Diversity and biomass of different species interacting within a defined type of habitat (Figs. 9.1, 9.2, 9.4, and 9.6)
Ecosystem	Flow of species' biomass and production among prey, predators and competitors from diverse communities across a range of habitats within a bounded region (Fig. 9.7)
Biosphere	Life on Earth (Plate 1 and Fig. 9.11)

In addition, the complexity of life is reflected over time and space by the biogeography of species (Figs. 1.6 and 6.1). For example, as Antarctica cooled and became thermally isolated during the Cenozoic (Chapter 6: Spreading Planet), organisms developed specialized adaptations and restricted distributions. With ocean temperatures that freeze freshwater, Antarctic fish became dominated by species in the suborder Nototheniodei that have a glycoprotein antifreeze (as in car radiators) to prevent their blood from becoming solid ice that would burst cells like filled water bottles in a freezer. Among the notothenioids, there also are icefish that certainly are evolutionary curiosities as the only vertebrates without red blood cells (hemoglobin) for carrying oxygen throughout their bodies. As a consequence of such adaptations, levels of endemism exceed 90% among the fish and other marine taxa living around Antarctica (Table 9.2).

Similarly, responding to the circumpolar circulation of the Southern Ocean, which has been operating since the late Oligocene (Fig. 6.5 and 8.3), marine species also evolved distributional patterns that ring the Antarctic continent (Fig. 9.1). Moreover, reflecting their evolution between deep-sea and coastal habitats— which are both cold, sheltered, and dark, with prolonged periods of low production—bottom-dwelling (benthic) species commonly have depth ranges exceeding 1000 meters across the Antarctic continental shelf.

In the open sea (pelagic) realm of the Antarctic marine ecosystem, there are micron-size viruses and bacteria along with various phytoplankton which are dominated by diatoms with more than 100 species among genera such as *Thalassiosira* and *Chaetoceros* (Fig. 9.2). These species are consumed by various zooplankton, including fish larvae, ctenophores, salps, arrow worms, polychaetes, and pteropods, as well as diverse crustacea among the ostracods, copepods, mysids, euphausids, and amphipods, which can be several centimeters long. The largest of the Antarctic zooplankton are jellyfish, some with tentacles extending many meters (Plate 6). Still larger free-swimming (nektonic) fish, squid, seals, and

TABLE 9.2   Percentages of Endemic Species among Marine Benthic
Groups South of the Antarctic Convergence [a]

Taxa[b]	Number of benthic species	Endemic species (%)
Plant Groups		
Green algae (Chlorophyta)	20	>16
Brown algae (Phaeophyta)	28	>41
Red algae (Rhodophyta)	55	>70
Animal Groups		
Sponges (Porifera)	300	50
Ascidia (Chordata)	129	56
Polychaeta (Annelida)	650	57
Bryozoa	310	58
Sea cucumbers (Echinodermata)	38	58
Isopoda and Tanaida (Arthropoda)	229	66
Brachiopoda	16	69
Molluscs[c]	800	75
Barnacles (Arthropoda)	37	76
Sea urchins (Echinodermata)	44	77
Sea spiders (Pycnogonida)	100	90
Amphipoda (Arthropoda)	470	90
Fish (Pisces)	202	95

[a] Adapted from Heywood and Whitaker (1984) and Picken (1985).
[b] Phyla are identified or noted in parentheses.
[c] Estimated from Arntz et al. (1997).

whales in the Antarctic marine ecosystem range in size up to the blue whale (*Balaenoptera musculus*, Table 2.1), which has a maximum length exceeding 30 meters and is the largest animal ever to inhabit the Earth.

Diverse and abundant assemblages also inhabit the Antarctic marine benthos on (epifaunal) as well as in (infaunal) the sediments (Plate 10). Microbenthic species include various algae and bacteria forming dense mats. There also are protozoans, single-celled animals with unique feeding adaptations, such as the foraminifera that glue sand grains together into filtering forms like small trees several centimeters high. Among the macrobenthic faunas, there are various molluscs, giant sea spiders, starfish that stretch 30 centimeters across, sea urchins, meterlong nemertean worms, crustaceans, and fish. At greater depths, which are more sheltered and less disturbed, there is an increase among the larger sedentary filterfeeding organisms, particularly the sea cucumbers, bryozoans, sponges, hydroids, soft corals, and tunicates.

In this adaptive interplay between species and their environments, fossil assemblages of extant species further reflect both environmental variability and biotic

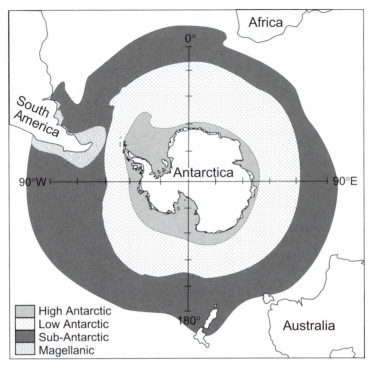

FIGURE 9.1   Generalized biogeographic zones (with tick marks at 10° latitude increments) based on the diversity of species in the Antarctic marine ecosystem (Fig. 9.2) that are strongly influenced by the circulation and historical development of the Southern Ocean (Figs. 6.5, 7.8, and 8.3). Modified from Hedgpeth (1969).

responses in the Earth system today (Plates 5 and 6). For example, guano deposits on emerged beaches reflect the population persistence of Adélie penguins in stable habitats along the Victoria Land Coast during the past 6000 years (Fig. 9.3). Similarly, living moss banks in the Antarctic Peninsula region and mats of primitive algae in permanently ice-covered lakes in the McMurdo Dry Valleys also have been thriving since the mid-Holocene—much like species in other habitats around the Earth (Chapter 7: Flowing Planet and Chapter 8: Breathing Planet).

With desert levels of precipitation (Fig. 8.7), Antarctic terrestrial species generally are restricted to ice-free coastal oases where there is a modicum of seasonal snowfall and melting. Algae have adaptations for dehydrating themselves as well as becoming insulated alive within sandstone rocks. There also are tiny mites, less than 3 millimeters in size with glycerol in their blood, nestling under rocks and in sand or other moistened habitats in temperatures below −30°C. Among these minute arthropods, which nonetheless are the largest animals on Antarctica, *Nanorchestes antarcticus* survives down to 85° south latitude as the southernmost terrestrial animal on Earth.

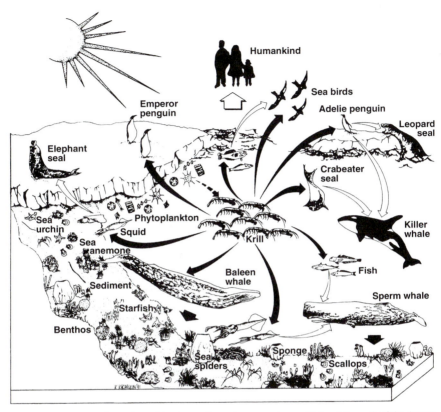

FIGURE 9.2   Illustration of the Antarctic marine ecosystem, which exists south of the Antarctic Convergence (Figs. 7.8 and 8.3), showing interactions among representative species groups at different trophic levels (Table 9.2; Fig. 9.7): from the phytoplankton in the sea-ice zone; to the zooplankton assemblages with krill (*Euphausia superba*) as the keystone species (dashed open arrows); to the whales, seals, birds, fish, and squid that consume the krill and other zooplankton species (solid arrows); to the killer whales (*Orcinus orca*) and leopard seals (*Hydrurga leptonyx*) that are the apex predators (open arrows). Ultimately, organic production flows from the pelagic food web onto the sea floor, where it is consumed and recycled by diverse assemblages of benthic species (large solid arrows). Humankind interrupts the flow of energy in the Antarctic marine ecosystem by permanently removing biomass from various trophic levels (large open arrow). Modified from Berkman (1992).

Antarctic terrestrial animals also include protozoans, rotifers, tardigrades, and nematodes, which live with the arthropods in impoverished soils as well as on incidental organic materials, exposed rocks, and ice surfaces. In permanently ice-covered lakes, planktonic animals (zooplankton) are dominated by rotifers with nematodes, tardigrades, and the occasional platyhelminth or annelid worm (Table 9.3). There even are a few planktonic crustaceans, including the copepod *Parabroteas sarsi,* which is the top predator in Antarctic lakes. In addition, Antarctic lakes contain benthic species, including bacteria, mosses, and green algae, as well

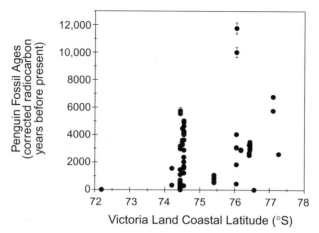

FIGURE 9.3   Persistence of Adélie penguin (*Pygoscelis adeliae*) rookeries along the Victoria Land Coast (Fig. 8.6), particularly in the vicinity of Terra Nova Bay, which have been radiocarbon-dated from cores of guano deposits (Plate 5). The radiocarbon ages have been corrected by subtracting the 1300-year age of Antarctic seawater (Berkman and Forman, 1996) that traveled through the deep sea from the North Atlantic and upwelled at the Antarctic Divergence (Figs. 7.8 and 7.9). Based on data from Baroni and Orombelli (1994) and adapted from Berkman (1997b).

as blue-green algae like the stromatolites that were among the most primitive photosynthesizers of oxygen in Earth's early atmosphere (Fig. 1.6). Antarctic terrestrial ecosystems also contain mosses, liverworts, lichens, fungi, and two species of flowering plants (Fig. 9.4).

Antarctica also holds promise for identifying adaptations that could support extraterrestrial life. Under the East Antarctic Ice Sheet, where water is maintained

TABLE 9.3   Terrestrial Life on the Antarctic Continent [a]

Faunal phylum	Number of species	Floral form	Number of species
Protozoa	68 [b]	Algae	360 [b]
Rotifera	13	Flowers	2
Tardigrada	6	Fungi	10
Nematoda	10	Lichens	400 [b]
Arthropoda	78 [b] 3 [c]	Liverworts	2
		Mosses	72

[a] Terrestrial life forms include plant and animal species as well as bacteria, which are not described in this table. Based on Block (1984).

[b] Uncertain number.

[c] Introduced species.

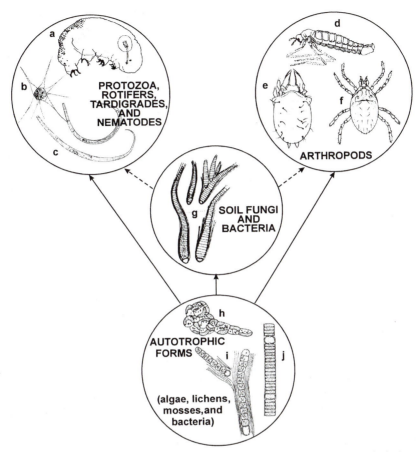

FIGURE 9.4 Diagram of the principal species groups and their trophic linkages in the impoverished terrestrial ecosystems of Antarctica (Table 9.3; Fig. 9.7). Organic materials and nutrients are added through seal and bird rookeries in some Antarctic coastal areas. Antarctic terrestrial taxa shown are with their species name, phylum and adult size in millimeters (mm), as available: a, *Hypsibius asper* (Tardigrada, 0.3 mm); b, *Teratocephalus tilbrooki* (Nematoda); c, *Astromoeba radiosa* (Protozoa, 0.02 mm); d, *Belgica antarctica* (Arthropoda, 1.5–2.5 mm); e, *Maudheimia petronia* (Arthropoda, 0.6 mm); f, *Stereotydeus delicatus* (Arthropoda, 0.4 mm); g, *Calothrix parietina* (Cyanophyceae, 0.01 mm); h, Chlorophyta (green algae); i, Cyanophyceae (blue-green algae/bacteria); and j, Cyanophyceae (blue-green algae/bacteria). Modified from Greene *et al.* (1969) with species from Block (1984) and Vincent (1988).

in its liquid phase because of the extreme pressures at depths below 3000 meters, there are nearly 70 lakes. The largest of these ancient and yet unexplored ecosystems (each of which may be several million years old) is Lake Vostok with a surface area around 14,000 square kilometers and water depths greater than 600 meters—placing it among the 15 largest lakes on Earth. The intrigue of Lake

Vostok is that primitive bacteria—with genetic fingerprints from DNA strands— have been discovered from the Vostok ice core (Fig. 7.4) in "lake ice" several hundred meters above the lake. Planning is underway to create an uncontaminated new hole with novel technologies, including "cryobots," to enter Lake Vostok and remotely sample this ecosystem as an analog for life in icy environments else- where in our solar system.

Antarctic marine and terrestrial ecosystems are classic contrasts. Despite the freezing temperatures and extreme seasonality, Antarctic marine life thrives in one of the richest ecosystems in the ocean (Table 9.2, Fig. 9.2). Conversely, Antarctic terrestrial life is the most impoverished of any continent, with only a handful of species eking out a sparse existence under environmental extremes not unlike those on lunar or Martian landscapes (Table 9.3, Fig. 9.4). Together, these Antarc- tic biota reveal habitat limitations that generally control the production of biomass in the Earth system.

LIMITING FACTORS

In circumstances where there are unlimited resources, populations tend to in- crease in a geometric fashion, with two individuals becoming four, then eight, then 16 and on upward (Fig. 9.5). In fact, as noted by Thomas Robert Malthus (1766– 1834) in his 1798 *Essay on the Principle of Population:* "It has been universally remarked that all new colonies settled in healthy countries, where there was plenty of room and food, have constantly increased with astonishing rapidity in their population." However, beyond the initial phase of colonization, some factor even- tually limits population growth like a weak link in a chain. These limiting fac- tors—which Malthus described for humans in terms of war, pestilence, famine, and "convulsions of nature"—become progressively more severe as populations approach the carrying capacity of their habitat. In contrast to geometric growth, limited populations tend to level off and form logistic or S-shaped growth curves (Fig. 9.5).

Population growth in all cases depends on the balance among births, deaths, immigrations, and emigrations, which influences recruitment. Conceptually, the per capita recruitment rates (r) can be combined with the initial population sizes (N) and maximal population sizes at the carrying capacity of the habitat (K) to deter- mine how the overall biomass or densities of population will change over time:

$$\text{Population growth rate} = r\,N\,\frac{(K - N)}{K} \qquad (9.1)$$

When population sizes are nearly zero, for example after a volcanic eruption or other "convulsion of nature," resources are effectively unutilized and there is an opportunity for geometric population growth. Conversely, as resources become limiting toward the carrying capacity of the habitat (when N approaches K), popu- lation growth rates become zero. If there are more individuals than the habitat can

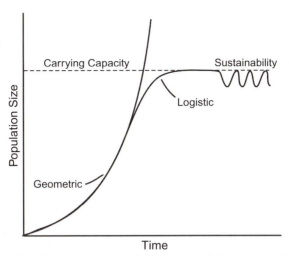

FIGURE 9.5 Population growth with unlimited resources is geometric and solely dependent on the per capita recruitment rate of new individuals into the population [Eq. (9.1)]. Maximum population growth rates occur at 50% of their carrying capacity. Resources in most habitats, however, are limited, with population growth becoming logistic or S-shaped as the carrying capacity of the habitat is approached. Ultimately, populations will decline or fluctuate as they approach the carrying capacity or over utilize the resources in their habitat beyond sustainable limits.

support (when N exceeds K), populations decline. In addition, for logistic growth, the maximum population growth rate occurs at a population size that equals 50% of its carrying capacity.

In the extremely seasonal polar ecosystems, light is a limiting resource for photosynthesis (Fig. 7.1). In general, planktonic plants (phytoplankton) float in the water at depths where there is sufficient sunlight for photosynthesis. This light corridor near the surface of aquatic ecosystems, called the euphotic zone, can extend several hundred meters in clear oceanic areas and only centimeters in turbid coastal areas (Fig. 8.7). In most water bodies, the lower limit of the euphotic zone is considered to be the depth where 1% of the incident solar radiation penetrates from the surface.

In the ice-covered marine and terrestrial ecosystems around Antarctica, however, the euphotic zone extends to depths where less than 0.1% of the incident radiation penetrates because aquatic algae have become adapted with specialized chlorophyll and complexes of accessory pigments. The distinct absorption spectra (e.g., Fig. 8.8b) of these pigments also enable Antarctic algae to utilize more deeply penetrating colors of light (Fig. 8.7). When these qualities and quantities of light become limiting—either at depths below the euphotic zone or as winter approaches—primary production ceases in polar ecosystems.

In many aquatic ecosystems, even with unlimited light, algal growth is limited by nutrients. Among the major nutrients, nitrogen and phosphorus contribute most to the utilization of carbon by photosynthetic species. Generally, the ratio of carbon, nitrogen, and phosphorus in the sea (C:N:P = 106:16:1)—known as the "Redfield ratio" after the 20th-century American scientist Alfred Redfield (1890–1983)—provides a useful baseline for determining when these nutrients become limiting. Silicon is another important nutrient because it is an essential ingredient for the pillbox-shaped frustules of diatoms, which are the most abundant algal forms in the Antarctic marine ecosystem. There also are micronutrients, notably iron, that may limit primary production even when the major nutrients are abundant.

Habitats with scarce nutrients, where plants grow poorly, are oligotrophic (scant nourishment), whereas habitats with abundant nutrients that stimulate plant production are considered to be eutrophic (good nourishment). For example, permanently ice-covered lakes on Antarctica tend to be oligotrophic because of limited nutrient inflows, unlike eutrophic areas in the Antarctic marine ecosystem near the Antarctic Divergence (Fig. 7.8) where nutrients are continually upwelling. Consequently, the amount of food available for larger animals is limited in Antarctic lakes compared to the adjacent marine ecosystem (Figs. 9.3 and 9.4). Outside of these aquatic environments, water becomes a limiting resource.

Resources also can become limiting as individuals compete with other organisms, either within their own species (intraspecific) or between other species (interspecific). In either case, the evolutionary outcome is to reduce competition so that organisms will have more resources available for their own production. As concisely stated by Hardin (1960): "Complete competitors cannot coexist." This statement implies that when competition is complete, organisms will be unable to coexist because some will dominate at the exclusion of others. Conversely, when organisms coexist, competition is minimal because the necessary resource is either unlimited or partitioned in some way among the organisms.

 How do organisms partition limited resources within and between species as well as over time and space?

An example of resource partitioning exists among competing marine mammals feeding in the Southern Ocean (Figs. 9.3 and 9.6). These mammals include seven species of baleen whales (suborder Mysticeti), such as the blue whale, which have large parallel comblike arrays in their mouth for sieving their prey from the seawater. There also are eight species of toothed whales (suborder Odontoceti) that occur south of the Antarctic Convergence. Toothed species include the killer whale (*Orcinus orca*) and the "great white leviathan" of Herman Melville's *Moby-Dick*—the sperm whale (*Physeter macrocephalus*), which has lengths exceeding 18 meters.

There also are six seal species in the Antarctic marine ecosystem from among the 36 on Earth (Fig. 9.2). The harem-forming southern elephant seal (*Mirounga leonina*) and Antarctic fur seal (*Arctocephalus gazella*) both colonize exposed coastal areas around the continental margin. In contrast, the crabeater seal (*Lobodon carcinophaga*), the predatory leopard seal (*Hydrurga leptonyx*), and the rare

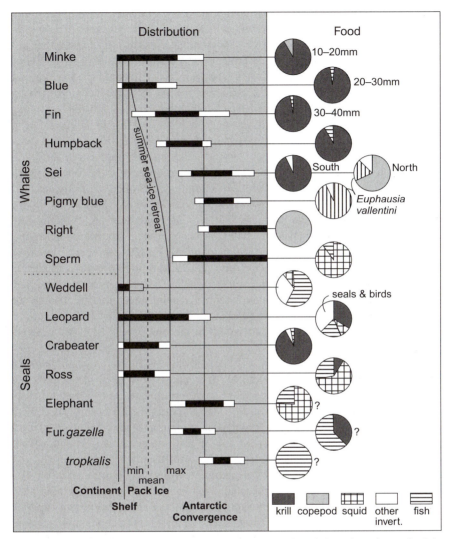

FIGURE 9.6   Resource partitioning among the eight whale and six seal species south of the Antarctic Convergence (Figs. 8.3), in the Antarctic marine ecosystem (Fig. 9.2). These marine mammals adjust their zonal distributions and migration patterns in relation to the seasonal sea-ice cycle to reduce their competitive overlap (Fig. 8.1). These species also reduce their competition for food by consuming different size classes of krill (*Euphausia superba*) and other common prey species. Modified from Laws (1977).

Ross seal (*Ommatophoca rossii*) are found among pack-ice flows and intervening open-ocean areas. The Weddell seal (*Leptonychotes weddelli*) is uniquely adapted to coastal habitats that are completely covered by sea ice, where they submerge for periods longer than an hour, dive to depths below 500 meters, and then return by echolocating breathing holes (Plate 7).

Most of these marine mammals feed principally on a small shrimplike herbivore called krill (*Euphausia superba*), which drifts in the plankton. The importance of krill in the Antarctic marine ecosystem derives from its circumpolar distribution and dense aggregations, or swarms, which can contain more than 50,000 individuals in a cubic meter of water with biomasses exceeding 15 kilograms. Viewed in three dimensions, each swarm has a relatively narrow edge, which enhances oxygen diffusion into the mass. The mechanisms behind this schooling behavior are not fully understood; however, it is known that individuals follow pressure changes associated with the wake of preceding individuals. The other species of *Euphausia* in the Antarctic marine ecosystem do not form dense aggregations, and in the absence of krill, the dominant zooplankton are copepods (primarily *Calananoides acutus, Calanus propinquus,* and *Rhincalanus gigas*).

Baleen whales minimize their interspecific competition for krill by occupying different zones south of the Antarctic Convergence and selecting different sizes of krill prey (Fig. 9.6). The baleen whales also stagger their southward migrations, with the blue whales arriving first, followed by the fin (*Balaenoptera physalus*), humpback (*Megaptera novaeangliae*), and sei (*Balaenoptera borealis*) whales. In addition, there are intraspecific differences in whale migrations by sex, age, and reproductive status. This timing and extent of annual whale migrations into the Antarctic marine ecosystem corresponds with the stored energy in their blubber, which ranges from 27% of the body mass in the blue whale to 17% in the sei whale.

The crabeater seal, with its specially adapted sievelike arrangement of teeth for filtering zooplankton, also is a principal krill predator. However, because crabeater seals feed on krill in the pack ice, they have minimal overlap with the baleen whales, which are feeding northward of the retreating ice edge (Fig. 9.6). These adaptations and the extreme krill abundances explain why the crabeater seal has a population size estimated between 15 and 30 million, accounting for about half of the global seal population and more than two-thirds of its biomass.

Squid also are important prey for mammals in the Antarctic marine ecosystem, especially among sperm whales and elephant seals. There are approximately 70 squid species that inhabit the Southern Ocean, generally below the euphotic zone and commonly deeper than 2000 meters. Many of these cephalopod mollusc species have mantle sacs that are less than 20 centimeters in length, but a few grow to very large sizes. In particular, *Mesonychoteuthis hamiltoni* can have total lengths exceeding 4 meters with weights greater than 150 kilograms. Competition for these squid as prey is minimized by elephant seals having their highest feeding activities during the austral winter, whereas the sperm whales mainly feed during the summer around Antarctica.

In addition, Antarctic marine mammals consume fish. Among the 270 Antarctic fish species, nearly 75% are bottom-dwelling. This benthic fish fauna generally occurs in coastal areas, whereas pelagic forms tend to occur at depths below 1000 meters. Moreover, the deep pelagic forms are dominated by 33 lanternfish species in the family Myctophidae, which is widely known for echoing human-generated sound pulses that distinguish "deep scattering layers" throughout the ocean.

Along with the marine mammals, penguins also compete for the krill, squid, and fish in the Antarctic marine ecosystem (Fig. 9.2). Among these flightless seabirds—which evolved exclusively in the Southern Hemisphere since the early Cenozoic—7 of the 18 extant species breed south of the Antarctic Convergence. King (*Aptenodytes patagonicus*) and rockhopper (*Eudyptes crestatus*) penguins breed on the peripheral islands surrounding Antarctica. Chinstrap (*Pygoscelis antarctica*), gentoo (*Pygoscelis papua*), and macaroni (*Eudyptes chrysolophus*) penguins breed in the maritime zone along the Antarctic Peninsula as well as on the peripheral islands. The Adélie (*Pygoscelis adeliae*) and emperor (*Aptenodytes forsteri*) penguins breed in the Antarctic Peninsula region as well as in the continental zone south of 65° south (Fig. 9.1, Plate 7).

An additional 31 species of flying seabirds also breed and feed south of the Antarctic Convergence. These include 4 albatross and 20 smaller petrel species as well as 7 species among the gulls, skuas, terns, and cormorants. Many of the smaller seabirds dwell in burrows that they excavate in loose rocks and moss banks. The larger species, which are better insulated and less affected by predation from other seabirds, have surface nesting sites. Most of these seabirds travel annually into the Antarctic region during the summer sea-ice retreat, some of which migrate great distances, as with Wilson's storm petrel (*Oceanites oceanicus*), which flies between the Arctic and Antarctic.

The top predators in the Antarctic marine ecosystem are the leopard seal and killer whale (Fig. 9.2). Leopard seals have pointed front teeth for grasping and tearing their prey and can grow to nearly 4 meters in length with weights over half a ton. Killer whales are much larger with lengths over 9 meters and weights over 7 tons. Both of these species prey on other large vertebrates, such as penguins and seals as well as fish and squid. Killer whales, which often hunt cooperatively in pods, also are known to feed on other whales. Overlap among these two top predators, however, is minimal since the killer whale is effectively unchallenged as the dominant predator at the apex of the Antarctic marine ecosystem (Fig. 9.2).

PYRAMID OF LIFE

Predators and prey transfer biomass through the Earth system in a cascade of biological activities. At the base of this organic (carbon-based) pyramid are the autotrophic (self-nourishment) organisms, which start the flow of food energy. These primary producers include plants, which photosynthesize basic sugars with light energy, as well as bacteria, which chemosynthesize sugars using chemical energy from sources such as the 350°C hydrothermal vents in the deep sea [Eq. (1.1)]. Above the primary producers, at all subsequent trophic levels, are the heterotrophic (different nourishment) organisms, which utilize organic matter synthesized by other organisms, up to the apex predator at the top of the trophic pyramid (Fig. 9.7). The shape of this pyramid indicates that available food energy, either in terms of biomass or the number of organisms, progressively decreases toward the higher trophic levels.

 Why are production and biomass fundamental concepts in interpreting ecological interactions?

At each trophic level above the primary producers (Fig. 9.7), food is consumed and allocated by animals for various life-sustaining functions (Fig. 9.8). Initially, much of the food energy is used simply for metabolism and other maintenance activities of the animal. Food energy also is lost through excretion with only a small amount of energy available for animals to increase in size or number. For example, we may only gain several ounces in weight after eating a 1-pound hamburger. Some of this assimilated food energy then can be allocated toward growth and reproduction, which together contribute to the biomass of the population.

The proportion of food that is converted into biomass reflects the ecological efficiency of transferring energy between trophic levels:

$$\text{Ecological efficiency} = \frac{\text{Production}_{\text{trophic level } n}}{\text{Production}_{\text{trophic level } n-1}} \qquad (9.2)$$

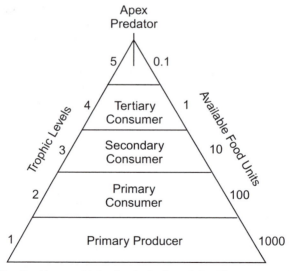

FIGURE 9.7 Trophic pyramid showing the feeding relationships among species in ecosystems (Figs. 9.3 and 9.4). At the base of the pyramid are the primary producers that synthesize carbohydrate energy [Eq. (1.1)], which is subsequently consumed by herbivores and various levels of carnivores up to the apex predator. In this example the ecological efficiency [Eq. (9.2)] for calculating the production at different trophic levels [Eq. (9.3)] is 10%.

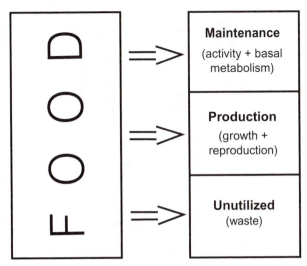

FIGURE 9.8   Generalized illustration of food energy that is consumed and partitioned by an organism for life-sustaining activities associated with its basic maintenance and production. Basic maintenance includes metabolic activities associated with respiration, digestion, and excretion, as well as any movement activities for obtaining the food. Food that is excreted and not assimilated for basic maintenance or production is unutilized waste. Production involves food energy that is converted into biomass through both growth and reproduction.

Based on the ecological efficiency (E, which varies from 0 to 1) and the biomass of the primary producers (B), the production (P) at any trophic level (n) then can be calculated:

$$P = B\,E^{n-1} \tag{9.3}$$

Figure 9.7 illustrates the application of Eq. (9.3) with an average ecological efficiency of 0.1, which indicates that 10% of the food energy is transferred into biomass at the next higher trophic level.

As reflected by species' growth rates, however, the amount of biomass produced within a population is variable. For example, the finely spaced shell bands of Antarctic scallops (*Adamussium colbecki*) provide detailed evidence about their growth (Fig. 9.9). Not only does scallop growth fluctuate on a seasonal cycle (as indicated by the pattern of relatively wide and narrow shell rings, like growth rings in trees), but their growth markedly decreases after the scallops reach sexual maturity. In fact, decadal mark-and-recapture experiments with the Antarctic scallop indicate that this benthic species grows less than a millimeter per year during adulthood—reaching sizes larger than 100 millimeters only after more than a century (Plates 5 and 6). Moreover, as illustrated by the sperm whale, there also can be differences between the growth of males and females because of their distinct energy requirements for reproduction (Fig. 9.10). Together, these growth patterns

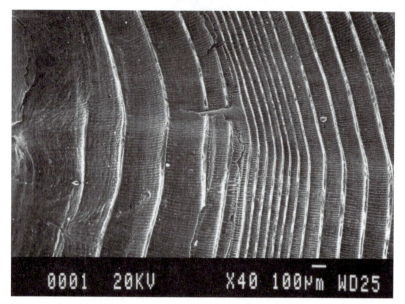

FIGURE 9.9 Antarctic scallop (*Adamussium colbecki*) shell growth that reflects its development over time like other accretionary structures (e.g., skeletons, teeth, trees, sediments, or ice cores). Imaged with a scanning electron microscope, the pattern of wide summer and narrow winter rings represent an annual growth cycle that extends across the shell during the century lifespan of this species (Plate 6). Increments between adjacent juvenile growth rings are relative to the 100 micrometer (0.0001 meter) scale bar. Adapted from Berkman (1997b).

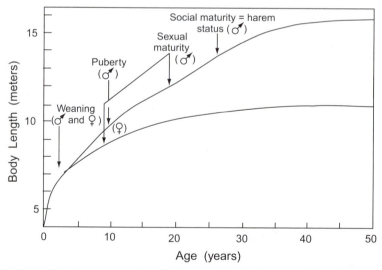

FIGURE 9.10 Average growth profiles for male and female sperm whales (*Physeter macrocephalus*) whose ages were determined by counting the annual layers in their teeth. Marked sexual dimorphism in growth rates and maximum sizes of this squid-eating toothed whale species (Fig. 9.6) reflects their different energy partitioning for growth and reproduction (Fig. 9.8). Modified from Brown and Lockyer (1984).

and adaptations reflect both the food availability and energy allocation among species and genders at different stages of their life histories.

Trophic dynamics across the Earth system, in response to sunlight (Fig. 7.1) and nutrient availability as limiting factors, can be illustrated by the cyclic production of phytoplankton and herbivorous zooplankton (Fig. 9.11). At low latitudes, where nutrient levels are low and solar radiation is constantly high throughout the year, there are relatively low-amplitude changes in the production of the primary producers and their consumers. In the mid-latitudes, taking advantage of winter nutrient accumulations, phytoplankton populations bloom with the return of spring. Subsequently, thriving zooplankton populations appear until they have depleted their food, at which point the phytoplankton can once again resume their production through winter onset.

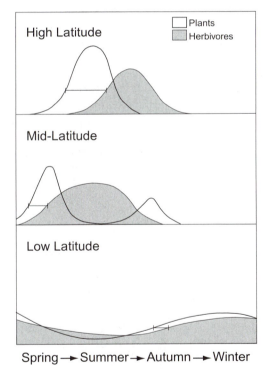

FIGURE 9.11   Generalized seasonal relationships between phytoplankton blooms and their subsequent consumption by herbivorous zooplankton—illustrating basic trophic dynamics (Fig. 9.7) across the Earth system. In the low latitudes, there is minimal seasonality in solar illumination (Fig. 7.1), temperature, and nutrient availability—all of which influence primary production. In the mid-latitudes, there are spring and fall phytoplankton blooms associated with solar variability as well relatively high nutrient levels. In the high latitudes, photosynthesis can occur only during the summer. Bloom amplitudes as well as the lag periods (horizontal bar) between primary and secondary production peaks decrease toward the lower latitudes. Adapted from Parsons and Takahashi (1973).

With the short pulse of summer sunlight in the high latitudes, like the seasonality of the region, there are bursts of phytoplankton and zooplankton production. Particularly in the Antarctic marine ecosystem, along with the advance and retreat of the sea ice (Fig. 8.1), there is a cascade of biological responses as herbivores up the trophic pyramid redirect their feeding strategies and energetics as photosynthesis turns completely on or off with the seasons (Figs. 9.3–9.10).

In addition to production cycles, trophic relationships [Fig. 9.7; Eq. (9.3)] provide a framework for interpreting the distribution of biomass throughout the world ocean. In general, there are three types of oceanic provinces that can be distinguished in relation to their underlying levels of primary production (Table 9.4). Oceanic areas, which cover the vast majority of the Earth's surface, generally are oligotrophic with exceedingly low nutrient concentrations for primary production. As a consequence, in these oceanic areas, many species are competing for limited energy that is inefficiently transferred across many trophic levels. Coastal marine habitats, which incorporate nutrients from terrestrial runoff, have higher levels of primary production with more efficient energy transfers among fewer trophic levels. However, the most productive marine habitats occur in upwelling areas where there are high nutrient concentrations for primary producers to support short efficient trophic pyramids.

Table 9.4 is particularly relevant because it reflects the nutritional sources from the sea that are utilized by humans. Based on the trophic level of the fish (which represents the food eaten directly by humans) and the ecological efficiency [Eq. (9.2)], it can be seen that less than 1% of the fish food from the sea is obtained from the open ocean—which accounts for 90% of the ocean area. In contrast, nearly half of the fish production comes from coastal areas. The amazing conclusion from Table 9.4 is that upwelling areas, which occupy less than one-tenth of

TABLE 9.4   Organic Production in Oceanic Provinces[a]

Ecosystem characteristics	Oceanic provinces		
	Oceanic	Coastal	Upwelling
Percentage of ocean	90	9.9	0.1
Oceanic province area (km^2)	326,000,000	36,000,000	360,000
Primary productivity (grams/m^2/year)[b]	500	1000	3000
Primary production (tons/year)[b]	163,000,000,000	36,000,000,000	1,080,000,000
Average trophic levels	6	4	2.5[c]
Average ecological efficiency	0.1	0.15	0.2
Fish production[d] (tons/year)[b]	1,630,000	121,500,000	129,600,000

[a] Adapted from Ryther (1969).

[b] Based on wet weights.

[c] Average value of two trophic levels (when the fish species are herbivorous, as among the anchovy) and three trophic levels.

[d] Derived from Eq. (9.3) $(P = BE^{n-1})$.

one percent of the total ocean area, account for more than half of the total fish production from the sea!

The principal upwelling areas in the ocean are associated with eastern boundary currents that carry cold polar waters equatorward along the west coasts of North America, South America, Africa, and Australia. Along with monsoonal upwelling along east Africa, these mid-latitude regions account for about 200,000 square kilometers of the estimated upwelling area in the ocean (Table 9.4). Conservatively, the remaining 160,000 square kilometers of upwelling area occurs around Antarctica (32,000-kilometer circumference), in a narrow zone that would cover an area around a quarter of the continent seaward for a distance of only 20 kilometers. These estimates suggest that the Antarctic marine ecosystem alone accounts for much more than 25% of the total production at the second and third trophic levels in the world ocean.

PART

I V

SUSTAINABLE
RESOURCE USE

RESOURCE ECONOMICS

Resources are everything biological or environmental that species use for their benefit. In a human context, resources are identified, utilized, and managed by diverse stakeholders as commodities that can be owned and sold. These commodities include living and nonliving resources, such as marine fisheries or mineral deposits, which have short-term commercial values that are limited by resource supply and demand. There also are resources that have long-term values, such as records of climate change that are necessary for charting the course of civilization centuries into the future. There even are abstract resources whose value is in the eye of the beholder, like the view of a pristine wilderness or the hut of an early explorer. The purpose of Part IV of this book is to examine the development and implementation of resource strategies in Antarctica as an example for balancing economic, scientific, government, and social interests in utilizing natural resources on a global scale (Antarctic Treaty Searchable Database: 1959–1999 CD-ROM).

On the broadest management level, the 1959 Antarctic Treaty created a dynamic framework for using the entire south polar region "exclusively for peaceful purposes" as a global resource "in the interest of all mankind." Through the Antarctic Treaty System (Chapter 5: International Stewardship), competing stakeholders have been able to identify common interests in continuously consulting and formulating resource management strategies (Box 5.3).

From the outset, the Antarctic Treaty Consultative Meetings (ATCM) provided forums for the international community to elaborate conservation strategies for Antarctic living resources (Table 5.2). In 1964, the Agreed Measures on the Conservation of Antarctic Fauna and Flora were adopted, creating specially protected areas as well as protected species. Recognizing the extensive exploitation of Antarctic seals during the 19th century and the potential for other human-induced reductions in species, the Antarctic Treaty nations signed the Convention on the Conservation of Antarctic Seals (CCAS) in 1972. However, seals along with most other species are part of interacting ecological systems, involving perspectives that focus beyond individual groups of species (Chapter 10: Ecosystem Conservation).

In the Antarctic marine ecosystem (Chapter 9: Living Planet), there also had been severe depletion of whale populations since the start of the 20th century with keystone species such as krill (*Euphausia superba*) as emerging commercial targets. Moreover, it became apparent that the krill alone could become a food staple exceeding the total harvest of all species from the sea, which is on the order of 100 million tons per year. Responding to these global concerns, the Antarctic Treaty nations signed the 1980 Convention on the Conservation of Antarctic Marine Living Resources (CCAMLR) to create an "ecosystem approach" for managing "harvested, related and dependent populations" in the Antarctic marine ecosystem.

These living resource regimes were fair-haired children of the Antarctic Treaty System compared to the Convention on the Regulation of Antarctic Mineral Resource Activities (CRAMRA), which was signed in 1988 (Table 5.2). Accommodations had to be reached among the claimant and nonclaimant nations—a divisive element in the Antarctic Treaty System. Interests in Antarctica as a "glittering prize" also were growing throughout the international community, especially after the *Wall Street Journal* speculated in 1974 on the extensive petroleum deposits on the Antarctic continental shelf. Moreover, there were concerns about lasting environmental impacts in Antarctic marine and terrestrial ecosystems. All of these issues were to have been resolved by CRAMRA as a "matter of urgency."

However, in 1989 the *Bahia Paraiso* oil spill in the Antarctic Peninsula region caused the Antarctic Treaty nations to abandon CRAMRA because of heightened concerns about mineral resource activities ever being *acceptable.* Despite 14 years of negotiating and elaborating criteria for acceptable mineral prospecting, exploration and development activities, CRAMRA was never ratified (Table 5.2). In its place, the 1991 Protocol on Environmental Protection to the Antarctic Treaty (PROTOCOL) simply prohibited "all mineral resource activities in Antarctica" for the next 50 years, at least, or until economic pressures overwhelm the current political consensus (Chapter 11: Environmental Protection).

The PROTOCOL also consolidated the resource management strategies from the first 30 years of the Antarctic Treaty System (Table 5.2). Beyond discrete environmental solutions, the PROTOCOL established that all Antarctic habitats—both marine and terrestrial—were linked as "dependent and associated ecosystems." Strategies for assessing the "minor or transitory" nature of environmental impacts were identified, particularly as they relate to the conservation of Antarctic fauna and flora. The PROTOCOL also identified environmental principles that included the "wilderness and aesthetic values" of Antarctica, as well as its intrinsic value as an area for conducting essential scientific research to understand the global environment.

Because of the increasing numbers of humans in Antarctica, either as part of national programs or commercial expeditions, guidelines for waste disposal and management were created. The PROTOCOL also instituted strategies for preventing marine pollution in the circumpolar Southern Ocean, since most of the human transport is by ship, especially by the tourist vessels that now transport more than 10,000 persons each year as the largest human contingent in the Antarctic region. In essence, because there are multiple uses of Antarctica—from science to tourism to resource exploitation—it was nec-

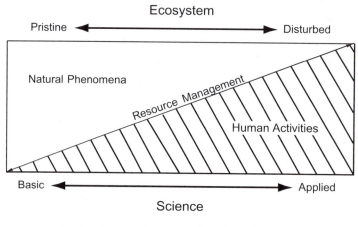

Scientific Research Continuum

FIGURE IV   Earth system science extends across a continuum from basic to applied research with a broad focus on ecosystem events, entities and phenomena over time and space on a planetary scale (Part I: Earth System Science). On the basic end of the spectrum are studies about the world around us just because of its wonder. On the applied end are studies, technologies, and enterprises for utilizing biological and environmental resources. Across the scientific continuum are insights about creating ecosystem management strategies that will perpetuate the rational use of our natural resources into the distant future. Modified from Berkman (1992).

essary to design a holistic blueprint for Antarctic area protection and management. Beyond the gentlemen's agreement among nations in the Antarctic Treaty, the PROTOCOL pertains to the shared responsibility of all entities in the Antarctic region—from national programs to commercial ventures to individuals.

The underpinning of resource management, whether in Antarctica or anywhere else in the Earth system, is the information available for understanding how humans affect natural systems. In this general context, the visionary international system in Antarctica is a model for designing resource policies that integrate information across the research continuum from basic to applied science (Fig. IV). Across this spectrum, basic science focuses on natural processes in pristine ecosystems, often without considering the ramifications of the research in a societal context. Conversely, applied science is directed toward analyzing human impacts in disturbed ecosystems, often without establishing the appropriate natural baselines. In essence, interpreting the relationship between natural processes and human impacts requires information that integrates both basic and applied science. The following chapters will highlight Antarctic examples for integrating scientific research and resource policies that are relevant to the future of humankind.

Humans, like all known life forms, are dependent on Earth's resources. Humans also have a unique capacity among Earth's species to modify land, ocean, and atmospheric systems along with the geological, physical, chemical, and biological processes that connect them (Fig. III). At a most fundamental level, understanding and being able to respond effectively to natural and human-induced environmental changes is essential for sustaining the development of societies throughout the Earth system into the distant future.

10

ECOSYSTEM CONSERVATION

*Each organic being is striving to increase in a geometrical
ratio . . . each at some period of its life, during some season of
the year, during each generation. . . .*
—*Charles Robert Darwin (1859),* On the Origin of Species

HARVESTING HISTORY

All species, as Darwin noted, are striving to survive and multiply in a "geometric ratio" (Fig. 9.5). *Homo sapiens* is no different from any other species,
particularly in view of our geometric population growth during the past several
centuries (Fig. II). Like other species—for fortune or survival—we also exploit
the largest and most accessible resources first before moving on to smaller, less
abundant resources. The history of resource exploitation by humans in Antarctica
has been no exception.

Since *Terra Australis Incognita* was first imagined, resources have been the
allure of Antarctica (Plate 2). Suggestions about Antarctica as a "tropical paradise" with masting timbers or grain crops had propelled nations southward (Chapter 3: *Terra Australis Incognita*). However, it was only after Cook's voyage south
of the Antarctic Circle in the late 18th century that humans began capitalizing on
the rich resources that actually existed in the region.

 **What determines the order in which species are harvested from
ecosystems?**

Around Antarctica, humans began with the seal and penguin species that could
easily be collected on patches of land around the continent. After diminishing

their populations, technologies were developed to effectively capture other marine living resources. The largest and most accessible animals—the whales—were exploited next. Following the progressive decline of the great whale species, fish and invertebrates now are the targets in the Antarctic marine ecosystem. This history of harvesting species in the Antarctic marine ecosystem can be used to illustrate the impacts of uncontrolled exploitation, the resilience of natural systems, and the challenges of sustaining our living resources for future generations.

Upon his return to England in 1775, Captain James Cook noted that there were extensive populations of the Antarctic fur seal (*Arctocephalus gazella*) on beaches throughout the subantarctic islands. These large marine animals represented an obvious and easily accessible source of capital, and by the end of the 18th century fur sealing had become a major commercial enterprise in the Southern Ocean (Fig. 10.1).

Fur sealing climaxed at South Georgia around 1800—within a mere 25 years of Cook's initial observation. By 1822, an estimated 1,200,000 seals already had been harvested, nearly wiping out the South Georgia population (Fig. 10.1). The sealers then moved to South Shetland Islands north of the Antarctic Peninsula, where there were additional abundant fur seal colonies, and within 3 years more than 320,000 fur seals had been harvested. The sealers than expanded their efforts to the South Orkney, South Sandwich, and other subantarctic islands. Again, populations of these seals were decimated, only more quickly because of the sealers' prior experience and improved technologies. When the sealers returned to these islands at the end of the century, after more than 50 years, the fur seal populations had not recovered (Fig. 10.1).

Elephant seals (*Mirounga leonina*) also were harvested during the 19th century, but not as relentlessly as the fur seal. Recognizing the consequences of un-

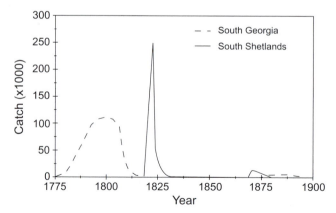

FIGURE 10.1   Estimated catches of Antarctic fur seals (*Arctocephalus gazella*) at South Georgia and the South Shetland islands demonstrate their rapid overexploitation and negligible population recovery during the 19th century. Modified from Holdgate (1984) and Berkman (1992).

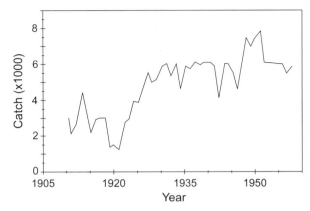

FIGURE 10.2　　Catches of elephant seals on South Georgia, which were licensed by the British government after 1910 at a limit of 6000 bull males per year (Table 10.5). This elephant seal licensing approach was the first conservation strategy for living resources in the Antarctic region. Modified from Bonner and Laws (1964) and Berkman (1992).

controlled seal harvesting, the British government began issuing quotas in 1910 for the exploitation of elephant seals on South Georgia. Only bull males were to be taken, and then only to the extent that sufficient numbers remained on the beaches to reproduce with their harems. These regulations, which were implemented as the first Antarctic resource conservation strategy, included a limit of 6000 bulls per year as well as specified sealing zones and seasons (Fig. 10.2). This elephant sealing industry continued until 1964, when it collapsed along with the Antarctic whaling industry.

　　None of the other four Antarctic seal species have been the focus of commercial harvesting. In view of harvesting the most abundant resources first, this absence of commercial interest is particularly interesting with respect to the crab-eater seal (*Lobodon carcinophaga*), which alone accounts for more than half of the seals on Earth. The Weddell seal (*Leptonychotes weddelli*) is the next most abundant Antarctic seal, with an estimated population size of 730,000 (Plate 7). Localized impacts on Weddell seal populations around Antarctica had occurred in relation to their utilization as food for dog teams until the late 1980s. The leopard (*Hydrurga leptonyx*) and Ross (*Ommatophoca rossii*) seals constitute slightly more than 2% of the Antarctic seal population and never have been harvested.

　　The presence of large rookeries in the vicinity of sealing and whaling enterprises, on subantarctic islands near the Antarctic Convergence (Fig. 8.3), also made penguins easily accessible targets. Penguins were killed to make clothing from their skins and fuel oil from their blubber, while their eggs were collected for food.

　　The king penguin (*Aptenodytes patagonicus*), because of its large size and thick layer of blubber, was harvested in great quantities. More than 400,000 king penguins were reported to have been killed in the Falkland Islands in 1867 alone. Similar levels of harvesting for the combined populations of king, macaroni (*Eudyptes chrysolophus*), and gentoo (*Pygoscelis papua*) penguins also have been reported for South Georgia.

However, the most extreme episode of penguin harvesting began on Macquarie Island in 1891 under a lease from the government of New Zealand. This industry initially focused on the king penguin and eventually shifted to the royal penguin (*Eudyptes schlegeli*). More than 150,000 penguins were killed per year on Macquarie Island until public outrage forced the New Zealand government to withdraw the lease in 1916.

Egg collecting also had an impact on penguin populations around Antarctica. On the Falkland Islands, for example, more than 13,000 rockhopper penguin (*Eudyptes chrysocome*) eggs were removed in a single day from a 2-kilometer stretch of cliff. Until recently, more than 10,000 gentoo penguin eggs have been collected each year by the people living on the Falkland Islands during the annual "egging picnic" on November 9th. As a consequence of harvesting the adults and collecting their eggs, penguin populations have been reduced or eliminated around Antarctica. These impacts are reflected in the populations of king penguins, which have greatly decreased on Macquarie Island, South Georgia, and the Kerguelen Islands and have completely vanished from the Falkland Islands.

Whaling in Antarctica began in 1904 with the establishment of a station at Stromness, South Georgia, by the Norwegian C. A. Larson. During the first year a single ship captured 195 whales (Fig. 10.3) from among more the million estimated in the Antarctic region (Table 10.1). The Antarctic whaling industry grew rapidly, and by 1912–1913 there were six land stations with 21 factory ships that captured 10,760 whales. All of the early Antarctic whaling was conducted in the Falkland Island Dependencies, which belonged to the United Kingdom (Chapter 3: *Terra Australis Incognita*).

To avoid government regulations, such as the licenses for elephant seals, a new type of whaling vessel was created in 1925. Whales could be brought onto ships by a slipway at the stern and then processed without returning to the land stations. This technological advance further increased whaling activity such that in 1930–31 more than 37,500 whales were taken by 205 catchers—yielding more than 570,000 tons of whale oil and causing the collapse of the world market for whale oil in 1931.

Initially, the humpback whale (*Megaptera novaeangliae*) was taken because of its abundance near islands—for much the same reason that the seals and penguins were first exploited. As the humpback populations declined, fishing for the blue (*Balaenoptera musculus*) and fin (*Balaenoptera physalus*) whales increased. The fishery for fin whales continued beyond the collapse of the blue whale populations until it also was replaced by fisheries for the sei (*Balaenoptera borealis*) and sperm (*Physeter macrocephalus*) whales. During the 1990s, Japan and Norway began harvesting the small minke whale (*Balaenoptera acutorostrata*) in opposition to the international moratorium on all commercial whaling activities that began in 1986.

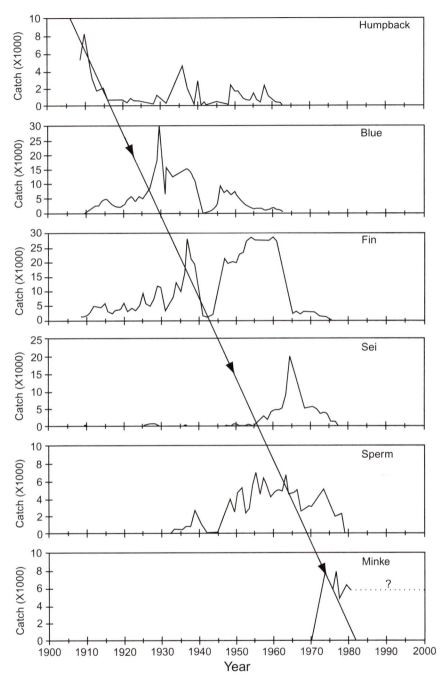

FIGURE 10.3 Annual catches of the great whales in the Antarctic marine ecosystem, showing the progressive depletion (diagonal line) of the different species during the 20th century. The whaling hiatus between 1940 and 1945 was due to World War II. These whaling activities have reduced the overall biomass among all whale species by more than 80% and among the humpback (*Megaptera novaeangliae*) and blue (*Balaenoptera musculus*) whales by more than 95% (Tables 10.1 and 10.2). The dashed line from the minke whale (*Balaenoptera acutorostrata*), among the smallest baleen whales, represents ongoing discussions about its future exploitation since the larger species no longer are commercially viable. Modified from Gambell (1985) and Berkman (1992).

TABLE 10.1   Estimates of Whale Populations before 1904[a,b]

Species	Whale characteristics			Whale food consumption		
	Population size	Animal weight (tons)	Population biomass (tons)	Krill (tons)	Squid (tons)	Fish (tons)
Blue	200,000	88	17,600,000	72,000,000	740,000	1,500,000
Fin	400,000	50	20,000,000	81,000,000	840,000	1,700,000
Humpback	100,000	27	2,700,000	11,000,000	1,110,000	200,000
Sei	75,000	19	1,425,000	6,000,000	60,000	100,000
Minke	200,000	7	1,400,000	20,000,000	200,000	400,000
Sperm	85,000	30	2,550,000	—	10,200,000	500,000
TOTAL	1,060,000	—	45,675,000	190,000,000	13,140,000	4,400,000

[a] Modified from May (1979).
[b] See Table 10.2 for current whale population estimates.

These continuous shifts in the target species and the progressive depletion of each stock (Fig. 10.3), except the new minke whale target, demonstrate that all whale fisheries have collapsed. This pattern of whale overexploitation occurred despite the regulatory strategies developed by the International Whaling Commission since its inception in 1946. These historical perspectives are strong evidence for the lack of human restraint in harvesting whales, with their extremely slow population turnover rates, to sustain any whale fishery now or in the future.

Combined, Antarctic whale stocks have been reduced by more than 80% (Tables 10.1 and 10.2). While the actual numbers may vary between estimates, there is agreement that the humpback and blue whale populations have been hit hardest, with stock sizes that have been diminished by over 95%.

TABLE 10.2   Estimates of Current Whale Populations[a,b]

Species	Whale characteristics			Whale food consumption		
	Population size	Animal weight (tons)	Population biomass (tons)	Krill (tons)	Squid (tons)	Fish (tons)
Blue	10,000	83	830,000	3,400,000	40,000	70,000
Fin	84,000	48	4,032,000	16,400,000	170,000	340,000
Humpback	3,000	27	81,000	300,000	—	—
Sei	41,000	18	738,000	2,900,000	30,000	60,000
Minke	200,000	7	1,400,000	19,800,000	200,000	410,000
Sperm	43,000	27	1,161,000	—	4,630,000	240,000
TOTAL	381,000	—	8,242,000	42,800,000	5,070,000	1,120,000

[a] Modified from May (1979).
[b] See Table 10.1 for pre-whaling population estimates.

Widespread reductions in large pelagic predator populations caused the commercial fisheries to consider new resources. Based on the diets of the whales species (Fig. 9.6) and their pre-exploitation population sizes, it is estimated that whale consumption of krill was around 190 million tons of krill each year (Table 10.1). After being exploited, it is estimated that whales only consumed around 43 million metric tons of krill (Table 10.2). As argued by the fishing industry from the Soviet Union, the 150 million-ton biomass of krill (*Euphausia superba*) that no longer was being consumed by whales provided a "surplus" that could be harvested by humans.

Consequently, after overharvesting the whales, humans then began targeting their krill prey because of its enormous biomass and dense concentrations in accessible swarms (Table 10.1). Locations of krill as well as other marine species have been identified within statistical fishing areas designated by the United Nations Food and Agriculture Organization for the Indian, Pacific, and Atlantic Ocean sectors in the Antarctic region (Figure 10.4).

The first recorded commercial catch of krill was in 1958–59, with a variable-depth trawl off a Soviet whaling vessel operating in the Atlantic Ocean sector of the Southern Ocean (Fig. 10.5). Between 1961 and 1979, the recorded catches of krill increased over five orders of magnitude, with the most marked changes occurring in the middle 1970s. This increased krill harvesting in the 1970s represents the added participation of Japan in 1971, Chile in 1974, Poland and West Germany in 1975, and Taiwan after 1977. In 1981–1982, just prior to the ratification of the Convention on the Conservation of Antarctic Marine Living Resources (CCAMLR), the krill harvest reached a peak at 528,000 tons. Afterward, krill harvesting fluctuated and then decreased markedly along with the diminished fishing pressure from Russia following the collapse of the Soviet Union in 1992.

Again—following the trend for the next most available resource—Antarctic fisheries began focusing on fish species. Antarctic fish species have been reported as potential commercial resources since the early 20th century. However, because of their relative inaccessibility and small biomasses compared to marine mammals, or krill, it was not until the end of the 1960s that Antarctic fish exploitation really began (Fig. 10.6).

Between 1969 and 1970, the Soviet Union harvested more than 403,000 tons of *Notothenia rossii* at South Georgia (Subarea 48.3) in an area where the total allowable catch for all of the fish species has been estimated to be only 50,000 tons per year (Figs. 10.4 and 10.6). Not surprisingly, *Notothenia rossii* populations at South Georgia declined rapidly and for the next several years only a few thousand tons of this species were harvested. Shortly afterward, Poland, Bulgaria, and West Germany began extending the finfish fishery along the Scotia Arc in the Atlantic Ocean sector with new target species and, by 1978, more than 150,000 tons of fish (primarily *Champsocephalus gunnari* with some *Notothenia rossii*) were being harvested annually.

Similar fishing efforts also have been exerted on the Kerguelen Plateau in the Indian Ocean sector (Fig. 10.4) where, in 1971, about 65% of the 229,500-ton

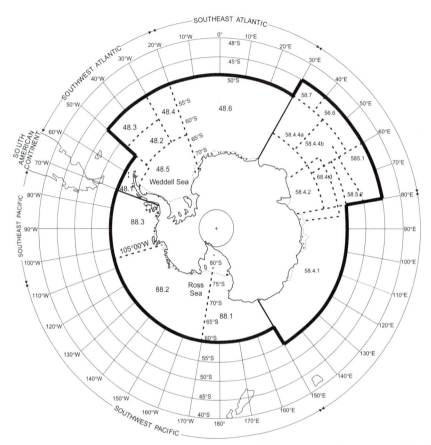

FIGURE 10.4 Sectors corresponding to statistical fishing areas that have been established under the auspices of the Food and Agriculture Organization of the United Nations (http://www.fao.org). The solid line around the Antarctic marine ecosystem represents the approximate position of the Antarctic Convergence (Figs. 7.8 and 8.3) and the northern jurisdictional boundary of the 1980 Convention on the Conservation of Antarctic Marine Living Resources (Antarctic Treaty Searchable Database: 1959–1999 CD-ROM).

harvest was *Notothenia rossii* (Fig. 10.6). Low *Notothenia rossii* catches followed, and the fishery refocused on *Champsocephalus gunnari* along with *Notothenia squamifrons*. In 1974 and 1977, these two species accounted for more than 75% of the 101,000 and 90,000 tons that were harvested, respectively. Again, the fish catch far exceeded the total allowable catch, which has been estimated to be only 20,000 tons per year for the Kerguelen Plateau area. Compared to the harvests in the Atlantic and Indian Ocean sectors, the fishing effort in the Pacific Ocean sector has been minor, with annual catches generally less than 100 tons.

By the late 1980s, after the *Champsocephalus gunnari* and *Notothenia rossii* stocks had been depleted, new fish species were becoming commercial targets,

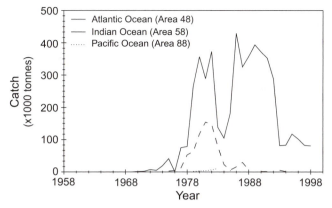

FIGURE 10.5   Harvesting of krill (*Euphausia superba*) in the Atlantic, Indian, and Pacific Ocean sectors of the Antarctic marine ecosystem (Fig. 10.4) based on data collected by the Scientific Committee of the 1980 Convention on the Conservation of Antarctic Marine Living Resources (http://www.ccamlr.org).

such as the myctophid *Electrona carlsbergi,* which had 75,000 tons harvested near South Georgia in 1990. Among the emerging Antarctic fisheries, the Antarctic cod (*Dissostichus mawsoni*) and particularly the Patagonian toothfish (*Dissostichus elegenoides*) have generated broad interest among Australian, Argentine, Chilean, French, Korean, New Zealand, Russian, South African, Ukranian, and United States industries. These industries also are expanding into new areas in the

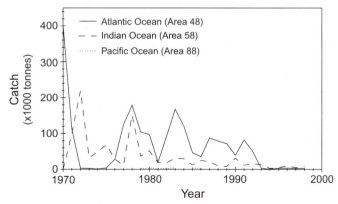

FIGURE 10.6   Finfish catches (from all species) in the Atlantic, Indian, and Pacific Ocean sectors of the Antarctic marine ecosystem (Fig. 10.4) based on data collected by the Scientific Committee of the 1980 Convention on the Conservation of Antarctic Marine Living Resources (http://www.ccamlr.org).

Atlantic, Indian, and even Pacific Ocean sectors around Antarctica (Fig. 10.4) where they reported capturing more than 11,000 tons of *Dissostichus elegenoides* in 1998.

Unfortunately, the largest catch among the current Antarctic fisheries is "illegal, unreported, and unregulated." In 1998 alone, it is estimated that more than 60,000 tons of Patagonian toothfish were traded (90% was exported to Japan and the United States)—exceeding the reported catches by a factor of 5 or 6. Moreover, some of this unregulated fishing comes from nations that are not under the jurisdiction of CCAMLR, such as the Seychelles, Faeroe Islands, and Belize. Considering that revenues from Patagonian toothfish (with a retail value exceeding seven dollars per kilogram in Japan) are upwards of $500 million, the ongoing challenge is to overcome short-term economic incentives and implement effective regulations that will sustain the harvested populations. Compliance is central to the effective implementation of any resource management strategy.

Another major problem with the longline fishery for Patagonian toothfish is the production of marine debris and incidental mortality (bycatch) of flying birds, marine mammals, and other marine species. Longlines, some of which extend more than 30 kilometers with more than 30,000 baited hooks, often are lost or abandoned. As a consequence, longlines are floating freely (ghost fishing) in the Antarctic marine ecosystem where marine species are being killed through entanglement or ingestion of the gear. Annual mortality of seabirds alone has been estimated by the CCAMLR to be between 50,000 and 100,000 in the late 1990s, mostly among the white-chinned petrel (*Procellaria aequinoctialis*), giant petrel (*Macronectes giganteus*), and black-browed albatross (*Diomedea melanophris*).

In addition to the species that already have been harvested, various algae, crustacea, molluscs, fish, and marine mammal species have been identified as potential living resources in the Antarctic marine ecosystem (Fig. 9.2, Table 10.3). In essence, the Food and Agriculture Organization of the United Nations has indicated that there are actual or potential fisheries at all trophic levels and localities in the Antarctic marine ecosystem. Motivations for developing these Antarctic fisheries are directly related to the commercial productivity of related industries in adjacent lower latitudes.

For example, interest in squid as an emerging living resource in the Southern Ocean stems from their wide occurrence in the diet of bird, seal, and whale species, which consume more than 30 million tons each year. Despite the lack of biological information on the squid in the Antarctic marine ecosystem, there have been a number of studies that have identified particular species for harvesting. These squid species include smaller forms, such as *Martialia hyadesi,* which are abundant in the surface waters, as well as the deep-dwelling giants, such as *Mesonychoteuthis hamiltoni,* which reaches several meters in length and is the principal food for the sperm whale. In the case of *Martialia,* 22,000 tons already have been caught incidentally along the Patagonian shelf of South America in conjunction with the *Illex argentinus* squid fishery. In 1996, more than 52 tons of *Martialia hyadesi* were captured in 7 days near South Georgia, signaling that it

TABLE 10.3 Living Resources with Actual and Potential Commercial Value in the Antarctic Marine Ecosystem[a,b]

Living resource group	Number of taxa	Collection method	Commercial use
Seaweeds	63	Mariculture, harvesting, bycatch	Human food, fodder, colloids, fertilizers, medical, pharmaceutical
Foraminifera[c]	Unknown	SCUBA	Medical
Benthic mollusks	17	Baited traps, dredging, trawling, bycatch	Human food
Benthic crustaceans	2	Baited traps, trawling, gillnetting, bycatch	Human food
Pelagic crustaceans	1	Trawling	Human food, fodder
Pelagic mollusks	20	Jigging, trawling, gillnetting, bycatch	Human food
Bivalves	9	Dredging, trawling, bycatch	Human food
Gastropods	8	Baited traps, bycatch	Human food
Cephalopods	20	Jigging, trawling, gillnetting, bycatch	Human food
Hagfishes and lampreys	2	Trawling, bycatch	Fodder
Sharks and skates	7	Trawling, bycatch	Human food
Bony fishes	50	Baited traps, trawling, gillnetting, long-lining, bycatch	Human food, fodder
Marine mammals[d]	21	Explosive harpoon, guns, bycatch	Human food, oil, skins, perfumes

[a] Within the statistical fishing areas that have been defined by the Food and Agriculture Organization of the United Nations that are being managed under the auspices of the 1980 Convention on the Conservation of Antarctic Marine Living Resources.

[b] Data from Fischer and Hureau (1985).

[c] Benthic protozoans that secrete a gluelike substances for binding sand grains have been identified as potential resources by United States and Australian scientists subsequent to the publication by Fischer and Hureau (1985).

[d] Capturing most species of marine mammals around Antarctica is prohibited by regulations under the 1946 International Convention for the Regulation of Whaling and the 1972 Convention on the Conservation of Antarctic Seals.

is possible to harvest commercial quantities of squid within the Antarctic marine ecosystem.

In addition to the swimming organisms (Figs. 10.1–10.3 and 10.5), there also is interest in harvesting Antarctic bottom-dwelling species. For example, near South Georgia in 1992—as a novelty—more than 299 tons of crabs (*Paralomis spinosissima* and *Paralomis formosa*) were harvested, representing more than 272,000 animals. In 1996, the South Georgia harvest of *Paralomis spinosissima* nearly doubled. Exploratory fisheries also have focused on bivalve mollusc species near other subantarctic islands.

How much of the harvest of marine species around Antarctica, as well as living resources worldwide, is driven by interests in economic gain rather than human survival?

Antarctic marine living resource activities mirror the exploitation of species throughout the sea during the last half of the 20th century (Table 10.4). Catches of the largest species, seals and whales, have decreased while the harvest of all other species groups has increased to a global yield from the sea that now exceeds 100 million tons per year. In addition on a global scale, fisheries for benthic species have increased at a faster rate than for pelagic species. As in the Antarctic marine ecosystem (Fig. 9.2)—with traditional commercial targets being progressively depleted, marine fisheries have been expanding to new species and into new areas throughout the ocean (Table 10.4).

As an upwelling zone (Fig. 7.8, Table 9.4), the Antarctic marine ecosystem supports an enormous biomass of krill, fish, squid, birds, seals, and whales. Natu-

TABLE 10.4   Global Harvest of Marine Species [a]

Marine species	Catch ($\times$ 1000 tons) [b]		
	1950	1975	1999
Seaweeds [c]	506.9	2,597.6	8,033.4
Benthic crustaceans [d]	220.0	566.2	1,609.8
Benthic molluscs [e]	955.4	2,826.2	10,742.4
Pelagic crustaceans [f]	413.1	1,359.8	4,124.8
Pelagic molluscs [g]	580.5	1,197.2	3,373.5
Diadromous fish [h]	88.6	216.6	488.6
Marine finfish	14,274.6	52,055.0	71,949.7
Turtles	1.7	8.2	87.6
Miscellaneous species [i]	181.3	839.2	4,272.1
Whales [j]	87,701	44,800	19,939
Seals [k]	810,148	578,617	426,326
TOTAL [l]	17,222.1	61,666	104,681.9

[a] Based on data from the Food and Agriculture Organization of the United Nations FAO FISH-STAT-PLUS ver. 2.3 (http://www.fao.org).

[b] Except whales and seals whose numbers are reported rather than biomasses.

[c] Includes brown, red, and green algae.

[d] Includes crabs and lobsters.

[e] Includes clams, mussels, scallops, oysters, abalone, and conch.

[f] Includes krill and shrimp.

[g] Includes octopus and squid.

[h] Marine species that migrate from the sea into freshwater and back.

[i] Includes corals, barnacles, echinoderms, sea squirts, sponges, and other species.

[j] Number of baleen and toothed whales.

[k] Number of seals and walruses.

[l] Total catch based on species' biomasses excluding whales and seals.

ral krill consumption by whales (Table 10.1)—as well as by seals, penguins, fish, and squid (Fig. 9.2)—reveals that the annual production of krill exceeds several hundred million tons. Considering that the worldwide harvest of species from the sea is around 100 million tons per year (Table 10.4), Antarctic krill could become humankind's single largest source of protein from the sea—potentially as large as all other marine fisheries from around the world combined.

INTERACTING ECOSYSTEMS

For the past two centuries, nations have been harvesting living resources in the Southern Ocean beyond the jurisdiction of any one nation. The larger more accessible resources, namely the seals and whales, were harvested first (Figs. 10.1–10.3). Smaller species of squid, fish, and krill subsequently were exploited, along with the decline of the larger animals and development of new harvesting technologies (Figs. 10.5 and 10.6). Although species were harvested independently, impacts from their depletion have propagated throughout the complex of relationships in Antarctic ecosystems (Figs. 9.3 and 9.4).

In particular, diminished baleen whale populations have increased the availability of krill (Fig. 10.3, Tables 10.1 and 10.2). With decreased competition for the keystone species in the Antarctic marine ecosystem (Chapter 9: Living Planet), fin and sei whales began feeding south of the Antarctic Convergence earlier each summer. Because of increased food availability, fin and sei whales decreased their mean ages at sexual maturity and increased their overall pregnancy rates along with those of the blue whale. Moreover, with fisheries selecting the larger, more accessible individuals first, population distributions and dynamics become skewed toward smaller and younger individuals. Fortunately for the harvested whale species, the decreased competition created a positive feedback for enhancing their average reproductive output and recovery (Figs. 10.7a and 10.7b).

The ecological vacuum created from depleting the whales has rippled through populations of competitor species at the same trophic level in the Antarctic marine ecosystem (Chapter 9: Living Planet). For example, prior to whaling, all of the seal species together consumed about one-third of the krill in the Antarctic marine ecosystem. Today, the seals (primarily the crabeater) have become the largest krill predators—annually consuming more than 80 million tons of krill, more than 1.5 times as much as the whales.

There also are suggestions that the crabeater seal has been reducing its age of sexual maturity (Fig. 10.7a) and increasing its circumpolar population size perhaps up to 40 million. Moreover, chinstrap (*Pygoscelis antarctica*) and Adélie (*Pygoscelis adeliae*) penguin populations appear to be increasing 3 to 12% per year around Antarctica (Plate 9). Population growth among these krill-eating species coincides with the diminished competition from whales and increased availability of their common prey.

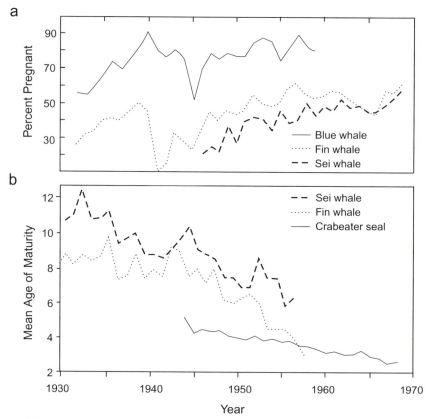

FIGURE 10.7 Changes in the reproductive capacity of marine mammals around Antarctica that were coincident with the human depletion of the great whale populations (Fig. 10.3). **(a)** Increased pregnancy rates among blue (*Balaenoptera musculus*), fin (*Balaenoptera physalus*) and sei (*Balaenoptera borealis*) whales. **(b)** Decreased ages of sexual maturity among fin and sei whales as well as crabeater seals (*Lobodon carcinophaga*). Modified from Laws (1977).

The most conspicuous population increase among krill predators has been with the Antarctic fur seal (*Arctocephalus gazella*) which nearly vanished around Antarctica during the 19th century (Fig. 10.1). On the South Georgia islands—where 1 to 2 million fur seals thrived prior to their exploitation—no seals were observed between 1907 and 1919. Following the whale population declines, however, fur seals began rebounding on these islands and across the Scotia Arc where major concentrations of the krill predators had overlapped (Fig. 9.6).

In 1930, 12 fur seal pups were found on South Georgia. By the early 1950s, there was a flourishing fur seal population on South Georgia with more than 5000 pups being produced each year. Between 1958 and 1972, the fur seal population increased nearly 17% per year with a doubling time around 4.5 years. Subsequently, the fur seal population on South Georgia has been expanding geometrically—over six orders of magnitude—to its current population size around 3 million individuals (Fig. 10.8). This recovery of the Antarctic fur seal, with its 20- to 30-year lifespan, is unprecedented among marine mammals.

Fur seals on South Georgia are the nucleus for about 96% of the species' pup production—generating impacts that now radiate from marine into terrestrial ecosystems. With such large populations on South Georgia, excretion by the fur seals is adding large quantities of nutrients to the lakes on South Georgia, which are changing their primary production levels and trophic dynamics. Moreover, the surging abundance of fur seals on South Georgia is now spilling onto millennium-old moss banks, which are being destroyed as the seal colonies expand across these terrestrial ecosystems (Fig. 9.4).

Impacts from whale harvesting (Fig. 10.3) are reverberating among Antarctic marine and terrestrial species at diverse ecological levels (Table 9.1). As experiments in progress, these impacts also illustrate the role of keystone species (Fig. 9.2) in the intertwined dynamics of dependent and associated ecosystems. Consequently, sustainable use of the krill, or any other living resource, requires realistic exploitation limits based on accurate predictions about how harvesting impacts propagate through ecosystems like ripples across a pond (Fig. 2.3).

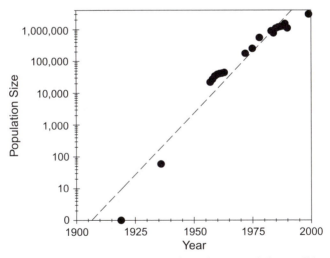

FIGURE 10.8   Remarkable recovery of the fur seal (*Arctocephalus gazella*) population on South Georgia, in the Atlantic Ocean sector (Fig. 10.4), after having been completely extirpated by overharvesting by 1907 (Fig. 10.1). Total fur seal population sizes were derived from pup production data (Payne, 1977; Boyd, 1993). The 1999 population size estimate was provided by J. P. Croxall (personal communication, 1999). The dashed line demonstrates the geometric increase (Fig. 9.5), across a logarithmic scale, of fur seal population sizes at South Georgia during the 20th century.

SUSTAINABILITY

Perspectives of Antarctic species as interconnected ecosystem elements have been elaborated in living resource management policies since the late 19th century. At the outset, however, harvesting activities were managed by individual nations establishing policies within specific areas for separate species (Table 10.5).

As represented by the elephant sealing on South Georgia (Fig. 10.2), early management strategies included scientific information. With bulls siring harems of elephant seals, it became apparent that harvesting quotas should be based on the number of males captured within specific periods and zones. Moreover, these

TABLE 10.5   Marine Living Resource Management Strategies Applied to Species in the Southern Ocean prior to the Antarctic Treaty System [a]

Year	Nation	Antarctic living resource management strategy
1881	United Kingdom	The Seal Fishery Ordinance, 1881
1902	Chile	Supreme Decree No. 3,310 Granting a Fishing Concession South of Terra Del Fuego
1905	United Kingdom	Permission to Norwegian Citizen for Whaling within Territorial Seas of the Falkland and South Georgia Islands
1906	United Kingdom	Whale Fishery Ordinance, 1906
1907	United Kingdom	License to Chilean Company for Whaling in the South Shetland Islands
1911	United Kingdom	United States Note Concerning a License to Take Sea Elephants off South Georgia Island
1911	United Kingdom	Lease to Danish Citizen of an Anchorage at South Georgia Island to Conduct Whaling
1912	United Kingdom	Lease to Operate a Whaling Station on Deception Island, South Shetland Islands
1921	United Kingdom	The Seal Fishery (Consolidation) Ordinance, 1921
1924	France	Decree Concerning a National Park for the Protection of Certain Species of Birds and Mammals
1926	New Zealand	The Ross Dependency Whaling Regulations, 1926
1928	Australia	Whaling Licenses in the Areas from Enderby to Queen Mary Lands
1928	Norway	Norwegian Provisional Regulations Forbidding the Hunting of Fur Seals
1931	International	International Convention for the Regulation of Whaling
1934	Australia	Imperial Whaling Industry Regulation Act, 1934
1935	New Zealand	Whaling Industry Act, 1935
1936	United Kingdom	Whale Fishery (Consolidation) Ordinance, 1936
1938	France	Decree Concerning a National Park for the Protection of Certain Species of Birds and Mammals
1946	International	International Convention for the Regulation of Whaling
1950	United Kingdom	Whaling Regulations
1951	Norway	Seal Fishery Law No. 1

[a] From Bush (1982).

early management strategies recognized the necessity for accurate record-keeping about the harvested animals, including their numbers, locations, dates, sexes, and sizes.

Since the 1930s, the traditional approach for managing living resources has been embodied in the concept of Maximum Sustainable Yield (MSY) for estimating the "total allowable catch" that can be taken without reducing the population size of a particular species. MSY is based on the assumption that population growth rates are logistic [Eq. (9.1)], initially increasing geometrically before decreasing as the "carrying capacity" is approached (Fig. 9.5).

In fisheries, there is the addition of a *fishing mortality rate,* which is described as the product of the fishing effort (F) and a constant catch coefficient (c). Fishing mortality rates have the same dimensions as per capita recruitment rates (r) so that their combined impact on population growth rates can by determined by slightly modifying Equation 9.1:

$$\text{Population growth rate} = r\, N\, \frac{(K - N)}{K} - c\, F\, N \qquad (10.1)$$

Consequently, the MSY occurs when net recruitment and fishing mortality are in equilibrium at 50% of the population's carrying capacity (Fig. 10.9).

Moreover, to sustain the population, a fishery would remove only large adults that already have contributed their reproductive output to the next generation. The size of the individuals is critical because only sexually mature adults can reproduce and support the recruitment of the population. Removing the smaller individuals, especially the immature juveniles, will both decrease the overall biomass and diminish the recruitment capacity.

This concept of sustainability is forward-looking, with a view toward balancing the utilization and perpetuation of natural resources. When living resources are harvested, there is an economic incentive to maximize the yield with the minimal amount of effort. Such commercial interests underlie short-term perspectives that generally lead to depletion of the populations at the heart of the enterprise. Maximizing the yield while maintaining the vitality of the harvested populations requires innovative solutions that bridge economics, science, and policy.

 How can living resources sustainably be harvested without diminishing the renewal capacity of their populations?

Despite the scientific underpinnings, resource management policies largely have been structured for economic and political purposes. For example, comments about the scandalous waste of raw whale materials (Mörch, 1908)—". . . About 1,600 carcasses were let adrift in one season! Mankind of to-day does not take kindly to wholesale waste of such proportions. . . ."—revealed strategies for increasing profits from whaling. Consequently, within a couple of years the United Kingdom began issuing licenses for utilizing entire whale carcasses rather than

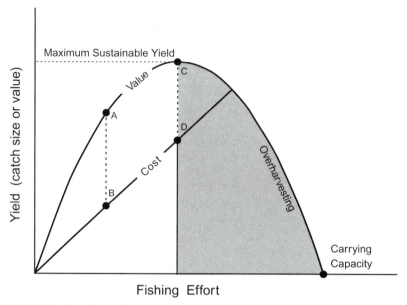

FIGURE 10.9 The parabola represents the logistic model of population growth [Eq. (9.1), Fig. 9.5] with the maximum sustainable yield (MSY) at 50% of a population's carrying capacity. In fisheries, the MSY is estimated to occur when net recruitment and fishing mortality rates are in equilibrium [Eq. (10.1)]. If the fishing impacts exceed the MSY and approach the population's carrying capacity, the population will be overharvested. Differences between the value and cost of the fishery, which reflect the return on investment (i.e., profit), are greatest at fishing effort levels (segment AB) that generate less than the maximum yield (segment CD).

just the blubber oil. These licenses, along with various leases, laws, regulations, conventions, and decrees, had the additional advantage of providing legal justifications for nations to assert their sovereignty over Antarctica (Fig. 3.5).

Even when resource management strategies reached international levels, as represented by the 1946 International Convention on the Regulation of Whaling, they still were structured with a view toward economic gain. This economic focus is classically reflected by the "blue whale unit" that was subsequently established: one blue whale was equated with two fin, two-and-a-half humpback, and six sei whales. As a result, with whalers free to pursue all whale species, capturing blue whales was encouraged because less cost-per-unit-of-effort was involved in achieving one "blue whale unit"—ultimately resulting in the greatest decimation among the blue whales (Fig. 10.3). Moreover, the very language of the convention is built on regulation (which highlights commercial dynamics) rather than conservation (which highlights species or ecosystem dynamics).

 What is conservation, and how is it related to ecosystem management?

When the Antarctic Treaty came into force in 1961, the marriage of policy with scientific and technical advice progressively expanded the focus on ecosystem conservation (Table 5.2; Antarctic Treaty Searchable Database: 1959–1999 CD-ROM). The first substantive conservation steps came with the Agreed Measures for the Conservation of Antarctic Fauna and Flora (Agreed Measures), which was annexed to Recommendation III–VIII from the Third Antarctic Treaty Consultative Meeting in 1964.

Beyond recognizing that "unique nature" of Antarctica fauna and flora, the Agreed Measures began integrating "protection, scientific study and rational use" within species' circumpolar ranges. The Agreed Measures, which only applied to the Antarctic Treaty area south of 60° South latitude, prohibited the introduction of "species of animal or plant not indigenous to that Area." The Agreed Measures also began a permit system for Specially Protected Species (such as the fur and Ross seals) and Specially Protected Areas because of their extreme "defenselessness and susceptibility" to human impacts. Importantly, the concept of "flora and fauna" went beyond individual species to the heart of the general trophic interactions that affect the dynamics of ecosystems (Chapter 9: Living Planet).

After adopting the Agreed Measures, the Antarctic Treaty nations implemented several recommendations regarding the vulnerability of Antarctic seals to commercial exploitation and the need for international conservation measures. These recommendations included a strategy for determining the maximum yields that could be sustainably harvested from various seal populations.

Following previous seal management efforts, with advice from the Scientific Committee on Antarctic Research (SCAR), the Antarctic Treaty nations signed the Convention on the Conservation of Antarctic Seals (CCAS) in 1972. CCAS expanded the permit system of the Agreed Measures and adopted a broad suite of conservation measures (Box 10.1). These conservation measures were designed to provide basic information on the density, size and gender distributions of seal populations over space and time with much more detail than had been involved in the earlier management of the elephant seals (as noted above). In addition, CCAS designed management strategies based on applied information about the gear, effort, and catch statistics of the fisheries. In general, these basic and applied data are essential for interpreting both natural variations and human impacts among harvested species (Fig. IV).

Concurrently, because of the potential value of krill as a global food source for humankind, SCAR established a subcommittee of its Biology Working Group in 1972 to broadly consider the marine living resources of the Southern Ocean. Four years later, SCAR started a 15-year coordinated international research program for the Biological Investigations of Marine Antarctic Systems and Stocks (BIOMASS). The primary objective of BIOMASS was to:

> ... gain a deeper understanding of the structure and dynamic functioning of the Antarctic marine ecosystem as a basis for the future management of potential living resources.

In the 1980–81 austral summer, the First BIOMASS Experiment (FIBEX) was carried out to investigate the physical, chemical, and biological characteristics of

BOX 10.1   1972 CONVENTION ON THE
CONSERVATION OF ANTARCTIC SEALS [a]

ARTICLE 3.1: ANNEXED MEASURES

. . . Measures with respect to the conservation, scientific study and rational and humane use of seal resources, prescribing inter alia:

a. permissible catch;
b. protected and unprotected species;
c. open and closed seasons;
d. open and closed areas, including the designation of reserves;
e. the designation of species areas where there shall be no disturbance
   of seals;
f. limits relating to sex, size, or age for each species;
g. restriction relation to time of day and duration, limitations of effort
   and methods of sealing;
h. types and specification of gear and apparatus and appliances which
   may be used;
i. catch return and other statistical and biological records;
j. procedures for facilitating the review and assessment of scientific
   information;
k. other regulatory measures including an effective system of
   inspection.

[a] From the Antarctic Treaty Searchable Database: 1959–1999 CD-ROM.

the Antarctic marine ecosystem (Fig. 10.10). These investigations were followed
by two phases of the Second BIOMASS Experiment (SIBEX I and II) in 1983–
84 and 1984–85.

Given the potential impacts of krill harvesting on the dependent species in the
pelagic food web (Fig. 9.2) and the need for coordinated international management
of Antarctic marine resources, the Antarctic Treaty System signed the Convention
on the Conservation of Antarctic Marine Living Resources (CCAMLR) in 1980.
CCAMLR followed from the scientific accomplishments of the BIOMASS program in the same way that the Antarctic Treaty succeeded the International Geophysical Year. In addition, the parallel structure of the Antarctic Treaty and SCAR
was extended to CCAMLR in the "legal personality" of a Commission and a
Scientific Committee.

Unlike the CCAS, which was associated with seal conservation only, CCAMLR
was designed to protect "fin fish, molluscs, crustaceans, and all other species of
living organisms, including birds" in the Antarctic marine ecosystem. CCAMLR
focused on the "complex of relationships of Antarctic marine living resources

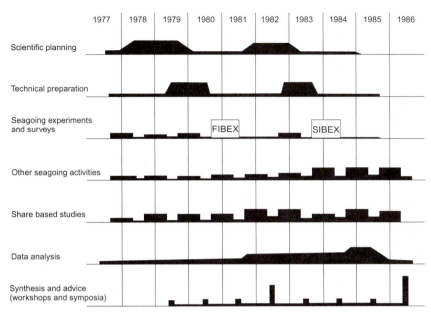

FIGURE 10.10   Illustration of the cooperative international scientific research timetable for the Biological Investigations of Marine Antarctic Systems and Stocks (BIOMASS) program, which was created by the Scientific Committee on Antarctic Research. Basic and applied information (Fig. IV) about the Antarctic marine ecosystem were collected and analyzed through a series of integrated activities: scientific planning, technical preparation, seagoing experiments, other seagoing activities, shore based studies, data analysis, synthesis, and advice, workshops, and symposia. The First BIOMASS Experiment (FIBEX) and the Second BIOMASS Experiment (SIBEX) are shown. Modified from El-Sayed (1977).

with each other" and "with their physical environment." Moreover, instead of being arbitrarily defined south of 60° south latitude (Table 5.2), the Antarctic marine ecosystem was constrained within ecological boundaries "south of the Antarctic Convergence" (Figs. 8.3 and 10.4).

In Article II (the ecological backbone of CCAMLR), conservation was defined in terms of "rational use" with the objective of maintaining the "ecological relationships between harvested, dependent and related populations." In addition, decreases in the "size of any harvested population to levels below which ensure their stable recruitment" would be prevented. Even the "risk of changes in the marine ecosystem which are not potentially reversible over two or three decades" would be prevented. Moreover, CCAMLR created an explicit goal of restoring depleted populations.

The concept of dependence, which is central to the ecosystem approach of Article II in CCAMLR, was expanded in the 1991 Protocol on Environmental Protection to the Antarctic Treaty (Protocol) to include "dependent and associated ecosystems." In the same sense that marine and terrestrial ecosystems are associated around Antarctica (as demonstrated by the fur seals), there also are associations with ecosystems beyond the Antarctic region as noted in Annex II for birds and mammals that are "indigenous to the Antarctic Treaty area or occurring there seasonally through natural migrations." In contrast to traditional marine resource management regimes, which focus on single species, CCAMLR and the Protocol have created "ecosystem approaches" for the rational use of all Antarctic living resources.

The principal challenges for managing ecosystems are related to accurately assessing species' demographics and variability. For example, populations of krill in the Antarctic marine ecosystem (Fig. 9.2) have been estimated to have a circumpolar biomass that ranges from less than 100 million to more than 7 billion tons, with an annual production that may exceed 1.3 billion tons. Clearly, such discrepancies preclude accurate MSY estimates. Moreover, the carrying capacities of populations also vary over time with changes in the ecosystem, indicating that optimal sustainable yields include environmental as well as species interactions.

In fact, the actual yield in a particular year can be quite variable, depending on environmental impacts that are unrelated to the fishery and affect natural mortality, growth, and recruitment processes throughout ecosystems (Fig. 10.11). To achieve this ecosystem objective, the CCAMLR Ecosystem Monitoring Program (CEMP) was created in 1984 to distinguish harvesting and environmental impacts on "critical components of the ecosystem" (Box 10.2)—acquiring information across the continuum from basic to applied research (Fig. IV).

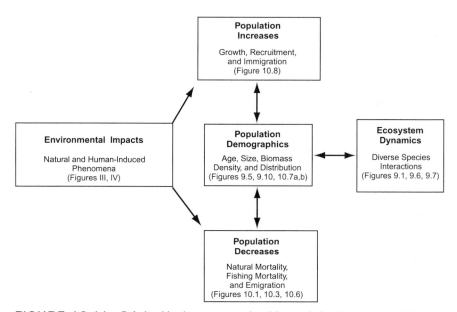

FIGURE 10.11   Relationships between natural and human-induced environmental impacts that, along with targeted harvesting, influence population variations. Resulting population demographics (densities, size frequencies, and biomasses) influence the dynamics of "dependent and associated ecosystems" and their feedbacks. Relevant figures are identified.

BOX 10.2   1980 CONVENTION ON THE
CONSERVATION OF ANTARCTIC MARINE
LIVING RESOURCES (CCAMLR)

**AIMS OF THE CCAMLR ECOSYSTEM MONITORING
PROGRAM (CEMP)**[a]

(i) to detect and record significant changes in critical components of
the ecosystem, to serve as a basis for the conservation of Antarctic
marine living resources; and

(ii) to distinguish between changes due to harvesting of commercial
species and changes due to environmental variability, both physical
and biological.

[a] From http:/www.ccamlr/org.

The classic example of omitting environmental variability in fisheries management strategies is the Peruvian anchovy industry, which had an estimated MSY of
9 to 10 million tons per year from 1964 through 1971. The Peruvian anchovy
(*Engraulis ringens*) was the world's largest marine fishery—until its sudden collapse in 1972. The problem was that fishery managers had overlooked the impact
of El Niño (Chapter 8: Breathing Planet), which is a periodic global ocean–atmosphere event that reduces the upwelling supply of nutrients for the phytoplankton prey of the anchovy along the Pacific Ocean coast of South America. As a
consequence of the impacts from El Niño, anchovy recruitment rates were reduced more than 85%. Unfortunately, because MSY remained the same without
compensating for the El Niño impact, the Peruvian anchovy population was dramatically overharvested.

Fisheries generate value in proportion to the balance between yield and effort
(Fig. 10.9). When populations are large with many big individuals, it is relatively
easy and inexpensive to generate large catch sizes. As populations are depleted,
leaving smaller individuals with a lower yield per recruit, more effort (i.e., greater
cost) is required to maintain a uniform catch size. In both cases, the greatest return
on investment (difference between the cost and yield value) for a fishery exists at
levels of effort that are below the MSY.

These *eco*nomic and *eco*logical aspects of living resource activities share the
"eco-" root associated with the "household" that is managed and studied, respectively. A key feature of household management is considering the ability to acquire necessary resources, commodities, or services. Access to goods is influenced
by supply and demand features, which determines their costs (Fig. 10.12), as classically recognized by Alfred Marshall (1842–1924).

Demand is related to quantities of a good that consumers are willing and able

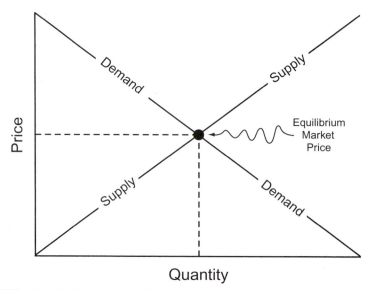

FIGURE 10.12   Prices and quantities of a marketable good or service in relation to consumer demands and producer supplies. The equilibrium market price represents the balance between supplies and demands, with higher prices leading to surpluses and lower prices leading to shortages of the good or service.

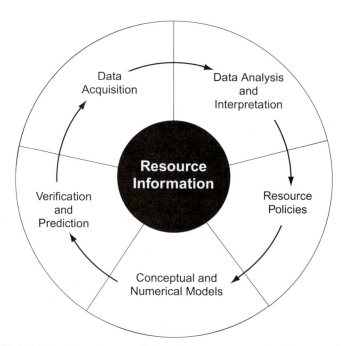

FIGURE 10.13   Managing natural resources, ecosystems, and environments in the Earth system requires scientific, economic, government, and societal information. Information itself embodies a dynamic process of iterative acquisition, assessment, and utilization of basic and applied data (Fig. IV) for the welfare of all stakeholders. Modified from the Earth System Sciences Committee (1988).

to buy at a given price based on their incomes, available alternatives, and personal tastes. Alternatively, supplies of a good relate to available quantities that a producer is willing and able to sell at a given price based on production costs, unexpected events, and competition. Equilibrium between consumer demands and producer supplies sets the market price (Fig. 10.12). Prices above the market price create surpluses; prices below the market price create shortages. As a consequence, excess supplies will force prices down, whereas excess demands drive price up, adjusting toward the equilibrium market price.

The challenge in managing our Earth "household" is to obtain sufficient information for creating farsighted policies that sustain ecosystems while promoting economic prosperity in the welfare of producers, consumers, and all other stakeholders (Fig. 10.13). This information is multifaceted, involving disparate types of data (e.g. Figs. 10.9–10.12) as well as diverse analytical strategies and feedbacks. Ultimately, on a global scale—as demonstrated by the Antarctic Treaty System since 1959—continuous consultation and "international cooperation in scientific investigation" are essential for generating the appropriate information for managing natural resources "in the interest of all mankind."

11

ENVIRONMENTAL

PROTECTION

When the Well's dry, we know the Worth of Water.
—*Benjamin Franklin (1746),* Poor Richard's Almanack

MULTIPLE-USE RESOURCES

Humans are intimately linked to the physical, geological, chemical, and bio-logical elements of the Earth's environment (Figs. II and III). We breathe the air and drink the water. We eat food from land and sea. We seek materials to clothe and shelter us. We build vast cities with technologies that are powered by diverse sources of energy. The resources for our civilization come from anywhere we find them—including remote and relatively inaccessible environments such as the deep sea, outer space, and Antarctica. The challenge of environmental protection is associated with managing distinct resource activities individually and collec-tively with a view centuries into the future.

Just as "no man is an island, entire of itself" (as noted by John Donne in the 17th century), resource activities are not conducted in isolation. When living resources are harvested, impacts propagate through dependent and associated ecosystems (Chapter 10: Ecosystem Conservation). When nonliving resources are exploited, impacts radiate through environments as well as ecosystems. Moreover, resource activities generate impacts that influence the dynamics of nations within the international community—extending beyond political boundaries across the Earth system.

 How can humankind exploit and protect natural resources at the same time?

In the international context of the Earth system, Antarctica is an ideal illustration of diverse stakeholders interacting with "multiple uses" of a region and its resources. As discussed earlier, for a couple of centuries, Antarctica has been affording humankind a rich bounty of living resources. Similarly, during the past 100 years, Antarctica has emerged as a unique international laboratory for humankind to generate scientific insights about the dynamics of myriad natural phenomena across time and space (Fig. 6.1). Over the past few decades, additional interest in using Antarctica and its resources has arisen. The coupled impacts among the environments, ecosystems, and stakeholders who use them in Antarctica have become visionary lessons with global implications.

A principal resource of Antarctica, for science and society, is its relatively pristine nature (Figs. III and IV). Since the International Geophysical Year (IGY) in 1957–58, Antarctica has been occupied continuously for "scientific investigation" within the scope of the Antarctic Treaty System (Chapter 4: Awakening Science and Chapter 5: International Stewardship). Among the 55 IGY research stations around Antarctica (Fig. 11.1), 12 were still in operation in 1998 (Fig. 5.2): Amundsen-Scott (United States), Davis (Australia), Dumont D'Urville (France), Esperanza (Argentina), General Bernardo O'Higgins (Chile), General San Martin (Argentina), McMurdo (United States), Mawson (Australia), Mirny (Russia), Scott (New Zealand), Syowa (Japan), and Vostok (Russia). "Active and influential presence in Antarctica" based on scientific investigation is further illustrated by the continuous commitment of nations such as the United States, which has the largest program on the continent (Fig. 11.2). Although science has remained as the essential ingredient for "international cooperation" in Antarctica, the principal human presence in Antarctica began shifting in the 1980s.

More people began visiting Antarctica, not for scientific investigation, but just for its aesthetic beauty—to gather only memories of viewing penguin and seal rookeries or pods of whales patrolling the ice edge, of icebergs from vast streaming glaciers near remote research stations, of historic monuments and other sites of special tourist interest. People also have been visiting Antarctica to set records of endurance because, as stated by Sir Edmund Hillary in 1968, "a demanding and constructive adventure is worthwhile for its own sake."

Beginning with the Argentine and Chilean cruises down to the Antarctic Peninsula in the 1950s, Antarctic tourism now ranges across the entire continent. According to the International Association of Antarctic Tour Operators, in 1999–2000 alone, there were tourists visiting Antarctica from at least 70 nations (Table 11.1). Moreover, the scope of Antarctic tourism has continued to expand geometrically, with nearly 15,000 individuals journeying southward each year at the dawn of the 21st century (Fig. 11.3). Consequently, tourism has become an enormous resource activity as the single largest source of human presence on Antarctica.

Nearly 99% of Antarctic tourists travel by ship, concentrating in coastal areas during the summer from November to March when there is minimal sea ice (Fig. 8.1) as well as access to open water for viewing the wildlife. Visits ashore generally are short (less than 3 hours) and moderate intensity (fewer than 100

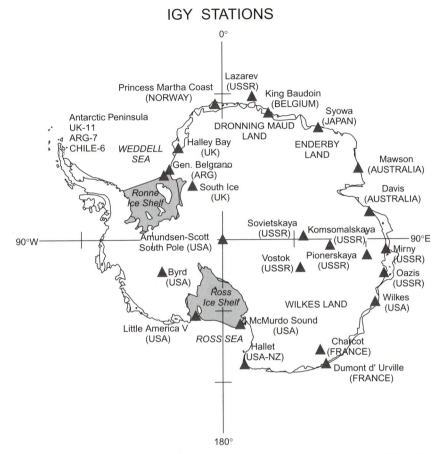

IGY STATIONS

FIGURE 11.1   Fifty-five research stations were operated around Antarctica (tick marks at 10° latitude increments) during the International Geophysical Year (IGY) in 1957–58 (Chapter 4: Awakening Science) by the 12 nations that became the original signatories to the 1959 Antarctic Treaty (Chapter 5: International Stewardship). Twelve of the IGY stations are among the 37 year-round research stations operated by 18 nations in the Antarctic region in 1998 (http://www.scar.org). Throughout, the Antarctic Peninsula has been the most crowded region (Fig. 11.4), in part because of the overlapping claims between Argentina, Chile, and the United Kingdom (Fig. 3.5).

people) with an average of eight landings per ship-based expedition. The majority of these visits are in the Antarctic Peninsula region where more than 150 sites, including 20 research stations, have been visited since 1989 (Fig. 11.4). Most of the visits, however, have been concentrated at fewer than 50 sites, with a handful of popular sites receiving 3000 to 4000 tourists each season. In addition, Chile and Argentina have established permanent outposts at their Antarctic Peninsula stations that are inhabited by small communities with banks, hotels, schools, and

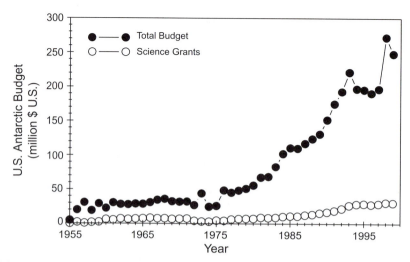

FIGURE 11.2 National commitment of the United States to maintain an "active and influential presence in Antarctica" (as stated in Presidential Memorandum 6646 signed by Ronald Reagan on 5 February 1982) with the National Science Foundation (NSF) as the lead coordinating agency—affirming the central role of "scientific activities" as the basis for international cooperation in the south polar region. The total NSF Antarctic budget and allocation for scientific grants increased along with international interest in Antarctica since before the International Geophysical Year in 1957–58 (Fig. 5.3). Data courtesy of the National Science Foundation, Office of Polar Programs.

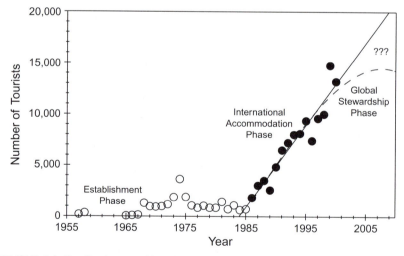

FIGURE 11.3 Tourism, as with nations entering the Antarctic Treaty System (Fig. 5.3), has expanded through an establishment phase into an international accommodation phase, which continues to involve increasing numbers of individuals from around the world (Table 11.1). The rate of future tourism growth (???) will influence the scope of environmental impacts, assessment strategies, and nongovernmental involvement in the Antarctic region during the global stewardship phase. Note that the accommodation phase for Antarctic tourism began around 1985, during the negotiations for the 1988 Convention on the Regulation of Antarctic Mineral Resources Activities. In contrast, the accommodation phase occurred for Antarctic Treaty nations a decade earlier (Fig. 5.3), when tourism initially peaked shortly after the oil embargo by the Organization of Petroleum Exporting Countries and the drilling activities of the *Glomar Challenger* in the mid-1970s (Fig. 6.4). Based on data from the International Association of Antarctic Tour Operators (http://www.iaato.org).

TABLE 11.1   Antarctic Commercial Activities among Different Nations

| Nation | Marine fisheries (%)[a] | Tourism[b] | |
		Tourists (number)	Operators (passengers)
Argentina	0.06	70	
Austria		107	
Australia	0.06	1124	819
Bahamas			2583
Belgium		110	
Bulgaria	0.03	10	
Canada		680	3881
Chile	1.90	12	
Estonia	3.16		
France	1.15	91	
Germany	0.02	1319	1779
Japan	28.71	432	
Korea, Republic of	0.41	4	
Latvia	0.66		
Lithuania	0.76		
New Zealand		112	89
Panama	0.04		
Poland	5.11	20	
Russian Federation	35.35	2	
South Africa	0.12	111	
Spain	0.02	69	
Switzerland		314	
Ukraine	22.34		
United Kingdom	0.05	1127	
United States	'fg0.06	7739	4094

[a] Percentages of the average annual yield from all Antarctic fisheries from 1990–97 (221,174 tons per year) based on data from the United Nations Food and Agriculture Organization (http://www.fao.org). See Chapter 10: Ecosystem Conservation.

[b] Number of Antarctic tourists from different nations in 1999–2000 excluding 1161 tourists from among the total 14,762 tourists from 70 nations (not shown). Number of passengers supported by principal operators from different nations in 1999–2000 (total 14,386) excluding 376 passengers who were supported by miscellaneous operators. Data from the International Association of Antarctic Tour Operators (http://www .iaato.org).

children being born as evidence of their "effective occupation" for asserting sovereignty (Chapter 3: *Terra Australis Incognita*).

Among the tourist flights to Antarctica, most land in the continental interior to launch adventure expeditions. There also are overflights of Antarctica that depart from Australia. However, the overall scope of Antarctic tourist flights has been diminished since 28 November 1979—when all 257 passengers on an Air New Zealand DC10 (Flight 901) crashed into Mt. Erebus, Ross Island, and were killed.

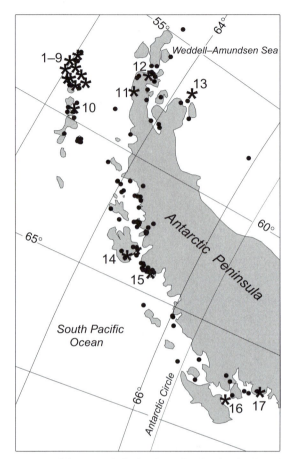

FIGURE 11.4   Map of the Antarctic Peninsula region showing the sites of year-round Antarc-
tic research stations (stars) in 1998 (http://www.usarc.usgs.gov): 1, Comandante Ferraz, Brazil; 2,
Arctowski, Poland; 3, Jubany, Argentina; 4, Bellingshausen, Russia; 5, Marsh/Frei, Chile; 6, Great
Wall, China; 7, Artigas, Uruguay; 8, King Sejong, South Korea; 9, Escudero, Chile; 10, Arturo Prat,
Chile; 11, Bernardo O'Higgins, Chile; 12, Esperanza, Argentina; 13, Marambio, Argentina; 14,
Palmer, United States; 15, Faraday/Vernadsky, United Kingdom/Ukraine; 16, Rothera, United King-
dom, and 17, San Martin, Argentina. Stations 1 through 9 are on King George Island alone. Sites of
tourist ship visits (circles) since 1989 also are shown (http://www.iiato.org).

In deep sorrow, the Antarctic Treaty nations adopted Recommendation XI-3 (Air
Disaster on Mt. Erebus) in 1981 to establish among all governments that "the site
on the northern slopes of Mount Erebus where the accident took place be declared
a tomb and that they ensure that the area is left in peace." The tragedy on Mt.
Erebus represents the larger challenge of anticipating consequences and developing effective guidelines for tourist and nongovernmental expeditions, which are
rapidly increasing in the Antarctic region (Fig. 11.3). As an example of proactive

policies, the Antarctic Treaty nations did adopt measures prior to the Mt. Erebus accident because of the inherent hazards of overflying Antarctica and the fact that "tourist overflight capacity exceeds existing capabilities of air traffic control" (Recommendation X-8).

 How can we avoid accidents and minimize the consequences when they happen?

Among the actual and potential resources, however, minerals alone electrified the focus of humankind on Antarctica. The economics of mineral exploitation in Antarctica had been considered since before the International Geophysical Year (IGY), as noted in 1958 by the Director of the United States IGY Antarctic Program, Laurence Gould: "The structure and geology of the rocks in west Antarctic suggest the possibility of oil. Traces of manganese, nickel, copper and other ores have been found. . . ." In fact, past connections with the other Gondwana continents (Fig. 6.3)—which do have mineral reserves that are being exploited (Fig. 11.5)—suggests that there are regions of Antarctica that also may contain mineral deposits.

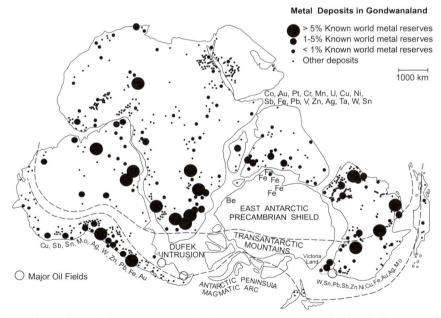

FIGURE 11.5 Reconstruction of the Gondwana supercontinent, showing the known metal deposits (see key) and major oil fields (open circles) among the Southern Hemisphere continents that were connected with Antarctica around 180 million years ago (Fig. 6.3). In addition, the relative locations of the Bushveld Complex in South Africa and the Dufek Complex in Antarctica are shown. Modified from Cook (1990).

For example, the Bushveld Complex in South Africa and the Dufek Complex in Western Antarctica share iron-rich magnetite characteristically associated with platinum-group metals. Similarly, gold deposits in southern Chile and traces of gold in the Antarctica Peninsula have been identified. In addition, traces of bismuth, chromium, cobalt, copper, lead, lithium, manganese, molybdenum, nickel, silver, tin, uranium, and zinc have been found in various areas around Antarctica (Fig. 11.5).

There also are nonmetallic minerals—particularly coal, which has been identified in exposed mountain seams areas around Antarctica (Fig. 3.1, *top*). These sedimentary deposits containing *Glossopteris* and other terrestrial plant fossils from 250 million years ago are similar to rocks in the Beacon Supergroup extending across other Gondwana continents (Fig. 3.1, *top*). It has been speculated that Antarctic coal deposits may exceed several hundred billion metric tons, although of low quality with high ash, sulfur, and tar characteristics.

However, it was only after the *Glomar Challenger* began drilling in the Ross Sea in 1972 that Antarctic mineral resources became a charged topic (Fig. 6.4). During this leg of the Deep Sea Drilling Program (now the Ocean Drilling Program), elevated gas ratios of ethane to methane were found in offshore sediments—indicators of potential petroleum. Coincidentally, the following year, the Organization of Petroleum Exporting Countries embargoed oil to Western Hemisphere nations and poignantly introduced the world to the fact that global hydrocarbon reserves are finite. Gasoline prices skyrocketed and consumers across nations waited in long lines for their rations of automobile energy.

Later in 1973, the United States Geological Survey noted in an internal circular that the *Glomar Challenger* data indicated that continental shelf regions adjacent to the Ross Ice Shelf and Filchner-Ronne Ice Shelf (Fig. 8.6) may have oil reserves on the order of 45 billion barrels. As a result of this government estimate, the *Wall Street Journal* heralded that "45 billion barrels of oil and 115 trillion cubic feet of natural gas could be recovered from the continental shelf of West Antarctica." For comparison, in 1982 the United States Department of Energy determined that proven reserves of oil in the hugely productive British sector of the North Sea were around 40 billion barrels. Despite the large gap in knowledge between known economic reserves and wishful thinking (Table 11.2), information from these projects, reports, and data interpretations was sufficient to generate worldwide interest in Antarctic mineral resources.

Petroleum products are vital for human activities across the Earth, but they also are a source of pollution impacts that are both extreme and frequent—particularly in the sea. On top of the extensive history of catastrophic marine oil tanker and well accidents, in 1998 alone there were 215 incidents that spilled nearly 32 million gallons (108,000 tons) of oil into the ocean. Because of global economics and the likelihood of such environmental impacts, world attention converged on Antarctica in the early 1970s as discussions about Antarctic mineral resources became a "matter of urgency."

Since 1968, global drilling programs have collected marine cores at more than

TABLE 11.2   General Classification Scheme for Describing Mineral Occurrences [a]

| Cumulative mineral production | Identified resources | | | Undiscovered resources |
| | Demonstrated | | | Hypothetical or speculative |
	Measured	Indicated	Inferred	
Economic	Reserves		Inferred reserves	
Marginally economic	Marginal reserves		Inferred marginal reserves	Wishful thinking
Subeconomic	demonstrated sub-economic resources		Inferred sub-economic resources	

[a] Developed by United States Geological Survey (USGS) and United States Department of Mines in 1976 and commonly called the "McKelvey Box," after Vincent McKelvey, who was the USGS Director.

1150 sites throughout the ocean to "explore the structure and history of the Earth as it is recorded in the basement rock and overlying sediments accumulated on the seafloor." Since 1972, more than 1000 marine sediment cores have been collected at more than 80 sites around Antarctica (Figs. 6.4 and 11.6). Many of these scientific drilling operations have been conducted in the ocean from sea-ice platforms as well as in coastal terrestrial environments under the auspices of the Scientific Committee on Antarctic Research (SCAR) through its Group of Specialists on Cenozoic Paleoenvironments of the Southern High Latitudes (Fig. 6.5).

Since 1978, more than 150,000 kilometers of multichannel seismic reflection data (Fig. 6.4) also have been collected around Antarctica by more than 13 nations (Fig. 11.7, Table 11.3). The institutions that are generating seismic profiles of the sea floor around Antarctica range from universities and national geologic survey programs to national oil corporations. Currently, all of these seismic data from the different institutions are being compiled by the SCAR through the Antarctic Offshore Stratigraphy Project (ANTOSTRAT), which began in 1988 (Table 11.3).

The broad objective of ANTOSTRAT, which includes archiving data in an international Antarctic Seismic Data Library System, is to openly share information that is essential for interpreting the history of Antarctic ice-sheet fluctuations in relation to global climate dynamics. Beyond scientific activities, which use Antarctica as a "natural laboratory" for studying the Earth system, ANTOSTRAT also provides a mechanism for sharing data and diffusing the economic considerations of proprietary information (Fig. 11.8).

Generally, mineral resources are nonliving and nonrenewable. One mineral resource exception would be icebergs, which are continuously calving from ice shelves, ice tongues, and glaciers in the polar regions. To discuss the feasibility of

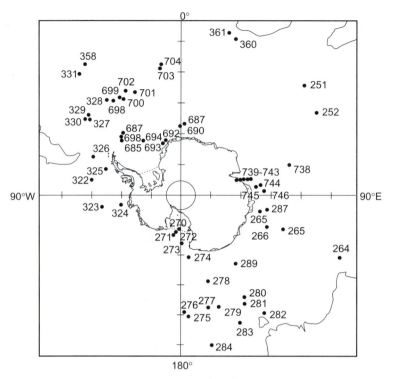

FIGURE 11.6   Drill site locations south of 30° south latitude (tick marks at 10° latitude incre-ments) where more than 1000 marine sediment cores (e.g., Fig. 6.4) have been drilled since 1972 by the international community as part of the Deep Sea Drilling Program (period: 1968–1985) and its successor, the Ocean Drilling Program (period: 1985–present). Since 1990, marine geological re-search around Antarctica has been conducted in coordination with the Scientific Committee on Ant-arctic Research (SCAR) Antarctic Stratigraphy Antarctic Offshore Stratigraphy Project (ANTOSTRAT), described in Figure 11.7 (http://www.antcrc.utas.edu /au /scar/antostrat). Modified from Webb and Cooper (1999).

utilizing this renewable mineral resource, the First International Conference and Workshop on Iceberg Utilization for Fresh Water Production, Weather Modifica-tion and Other Applications was convened in 1977 at Iowa State University with participants from 18 countries. Based on this meeting, it was estimated that about 800 cubic kilometers of icebergs could be utilized each year from Antarctica as a potentially significant contribution to the 3100-cubic-kilometer consumption of freshwater worldwide. Eventually, recognizing that the "Antarctic represents the world's largest freshwater reserve," Recommendation XV-21 was adopted in 1989 to consider the "feasibility of commercial exploitation of icebergs, relevant technologies and possible environmental impacts."

Recognizing potential environmental and political repercussions from the "ex-ploration and exploitation of mineral resources" around Antarctica, the Conven-

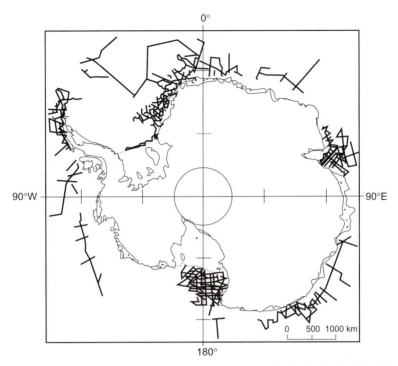

FIGURE 11.7   More than 150,000 kilometers of multichannel seismic reflection data (Fig. 6.4), acquired around Antarctica (tick marks at 10° latitude increments) by universities and institutions from different nations since 1978 (Table 11.3). Since 1988, these seismic data have been compiled by the Scientific Committee on Antarctic Research (SCAR) through the Antarctic Offshore Stratigraphy Project (ANTOSTRAT), for the purpose of providing open access to marine geophysical data for interpreting the environmental history of Antarctica since the breakup of Gondwana (Fig. 6.3). The implementation of ANTOSTRAT helps to diffuse the economic issue of shared versus proprietary information (Fig. 11.8). Modified from Behrendt (1990).

tion on the Regulation of Antarctic Mineral Resources (CRAMRA) was signed in 1988 after 6 years of urgent negotiation to "ensure that Antarctica shall continue forever to be used exclusively for peaceful purposes and shall not become the scene or object of international discord." In supporting this visionary objective of peaceful use—which the 1959 Antarctic Treaty instituted as humankind's primary use—CRAMRA identified environmental protection as a common goal of all resource activities around Antarctica (Box 11.1). Beyond protecting against environmental impacts, CRAMRA further recognized that resource activities could affect each other and that additional strategies were required to protect the multiple uses of Antarctica (Box 11.2).

Despite the development of CRAMRA, on 28 January 1989, the Argentine supply vessel *Bahia Paraiso* ran into Full Astern Reef along the coast of the Antarctic Peninsula—spilling 600,000 liters of oil into Arthur Harbor. This Antarctic

TABLE 11.3   Acoustic Surveys of Marine Sediments around Antarctica Conducted by the International Community [a]

Nation	Organization(s)	Antarctic Regions [b]				
		AP	RS	WL	PB	WS
Australia	Australian Geological Survey Organization				X	
Brazil	National Committee on Antarctic Research	X				
China	Guangzhou Marine Geological Survey	X				
France	Institut Français du Petrole		X	X		
Germany	Alfred Wegener-Institut für Polar- und Meeresfor- schung, Bundesanstalt für Geowissenschaften und Rohstoffe, Institut für Geophysik	X	X			X
Italy	Osservatorio Geofisico Sperimentale	X	X			
Japan	Geological Survey of Japan, Japan National Oil Corporation	X	X	X	X	X
Korea	Korean Ocean Research Development Institute	X				
Norway	University of Bergen					X
Poland	Polish Academy of Sciences	X				
Russia	Joint Stock Marine Arctic Geological Expedition	X	X		X	X
Spain	Instituto Español de Oceanografia, Universidad de Granada	X				
United Kingdom	British Antarctic Survey	X				
United States	Rice University, United States Geological Survey	X	X	X		

[a] See Fig. 6.4.

[b] AP, Antarctic Peninsula (80–35°W); RS, Ross Sea (160°E–165°W); WL, Wilkes Land (100–160°E); PB, Prydz Bay (60–90°E); and WS, Weddell Sea (60°W–5°E). Based on Cooper *et al.* (1995).

oil spill was two orders of magnitude smaller than the *Exxon Valdez* accident, which released nearly 40 million liters of crude oil into Prince William Sound, Alaska, on 24 March 1989. Nonetheless, concerns about environmental impacts from Antarctic mineral resource activities were galvanized, and during this period France and Australia signaled their unwillingness to ratify CRAMRA. With-

Economic Litmus Test

(based on access to information)

Science		Industry
↑↓	*versus*	↑↓
Shared Information		**Proprietary Information**

FIGURE 11.8   Litmus test for distinguishing scientific and economic interests in natural resources based on whether access to the data is open or restricted, respectively.

BOX 11.1 1988 CONVENTION ON THE REGULATION OF ANTARCTIC MINERAL RESOURCE ACTIVITIES (CRAMRA)[a]

ARTICLE 2: OBJECTIVES AND GENERAL PRINCIPLES

3. In relation to Antarctic mineral resource activities, should they occur, the Parties acknowledge the special responsibility of the Antarctic Treaty Consultative Parties for the protection of the environment and the need to:

   a. protect the Antarctic environment and dependent and associated ecosystems;
   b. respect Antarctica's significance for, and influence on, the global environment;
   c. respect other legitimate uses of Antarctica;
   d. respect Antarctica's scientific value and aesthetic and wilderness qualities;
   e. ensure the safety of operations in Antarctica;
   f. promote opportunities for fair and effective participation of all Parties; and,
   g. take into account the interests of the international community as a whole.

[a] From the Antarctic Treaty Searchable Database: 1959–1999 CD-ROM.

BOX 11.2 1988 CONVENTION ON THE REGULATION OF ANTARCTIC MINERAL RESOURCE ACTIVITIES (CRAMRA)[a]

ARTICLE 15: RESPECT FOR OTHER USES OF ANTARCTICA

1. Decisions about Antarctic mineral resource activities shall take into account the need to respect other uses of Antarctica, including:

   a. the operation of stations and their associated installations, support facilities and equipment in Antarctica;
   b. scientific investigation in Antarctica and cooperation therein;
   c. the conservation, including rational use, of Antarctic marine living resources;
   d. tourism;
   e. the preservation of historic monuments; and
   f. navigation and aviation;

that are consistent with the Antarctic Treaty system.

[a] From the Antarctic Treaty Searchable Database: 1959–1999 CD-ROM.

out the required unanimous support of the Antarctic Treaty Consultative Parties (Table 5.1), the minerals regime was abandoned (Table 5.2).

Ensuing from the CRAMRA, the Antarctic Treaty nations adopted the concept of Multiple-Use Planning Areas at the 15th Antarctic Treaty Consultative Meeting in 1989 (Recommendation XV-11):

> ... to ensure that on-going and planned human activities in Antarctica, through their combined or cumulative effects, do not result in mutual interference or in adverse impacts upon the Antarctic environment.

This concept of multiple uses goes beyond "mutual interference" to the heart of protecting and maintaining the unique values of Antarctica.

In addition, emerging quickly from CRAMRA, the 26 consultative nations of the Antarctic Treaty System signed the Protocol on Environmental Protection to the Antarctic Treaty (Protocol) in Madrid, Spain, in 1991 (Tables 5.1 and 5.2). Seven years later, after being ratified unanimously, the Protocol came into force as the comprehensive regime for assessing, preventing, and mitigating "combined or cumulative" impacts from the multiple uses of Antarctica (Box 11.3).

IMPACT ASSESSMENT

The Protocol (Article 3) institutes a broad framework for planning and conducting activities around Antarctica based on

> ... information sufficient to allow prior assessments of, and informed judgments about, their possible impacts on the Antarctic environment and dependent and associated ecosystems and on the value of Antarctica for the conduct of scientific research.

Utilizing scientific insights about the Earth system (Figs. III and IV), the Protocol further establishes general categories of natural phenomena that are of fundamental importance in protecting the Antarctic environments and ecosystems (Box 11.3).

 What information is needed to distinguish human impacts from natural variability (Fig. IV)?

With foresight and a view toward proactive information gathering (Protocol, Article 3), "prior assessments" can be generated with "key environmental parameters and ecosystem components so as to identify and provide early warning of any adverse effects. . . ." Such environmental and ecosystem "sentinels" are being used widely throughout the world in research efforts such as the International Mussel Watch Program, which is being applied in Antarctica with the circumpolar scallop (*Adamussium colbecki*) and clam (*Laternula elliptica*) (Plate 6). General characteristics of key indicator organisms are described in Box 11.4.

However, "prior assessments" of human impacts on species, ecosystems, and environments often are unavailable because they were unanticipated. To play

BOX 11.3 1991 PROTOCOL ON
ENVIRONMENTAL PROTECTION TO THE
ANTARCTIC TREATY (PROTOCOL)[a]

ARTICLE 3. ENVIRONMENTAL PRINCIPLES

1. The protection of the Antarctic environment and dependent and associated ecosystems and the intrinsic value of Antarctica, including its wilderness and aesthetic values and its value as an area for the conduct of scientific research, in particular research essential to understanding the global environment, shall be fundamental considerations in the planning and conduct of all activities in the Antarctic Treaty area.

2. To this end:

   a. activities in the Antarctic Treaty area shall be planned and conducted so as to limit adverse impacts on the Antarctic environment and dependent and associated ecosystems;
   b. activities in the Antarctic Treaty area shall be planned and conducted so as to avoid:
      i.   adverse effects on climate or weather patterns;
      ii. significant adverse effects on air or water quality;
      iii. significant changes in the atmospheric, terrestrial (including aquatic), glacial or marine environments;
      iv. detrimental changes in the distribution, abundance or productivity of species or populations of species of fauna and flora;
      v.   further jeopardy to endangered or threatened species or populations of such species; or
      vi. degradation of, or substantial risk to, areas of biological, scientific, historic, aesthetic or wilderness significance;

[a]From the Antarctic Treaty Searchable Database: 1959–1999 CD-ROM.

catch-up, such baselines can be generated from the growth structures of organisms (such as teeth or shell growth bands) that continuously record ambient environmental variations during their lifetimes (e.g., Fig. 9.9). Baselines also can be generated from geological, chemical and fossil archives that reflect the natural dynamics of the Earth system unambiguously from periods before any human impacts (Figs. 6.5, 7.4, 8.10, and 9.3).

In addition to assessments, the Protocol created guidelines that are both objective and subjective for making "informed judgements" about whether human activities should proceed (Box 11.5). Whereas "minor" is a subjective term, "transitory" can be objectively related to the recovery capacity of species and ecosystems. In one sense, the time frame of a "transitory" human impact already is defined in Article II of the 1980 Convention on the Conservation of Antarctic

---

BOX 11.4   CRITERIA OF KEY INDICATOR SPECIES[a]

(a) Basic biology is known
(b) Reflects environmental variability
(c) Broadly common in habitats
(d) Large, abundant, and easy to collect
(e) Comparable baselines from different times and locations
(f) Easy to manipulate in field and laboratory experiments
(g) Sensitive to human impacts

[a] Modified from Berkman (1998).

Marine Living Resources (CCAMLR), which discusses the prevention of ecosystem changes that are not "potentially reversible over two or three decades." This CCAMLR time frame was based on the general lifespan of Antarctic seals, which further suggests applications of key indicator organisms (Box 11.4) for assessing "transitory" impacts in ecosystems.

BOX 11.5   1991 PROTOCOL ON ENVIRONMENTAL PROTECTION TO THE ANTARCTIC TREATY (PROTOCOL)[a]

ARTICLE 8: ENVIRONMENTAL IMPACT ASSESSMENT

1. Proposed activities referred to in paragraph 2 below shall be subject to the procedures set out in Annex I for prior assessment of the impacts of those activities on the Antarctic environment or on dependent or associated ecosystems according to whether those activities are identified as having:

   a. less than a minor or transitory impact;
   b. a minor or transitory impact; or
   c. more than a minor or transitory impact.

2. Each party shall ensure that the assessment procedures set out in Annex I are applied in the planning processes leading to decisions about any activities undertaken in the Antarctic Treaty area pursuant to scientific research programmes, tourism and all other governmental and non-governmental activities in the Antarctic Treaty area for which advance notice is required under Article VII (5) of the Antarctic Treaty, including associated logistic support activities.

[a] From the Antarctic Treaty Searchable Database: 1959–1999 CD-ROM.

Beyond merely monitoring changes, quantitative approaches for assessing "minor or transitory impacts" in ecosystems involve experiments for interpreting impact durations and magnitudes as well as biological responses (Fig. 11.9). Assessed across gradients (Chapter 2: Conceptual Integration), with the appropriate controls or baselines, experiments provide frameworks for relating pollutants or other habitat perturbations from being small and confined to large and dispersed. Similarly, impacts could be related from acute and short-term to chronic and long-term. Ultimately, however, environmental or ecosystem impacts are reflected by changes in biological production (Chapter 9: Living Planet) across gradients from sublethal to lethal. Together, such impact gradients illustrate the matrix of information that could be generated for measuring, interpreting, and judging whether human activities have "minor or transitory impacts" in "dependent and associated ecosystems."

For example, the total magnitude of impacts from research stations across the 14 million square-kilometer area of the Antarctic continent (Figs. 11.1 and 11.4) can be considered in relation to human populations on any other continent. If this sparce distribution of stations was superimposed on North America, there might be a station in Los Angeles with a few others dotted northward along the West Coast, a few scattered across Canada, perhaps a concentration of sites in New England, and a handful in interior localities such as Philadelphia or Washington, D.C. In addition to being widely separated, the maximum size of Antarctic research stations is comparable to a tiny town, as represented by McMurdo with

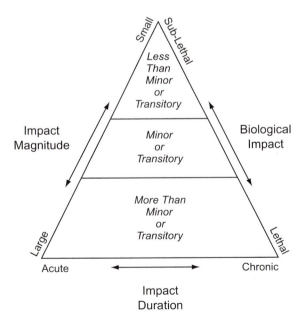

FIGURE 11.9   Impact gradient matrix for quantifying impact durations and magnitudes as well as biological responses to assess "minor or transitory impacts" as prescribed by the 1991 Protocol on Environmental Protection to the Antarctic Treaty (Box 11.5).

1500 persons during the austral summer (Fig. 5.2a). Moreover, the majority of Antarctic research stations involve fewer than 100 persons—indicating that Antarctic station impacts are "minor" by any measure on a continental scale (e.g. Figs. 5.2b and 5.2c).

Since the heroic age (Chapter 3: *Terra Australis Incognita*), however, most Antarctic stations have been located in coastal areas that are ice-free and accessible compared to the 98% of Antarctica that is ice-covered (Figs. 11.1 and 11.4). Moreover, since the IGY, the highest concentration of coastal stations has been in the Antarctic Peninsula region, with nine stations on the 1450-square-kilometer area of King George Island alone (Fig. 11.4). Importantly, exposed coastal areas are where most of the terrestrial life on the continent ekes out its existence (Fig. 9.4, Table 9.3).

Localized impacts at coastal stations range from discarded materials (such as buildings and drums at abandoned stations) to displacement of natural assemblages (such as the Adélie penguin rookery near the French station at Dumont D'Urville, which was replaced by an aircraft runway in the 1980s). There also are research stations that have been operating continuously since the IGY that have become point sources of chronic pollution impacts, such as the United States' research facility at McMurdo Station (Fig. 5.2a and 11.1).

Adjacent to the McMurdo Station in Winter Quarters Bay, with its ice wharf for docking vessels near a former dump site, there is intense and localized pollution within a 0.1-square-kilometer area (Fig. 5.2a). Hydrocarbon concentrations in the sediments range to 4500 parts per million in the back part of Winter Quarters Bay and decrease several orders of magnitude within a couple of hundred meters toward McMurdo Sound (Fig. 3.1b). Similarly, polychlorinated biphenyls (PCBs) and other synthetic organic compounds, including dichlorodiphenyltrichloroethane (DDT), show significantly higher concentrations in Winter Quarters Bay than background concentrations in McMurdo Sound. Across this pollution gradient, infaunal species (polychaete worms and bivalve molluscs) as well as epifaunal species (starfish, sea urchins, and nemertean worms) increase in abundance as concentrations of hydrocarbons and chlorinated compounds decrease from the station point source.

The *Bahia Paraiso* oil spill near Palmer Station (Fig. 11.4) in 1989 is a poignant example of a localized acute ecosystem perturbation. The spill was confined by small islands within a 100-square-kilometer area with limited wind-and-wave dispersal across the sea ice and open water. The type of oil spilled was diesel fuel antarctic (DFA), which is semi-volatile with low concentrations of toxic aromatic hydrocarbons that weather quickly compared to unrefined crude oil. Nonetheless, the oil was spilled in a polar environment where cold temperatures slow the bacterial decay of all organic matter, as demonstrated by the persistence of fuel oil residues in marine sediments dating back to the beginning of the 20th century near the Stromness whaling station on South Georgia.

Most of the 600,000 liters of DFA from the *Bahia Paraiso* oil spill washed into the intertidal zone where limpets (*Nacella concinna*) grow on the rocks as food for the kelp gull (*Larus dominicanus*). Within weeks, there was greater than 50%

mortality among the nearby limpet populations, with hydrocarbon concentrations in their tissues exceeding 125,000 parts per billion. High concentrations of hydrocarbons (greater than 17,000 parts per billion) also were observed in clams near the spill and at lower levels (less than 1300 parts per billion) a couple of kilometers away. Following the oil spill there was high reproductive failure among the south polar skua (*Catharacta maccormicki*), Adélie penguin, and cormorant (*Phalacrocorax atriceps*) populations in the vicinity. Fatalities among cormorant adults also opened up space in rookeries, which exposed surviving chicks to increased predation from skuas, eventually causing the number of nests on Cormorant Island to decline from nearly 400 to zero.

In addition to chemical or physical impacts, Antarctic ecosystems also are being disturbed by nonindigenous species transported by humans. The alarming concern and reality about invading species is that they cause structural and functional changes in native biotic assemblages. Because of the huge magnitude of invasive species being introduced by humans around the world (the Office of Technology Assessment estimates nearly 6300 alien species in the United States alone), measures to mitigate their impact have been adopted repeatedly since the first Antarctic Treaty Consultative Meeting (Recommendation I-VIII) in 1961.

Most of the alien species in the Antarctic region have been introduced on islands in "associated ecosystems" that are north of the 60° south latitude jurisdiction of the Antarctic Treaty System. Among the 42 vascular plants on Marion Island, for example, 18 are a result of human introduction (Table 11.4). In addition, many of the exotic biota, such as the Norway rat (*Rattus norvegicus*), came

TABLE 11.4   Alien Vascular Plants on Marion Island (47°52′ S, 37°51′ E)

Species name	Year of introduction
Agrostis castellana	1975
Agrostis gigantea	1994
Agrostis stolonifera	1965
Agropyron repens	1965
Alopecurus australis	1965
Avena sativa	1965
Cerastium fontanum	1873
Festuca rubra	1966
Holcus lanatus	1953
Hypochoeris radicata	1953
Plantago lanceolata	1965
Poa annua	1948
Poa pratensis	1965
Rumex acetosella	1953
Sagina procumbens	1965
Stellaria media	1873

[a] Based on Gremmen (1997).

TABLE 11.5   Introduced Animals on Subantarctic Islands

Introduced species	Common name	Year of introduction
Calliphora vicina	Blowfly	1978
Felix catus	Cat	c. 1820
Mus musculus	House mouse	1800s
Oopterus soledadinus	Beetle	1939
Oryctolagus cuniculus	Rabbit	c. 1850
Ovis ammon	Mouflon	1957
Ovis aries	Sheep	1909
Rangifer tarandus	Reindeer	1911
Rattus norvegicus	Norway rat	c. 1800
Rattus rattus	Black rat	1800s

[a] Based on Leader-Williams (1985) and Chevrier et al. (1997).

down with the early explorers at the start of the 19th century (Table 11.5). Along with the rats, rabbits (*Oryctolagus cuniculus*) and cats (*Felix catus*) have been responsible for local elimination of various native birds on subantarctic islands. In the case of Macquarie Island (54°40′S, 158°55′E), two endemic bird species—a banded rail (*Rallus philippensis*) and a parakeet (*Cyanorhampus novaezelandiae*)—even became extinct between 1880 and 1894 because of species introductions.

Invading species also have extended into the Antarctic region, including an insect and two spider species (Table 9.3). In 1997, Australian scientists also identified antibodies to an avian pathogen from domestic chickens (*Gallus domesticus*) that had been incorporated into 2% of the Adélie penguins and up to 63% of the emperor penguins (*Aptenodytes foresteri*) near Mawson Station (Fig. 11.1). This infectious bursal disease virus (IBDV), which is transmitted through waste materials, is known to affect the immune systems of chicks and retard their growth. However, around Antarctica, there is scarce information on the impacts and continental extent of such diseases and other nonindigenous introductions.

In contrast to localized human impacts, there also are global impacts around Antarctica from remote sources. For example, during the 1960s, DDT and other human-synthesized compounds began accumulating in Antarctic ice, lakes, and species—in the most remote and isolated regions of the Earth system. Two decades later, emissions of chlorofluorocarbons (predominantly from the Northern Hemisphere) were found to be inducing the "ozone hole" in the remote atmosphere over Antarctica (Figs. 8.11a and 8.11b). Moreover, since the late 19th century, combustion of organic materials has contributed to the increasing concentrations of carbon dioxide in the global atmosphere that have been found in ice cores (Figs. 8.9 and 8.10). Like messengers, such transboundary pollutants have been dispersing with the ocean and atmosphere (Figs. 7.8, 7.9, and 8.5)—connecting resource activities among nations and environments throughout the Earth system in an international context.

ACCOMMODATING VALUES

In addition to objective features that can be quantified, Antarctic environmental protection involves values that are shared among diverse stakeholders. In 1959, these shared values were expressed in terms of "common interests" (Box 5.3) among the claimant and nonclaimant nations who originally signed the Antarctic Treaty (Fig. 3.5, Table 5.1)—providing a "firm foundation" for the "internal accommodation" of nations in the Antarctic Treaty System (Chapter 5: International Stewardship).

 How are the values of the Antarctic Treaty System relevant to humanity?

As the Antarctic Treaty System evolved with new situations and stakeholders (Figs. 5.3 and 11.1–11.4, Tables 5.1, 5.2, 11.1, and 11.3), specific values were identified by the consultative nations in relation to the Antarctic environment "in the interest of all mankind." In 1975, the remote and pristine nature of the Antarctic environment was characterized in terms of its "value for global baseline monitoring purposes" (Box 11.6). As discussions about Antarctic mineral resources began escalating in 1979 (Recommendation X-1), the "importance of Antarctica to the world environment" was further described in terms of its "unique

---

BOX 11.6   1985 RECOMMENDATION VIII-13[a]

THE ANTARCTIC ENVIRONMENT

The Representatives,

Recognizing that prime responsibility for Antarctic matters, including protection of the Antarctic environment, lies with the States active in the area which are parties to the Antarctic Treaty;

Noting the vulnerability of the Antarctic environment to human interference and that the consequences of major alterations would be of global significance;

Noting the distance of the Antarctic from the main sources of environmental pollution and hence its value for global baseline monitoring purposes; . . .

[a]From the Antarctic Treaty Searchable Database: 1959–1999 CD-ROM.

TABLE 11.6   Antarctic Area Classification [a,b]

Antarctic Treaty Area

Adoption:	Antarctic Treaty, Article VI (1959)
Scope:	". . . Area south of 60^0 South Latitude, including all ice shelves, but nothing in the present Treaty shall prejudice or in any way affect the rights, or the exercise of the rights, of any State under international law with regard to the high seas within that area."
Designation:	Continent-wide

Historic Sites and Monuments

Adoption:	Recommendation I-9 (1961), Recommendation V-4 (1968)
Scope:	"Tombs, buildings or objects of historic interest"
Designation:	74 Historic Sites or Monuments

Special Conservation Area

Adoption:	Recommendation III-8, Agreed Measures for the Conservation of Antarctic Fauna and Flora Preamble (1964)
Scope:	Status applied to the Antarctic Treaty area
Designation:	continent-wide

Specially Protected Areas (SPA)

Adoption:	Recommendation III-8, Agreed Measures for the Conservation of Antarctic Fauna and Flora Preamble (1964)
Scope:	"Areas of outstanding scientific interest . . . shall be accorded special protection . . . in order to preserve their unique natural ecological system"
Designation:	29 SPA

Sites of Special Scientific Interest (SSSI)

Adoption:	Recommendation VII-3 (1972), Recommendation VIII-3 (1975)
Scope:	Sites where "scientific investigations may be jeopardised by accidental or wilful interference" that are of "exceptional scientific interest and therefore require long-term protection from harmful interference" and are of "non-biological interest"
Designation:	37 SSSI

Seal Reserves

Adoption:	Convention on the Conservation of Antarctic Seals, Annex 1, Article 3 (1972)
Scope:	"Open and closed areas, including the designation of reserves" and the "designation of special areas where there shall be no disturbance of seals"
Designation:	Three Seal Reserves

Areas of Special Tourist Interest (ASTI)

Adoption:	Recommendation VIII-9 (1975)
Scope:	Areas designated for tourist visits
Designation:	None designated

Antarctic Marine Ecosystem Area

Adoption:	Convention on the Conservation of Antarctic Marine Living Rresources (CCAMLR) Article 1 (1980)
Scope:	"Area south of 60° South latitude and to the . . . area between that latitude and the Antarctic Convergence which form part of the Antarctic marine ecosystem"
Designation:	Continent-wide

Tomb

Adoption:	Recommendation XI-3 (1981)

(continues)

TABLE 11.6   *(Continued)*

Scope:	"Northern slopes of Mount Erebus where the [1979 airplane] accident took place be declared a tomb and that they ensure that the area is left in peace"
Designation:	1 Tomb

Marine Sites of Special Scientific Interest (MSSSI)

Adoption:	Recommendation XIV-6 (1987)
Scope:	"Protect marine scientific investigations which might suffer from wilful or accidental interference and inshore marine sites of scientific interest where harmful interference is generally recognized to be likely"
Designation:	2 MSSSI

Multiple-Use Planning Areas (MPA)

Adoption:	Recommendation XV-11 (1989)
Scope:	"Coordinating human activities in those areas where such activities pose identified risks of mutual interference or cumulative environmental impacts"
Designation:	None designated

Natural Reserve

Adoption:	Protocol on Environmental Protection to the Antarctic Treaty (Protocol), Article 2 (1991)
Scope:	Antarctica designated as a "natural reserve, devoted to peace and science"
Designation:	Continent-wide

Antarctic Specially Protected Areas (ASPA)

Adoption:	Protocol, Annex V: Protected Area System, Article 3 (1991)
Scope:	"Any area, including any marine area, may be designated . . . to protect outstanding environmental, scientific, historic, aesthetic or wilderness values, any combination of those values, or ongoing or planned scientific research."
Designation:	None designated

Antarctic Specially Managed Areas (ASMA)

Adoption:	Protocol, Annex V: Protected Area System, Article 4 (1991)
Scope:	"Areas where activities pose risks of mutual interference or cumulative environmental impacts"
Designation:	None designated

CCAMLR Ecosystem Monitoring Program (CEMP) Sites

Adoption:	CCAMLR Commission Conservation Measure 18/XIII (1994)
Scope:	Protect against "accidental or wilful interference" at CEMP Sites
Designation:	2 CEMP Sites

[a] See Antarctic Treaty Searchable Database: 1959–1999 CD-ROM.
[b] See Table 5.2.

ecological and scientific value." With discussions about mineral resources, the Antarctic Treaty System began regarding "data and information of commercial value" (CRAMRA, Article 16). Moreover, in 1989, because of growing concerns about commercial interests and multiple uses, the Antarctic Treaty System developed comprehensive measures for environmental protection (Recommendation XV-11) in relation to the "unique biological, geological, glaciological, geomorphological, ecological, scientific, historic, aesthetic, scenic and wilderness values of Antarctica." Through the Protocol and its unifying annexes (Table 5.2),

Annex I: Environmental Impact Assessment;
Annex II: Conservation of Antarctic Fauna and Flora;
Annex III: Waste Disposal and Management;
Annex IV: Prevention of Marine Pollution
Annex V: Area Protection and Management
Annex VI: Liability (?)

the "intrinsic," "special," and "natural" values of Antarctica have became integral to planning and conducting human activities in the Antarctic Treaty area (Boxes 11.3 and 11.6).

Emergence of the Antarctic Treaty System as an international cooperation precedent for "all mankind" is reflected by the values and accommodations of its diverse stakeholders. Initially, the "internal accommodation" between claimant and nonclaimant signatories fostered the "establishment phase" of the Antarctic Treaty System (Fig. 5.3) until the mineral issue became a "matter of urgency." With awakened focus, the signatory nations then began developing an "external accommodation" with the rest of the international community under the auspices of the Antarctic Treaty:

> . . . ensuring the use of Antarctica for peaceful purposes only and the continuance of international harmony in Antarctica [to] further the purposes and principles embodied in the Charter of the United Nations.

During this "international accommodation phase" (Fig. 5.3) the Antarctic Treaty System membership grew more than 500% before entering the "global stewardship phase" in 1991, when the Protocol was signed (Fig. 5.2).

Similar phases of involvement among the multiple users of Antarctica also appear in the commercial sector with tourism (Fig. 11.3) and in the science sector, as demonstrated by the continuous commitment of nations operating research programs in Antarctica since the IGY (e.g., Fig. 11.2).

In addition, interests of all users have been accommodated by the diverse types of areas reserved for protection and preservation around Antarctica (Table 11.6). Since 1959, more than 70 measures have been adopted by the Antarctic Treaty Consultative Parties regarding protected areas. In addition, more than 150 sites and associated management plans have been approved within 11 of the 15 protected area categories. Moreover, with a view toward implementation and representation, there has been an ongoing "review of the protected area system" since 1972 (Recommendation VII-2)—unifying the previous measures into the Protocol, Annex V on Area Protection and Management.

Environmental protection in Antarctica embodies scientific, economic, government, and social values and accommodations among nations and diverse stakeholders. In the "interest of all mankind," the design and implementation of such strategies are fundamental to using Antarctica and the Earth system "for peaceful purposes only" (Chapter 12: The Science Keystone).

PART

V

OUR GLOBAL COMMONS

PRECEDENT FOR HUMANITY

During the second half of the 20th century, as a civilization, we have walked with Neil Armstrong on the Moon and driven in a robotic vehicle across the Martian surface. We have sent manned submerbles to the bottom of the deepest ocean trenches and space vehicles toward the limits of our solar system. We have space borne telescopes that are beginning to peer into the universe billions of light years beyond and satellites scanning the Earth in minutes across distances that took explorers centuries to scope. We extract sediment and ice cores, revealing the Earth's history by geochemical assays with minute detection levels—often less than one part in a trillion. We are discovering biological fragments locked in rocks that reflect the emergence and extinction of species over millions of years. In the process of learning about the world around us, as the only species ever to step beyond the atmosphere and view the Earth system from outside we are beginning to understand our dimensions in nature across time and space (Part I: Earth System Science).

Spreading across the Earth since the dawn of our evolution, the human population finally reached 1 billion near the beginning of the 19th century. By the first half of the 20th century, the human population already had doubled and by the end of the century exceeded 6 billion persons. During this later period, India alone grew from 345 million persons in 1947 to a billion persons in 1999—an increase in one country within 50 years that the entire human population achieved across the planet in 500 years from 1350 to 1804 (Part II: Progress of All Mankind).

Understanding the relationship between human population production and Earth system variability is as vital today as it was when our ancestors were living in caves. Now, we can survive beyond our biological adaptations, in otherwise inhospitable environments such as Antarctica, the deep sea, or outer space. However—in all cases—we still need food, energy, and material resources from the Earth. Satisfying these basic biological needs, in view of our growing global population, will increasingly involve solutions that extend across the planet (Part III: Our Dynamic Planet).

Expansion of our civilization is an Earth system phenomenon affecting resources and habitats on a planetary scale. We have created agriculture, eliminated forests, and transformed landscapes. We have overexploited species on land and in the sea, even in the most remote parts of the planet. We have industrialized and produced chemicals that are being dispersed globally by the atmosphere. Compared to other species on Earth, the consequences of our production have extended from local to global scales over exceptionally brief periods (Part IV: Sustainable Resource Use).

Antarctica is analogous to the Earth system itself. As a system, Antarctica reflects the time and space dimensions that are fundamental to understanding natural phenomena across the Earth, from the tectonic separation of continents over millions of years to the fluctuation of environments over seasons. Antarctica, with its ice sheets and climatic relation to sea level, also underscores the land–ocean–atmosphere coupling that cycles water around the Earth across glacial–interglacial periods as well as shorter periods. These habitat dynamics represent geological and ecological time scales associated with the evolution of species and persistence of their populations.

Antarctica also is a microcosm of the Earth system with its inter-

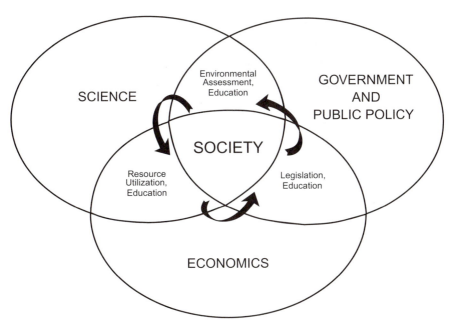

FIGURE V   Integration of scientific, economic, governmental, and public policy perspectives for promoting and sustaining the common welfare of our global society. These interdisciplinary connections (Fig. 2.1) are at the heart of the Antarctic Treaty System and its international precedent in managing an entire continent for "peaceful purposes only" (Plate 8). Modified from Berkman (1997a).

national aspects—representing a compressed history of the developmental stages in our civilization (Fig. 5.3). As *Terra Australis Incognita,* nations imagined the riches and spices of an uncharted "new world." With advances in ships (new technologies of the era) nations began racing for priority—to be first—in the discovery of lands and resources (which were first seen around Antarctica by James Cook near the end of the 18th century). When finally discovered, nations quickly identified avenues of commercial gain as they exploited the largest, most accessible, and most profitable resources first, with species such as the Antarctic fur seal quickly being overexploited.

To protect their resources, nations soon extended their jurisdictions by asserting territorial claims (as among the seven Antarctic claimants). Although claimant boundaries have been mapped around Antarctica—like the sovereign territories that jigsaw across all other continents—there is no "basis for asserting, supporting or denying" those claims as long as the 1959 Antarctic Treaty remains in force. More importantly, with a view toward "international harmony" and the "progress of all mankind," the Antarctic Treaty System has created a common vision among nations representing more than 70% of the Earth's human population.

Human population and Earth system dynamics are global issues, embracing the inclusive interests of diverse stakeholders across the planet (Fig. V). Like a beacon, worldwide involvement and cooperation in Antarctica are precedents for humankind—radiating toward international stewardship of our global civilization.

12

THE SCIENCE KEYSTONE

Imagine all the people, living life in peace . . .
Imagine all the people, sharing all the world.
—John Lennon (1971), "Imagine"

INSPIRING PERSPECTIVE

Coldest, windiest, driest, most isolated, least populated, most pristine, and most peaceful—Antarctica is a land of extremes, offering precious perspectives on the Earth system and its relation to humankind (Fig. IV). These insights about Antarctica and the Earth system largely emanate from scientific investigations (Fig. III). Moreover, in Antarctica, science has the added value of being a central pillar for the "firm foundation" of international cooperation (Fig. V). Essentially, science offers a method and philosophy for studying and managing the world we live in.

The scientific method starts with a question, which grows into hypotheses that are objectively tested to reveal likely answers. Rooted in inquiry, this experimental process is fundamental to the "progress of all mankind" through the identification of resources and development of basic tools, technologies, and industries (Chapter 4: Awakening Science). After letting the genie out of the bottle, science further contributes to the design of strategies for assessing, controlling, and mitigating impacts from our progress (Chapter 11: Environmental Protection).

Beyond its quantitative mien—which is paradoxically perceived with awe and disdain—science offers humankind common ground in searching for answers about the past, present, and future. In fact, the further we project backward or forward, the more central science becomes.

Why is understanding the Earth as a system relevant to the world we live in?

Perspectives of time and space—which are fundamental to science—place events, entities, and phenomena in context across gradients and continua: bigger or smaller, faster or slower, older or younger. In essence, science provides objective references for integrating information and for understanding the complexities of our world (Chapter 2: Conceptual Integration).

Since its origin 4 to 5 billion years ago, the Earth has produced continents that slowly move horizontally and vertically across the planet surface. Antarctica, as a keystone fragment of the Gondwana supercontinent, provides a focal point for describing continental motion at various intervals during the past 200 million years.

During the past 65 million years, as Antarctica became isolated and glaciated, the Earth system began cooling (Chapter 6: Moving Planet). Superimposed on this long-term cooling trend are relatively short-term excursions when the Earth warms and cools. Water—cycling from the ocean through the atmosphere onto the continents and back—has been preserved in records that reflect glacial–interglacial climate shifts with millennial frequencies during the past half-million years. During the past 17,000 years, since the Last Glacial Maximum, sea level has risen more than 120 meters—further underscoring the driving dynamics of the hydrologic cycle in the Earth system (Chapter 7: Flowing Planet).

Telescoping toward the present, fossil assemblages along with sediment and ice cores reveal relatively stable environmental conditions during the past 6000 years—coincident with the global proliferation of calendars and written languages throughout our civilization. Over the past millennium, ice cores further document atmospheric carbon dioxide concentrations markedly increasing along with human populations throughout the world during the past two centuries (Fig. II). Pesticides in Antarctic snow and species as well as the seasonal creation of the "ozone hole" over Antarctica further demonstrate the global reach of human impacts during the late 20th century. Together, these records from Antarctica and elsewhere underscore the dynamics of the Earth system which connects humankind on a global scale (Chapter 8: Breathing Planet and Chapter 9: Living Planet).

Antarctica also reveals basic human nature in utilizing resources in the Earth system—biggest and easiest with largest economic potential first. In the late 1700s, fur seals were captured along accessible Antarctic coastlines. As populations were depleted new seal rookeries were identified. After these Antarctic marine living resources had been exhausted, baleen whales were next. One species after another was diminished as new technologies, such as the explosive harpoon, moved them toward the limit of extinction. This wake of declining marine populations now is evident among smaller living resources, particularly Antarctic fish. The challenge is learning from past activities to prevent overexploitation of resources, such as krill, that have global value for "all of mankind" (Chapter 10: Ecosystem Conservation).

At all levels, from local communities to the entire planet, understanding Earth system phenomena involves science (Fig. III). Science is conducted for basic purposes because nature is inherently interesting and because humans are innately curious (Fig. IV). Science also is conducted for applied purposes to identify resources and develop technologies (Fig. V). Broadly, science has been central in the development of our civilization.

Across generations, science has stimulated continuity in our world by building on an ever expanding base of knowledge. However, beyond understanding the Earth system or even human tendencies, it is the "common ground" feature of science that is most important in our society—providing an objective framework for dialogue among diverse stakeholders. Such dialogue becomes essential in the international arena, where national security interests can escalate into isolation and confrontation. In this context, Antarctica is a unique example in the history of our civilization, where science continuously has fostered cooperation among nations with diverse cultural, economic, and political orientations (Chapter 5: Global Stewardship).

EMERGING COMMON INTERESTS

Picture a grass pasture where different herders are grazing their sheep. There is plenty of grass, but there are more sheep than the pasture can support at once. Together, the group of herders could rotate their use of the common pasture over time and space so that all sheep could feed sufficiently on a continuous basis. Conversely, an individual herder could let his or her sheep graze maximally, ignoring cooperative interests at the expense of the grass pasture as well—a situation classically known as the "tragedy of the commons." What should the individual herder do?

This classic dilemma applies broadly to living and nonliving resources that are used collectively by different stakeholders in communities and nations across the Earth. Moreover, when resources are in limited supply, dominant competitors are favored to the exclusion of all others. These resource issues we face as a civilization parallel those of any other species—*complete competitors cannot coexist* (Chapter 9: Living Planet).

Beyond direct resource utilization, human productivity also has indirect consequences through habitat pollution and modification. Fortunately, by the end of the second millennium in the "common era," nations began reaching across borders to reduce their impacts in the Earth system. In fact, from the vantage of the future, historians will be able to look back on the 20th century and demonstrate substantial contributions from simply recognizing that human development can impact species and their environments beyond national jurisdictions (Table 12.1). Moreover, the emergence of international agreements for ecosystem and environmental protection clearly shows the growing need among nations to resolve common issues cooperatively (Fig. 12.1).

TABLE 12.1   History of International Ecosystem and Environmental Protection [a]

Year [b]	Convention or treaty
1933 (1936)	Convention Relative to the Preservation of Fauna and Flora in their Natural State
1940 (1942)	Convention on Nature Protection and Wild Life Preservation in the Western Hemisphere
1946 (1948)	International Convention for the Regulation of Whaling
1949 (1950)	Convention for the Establishment of an Inter-American Tropical Tuna Commission
1950 (1963)	International Convention for the Protection of Birds
1951 (1953)	Convention for the Establishment of the European and Mediterranean Plant Protection Organization
1951 (1952)	International Plant Protection Convention
1952 (1953)	International Convention for the High Seas Fisheries of the North Pacific Ocean
1954 (1958)	International Convention for the Prevention of Pollution of the Sea by Oil
1957 (1957)	Interim Convention on Conservation of North Pacific Fur Seals
1958 (1962)	Convention on the High Seas
1958 (1964)	Convention on the Territorial Sea and the Contiguous Zone
1958 (1964)	Convention on the Continental Shelf
1958 (1966)	Convention on Fishing and Conservation of the Living Resources of the High Seas
1959 (1961)	Antarctic Treaty [c]
1959 (1963)	North-East Atlantic Fisheries Convention
1959 (1960)	Convention Concerning Fishing in the Black Sea
1961 (1968)	International Convention for the Protection of New Varieties of Plants
1962 (1963)	Convention on the African Migratory Locust
1963 (1963)	Treaty Banning Nuclear Weapon Tests in the Atmosphere, Outer Space and Under Water
1964 (1966)	Fisheries Convention
1964 (1968)	Convention for the International Council for the Exploration of the Sea
1966 (1969)	International Convention for the Conservation of Atlantic Tunas
1967 (1968)	Phyto-Sanitary Convention for Africa
1967 (1967)	Treaty on Principles Governing the Activities of States in the Exploration and Use of Outer Space, Including the Moon and other Celestial Bodies
1968 (1969)	African Convention on the Conservation of Nature and Natural Resources
1968 (1971)	Convention on the Conservation of the Living Resources of the Southeast Atlantic
1971 (1972)	Treaty on the Prohibition of the Emplacement of Nuclear Weapons and other Weapons of Mass Destruction on the Sea-bed and the Ocean Floor and in the Subsoil thereof
1971 (1975)	Convention on Wetlands of International Importance Especially as Waterfowl Habitat
1972 (1975)	Convention for the Protection of the World Cultural and Natural Heritage
1972 (1974)	Convention on the Prevention of Marine Pollution by Dumping from Ships and Aircraft
1972 (1975)	Convention on the Prevention of Marine Pollution by Dumping of Wastes and Other Matter
1972 (1978)	Convention on the Conservation of Antarctic Seals
1973 (1975)	Convention on International Trade in Endangered Species of Wild Fauna and Flora
1973 (1974)	Convention on Fishing and Conservation of the Living Resources in the Baltic Sea and the Belts
1973 (1983)	International Convention for the Prevention of Pollution from Ships
1974 (1976)	Convention on Registration of Objects Launched into Outer Space
1974 (1980)	Convention on the Protection of the Marine Environment of the Baltic Sea Area

(*continues*)

TABLE 12.1   *(Continued)*

Year[b]	Convention or treaty
1974 (1978)	Convention for the Prevention of Marine Pollution from Land-Based Sources
1978 (1979)	Kuwait Regional Convention for Cooperation on the Protection of the Marine Environment from Pollution
1976 (1978)	Convention for the Protection of the Mediterranean Sea Against Pollution
1976 (1990)	Convention on Conservation of Nature in the South Pacific
1978 (1980)	Treaty for Amazonian Cooperation
1978 (1979)	Convention on Future Multilateral Cooperation in the Northwest Atlantic Fisheries
1979 (1983)	Convention on the Conservation of European Wildlife and Natural Habitats
1979 (1982)	Convention for the Conservation and Management of the Vicuna
1979 (1983)	Convention on the Conservation of Migratory Species of Wild Animals
1979 (1983)	Convention on Long-Range Transboundary Air Pollution
1980 (1982)	Convention on the Conservation of Antarctic Marine Living Resources
1980 (1982)	Convention on Future Multilateral Cooperation in the North-East Atlantic Fisheries
1981 (1984)	Convention for Co-Operation in the Protection and Development of the Marine and Coastal Environment of the West and Central African Region
1981 (1984)	Convention for the Protection of the Marine Environment and Coastal Area of the South-East Pacific
1982 (1983)	Convention for the Conservation of Salmon in the North Atlantic Ocean
1982 (1983)	Benelux Convention on Nature Conservation and Landscape Protection
1982 (1985)	Regional Convention for the Conservation of the Red Sea and Gulf of Aden Environment
1982 (1994)	United Nations Convention on the Law of the Sea
1983 (1989)	Agreement for Co-Operation in Dealing with Pollution of the North Sea by Oil and Other Harmful Substances
1985 (1988)	Vienna Convention for the Protection of the Ozone Layer
1986 (1990)	Convention for the Protection of the Natural Resources and Environment of the South Pacific Region
1989 (1991)	Convention for the Prohibition of Fishing with Long Driftnets in the South Pacific
1989 (1992)	Basel Convention on the Control of Transboundary Movement of Hazardous Wastes and their Disposal
1991 (1997)	Convention on Environmental Impact Assessment in a Transboundary Context
1991 (1998)	Protocol on Environmental Protection to the Antarctic Treaty
1992 (1993)	Convention on Biological Diversity
1992 (1994)	United Nations Framework Convention on Climate Change
1992 (1996)	Convention on the Protection and Use of Transboundary Watercourses and International Lakes
1994 (1996)	United Nations Convention to Combat Desertification in those Countries Experiencing Serious Drought and/or Desertification, Particularly in Africa
1994 (1996)	Lusaka Agreement on Co-operative Enforcement Operations Directed at Illegal Trade in Wild Fauna and Flora

[a] International (more than two nations) conventions and treaties that have come into force, excluding subsequent agreements and protocols such as the 1990 Montreal Protocol on Substances That Deplete the Ozone Layer for the 1985 Vienna Convention for the Protection of the Ozone Layer. Compiled from legal databases of the United Nations (http://www.un.org/Depts/Treaty), Fletcher School of Law and Diplomacy, Tufts University (http://www.tufts.edu/fletcher), and the Consortium for International Earth Science Information Network (http://sedac.ciesin.org/pidb).

[b] Year signed (year entered into force).

[c] Complete texts of all legal instruments adopted by the Antarctic Treaty Consultative Parties are in the Antarctic Treaty Searchable Database: 1959–1999 CD-ROM.

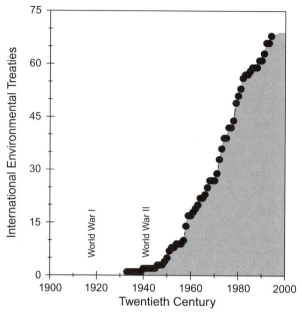

FIGURE 12.1 Cumulative development of international ecosystem and environmental protection conventions and treaties during the 20th century. In stark contrast to the international hostilities of the two world wars during the first half of the 20th century, nearly 95% of the 68 legal instruments of international cooperation have come into force since 1950 (Table 12.1).

How do we balance economic, governmental and scientific perspectives in managing resources for the common good (Fig. V)?

Treaties, conventions, agreements, and protocols among nations provide legal instruments for managing common resources. National interests can be regional in scope across continents, such as Europe, or ocean areas, such as the North Atlantic. National interests also can target specific natural or anthropogenic impacts such as the migration of locusts across Africa or pollution in the Mediterranean Sea. In each instance, within these regional agreements, international aspects only involve several of the nearly 200 nations around the Earth (Table 12.1).

Nations also share interests in ecosystem and environmental phenomena that transcend national jurisdictions. For example, movement of the global atmosphere and ocean around the Earth (Figs. 7.9 and 8.4) has influenced the creation of legal strategies to manage transboundary pollutants that originate within specific regions but which affect the welfare of nations across the planet, such as ozone depletion (Fig. 8.11). Global interests among nations also include environmental changes associated with Earth's climate variability (e.g., Figs. 7.4, 7.6, 8.9, 8.10, and 9.2), which now is influenced by natural and human-induced phenomena.

Common interests in these Earth system agreements are represented by broad international involvement (Table 12.1).

International oversight also has extended to all of humanity—beyond the jurisdiction of any nation—with regard to the high seas and deep sea bed; outer space, the Moon, and celestial bodies; and Antarctica. However, managing these "common spaces" for the "benefit of mankind" is enormously complicated because of the diversity of cultures, philosophies, religions, histories, industries, and government structures among nations. In the words of Hugo Grotius (1583–1645), a Dutchman who wrote about international society during the 17th century, "Love is not due all in the same degree . . . a greater love is due a father than a stranger." Grotius' idea suggests that even with international legal frameworks in place, there will be a greater tendency for cooperation among nations who have identified common interests. This concept of international regions and resources also presents a grand paradox in that the rights of nations belong to everyone (*res communis*) and no one (*res nullius*) at the same time.

 What are the common interests of nations around the Earth?

The legal status of the ocean, for example, had long been considered in terms of national jurisdictions when Grotius crafted *Mare Liberum* in 1609 to explain international "freedoms of the seas." Four centuries later, these collective freedoms and responsibilities of nations matured into the "common heritage of mankind" principle, which was introduced to the United Nations in 1967 by the Ambassador to Malta, Arvid Pardo (1914–1999).

Fifteen years later, the "common heritage of mankind" became the centerpiece of the 1982 United Nations Convention on the Law of the Sea (UNCLOS)—establishing an international regime for using the deep sea bed and its potential resources (such as manganese nodules) beyond the continental shelf zones of coastal nations (Box 12.1). UNCLOS also reinforced earlier freedoms for fishing, laying submarine cables, navigating, overflying, constructing installations, and conducting scientific investigation through the "high seas" beyond the 200-mile "exclusive economic zones" of coastal nations (Fig. 12.2). Although "equitable and efficient utilization" of resources is enigmatic, the evolving legal principle of the "common heritage of mankind" has proved farsighted by inspiring the common interests of "peace, security, co-operation and friendly relations among all nations" for present and future generations.

Similarly, "common interests of all mankind" had been identified in the 1967 Treaty on Principles Governing the Activities of States in the Exploration and Use of Outer Space, Including the Moon and other Celestial Bodies (Box 12.2), as well as the 1959 Antarctic Treaty (Box 5.1). Like UNCLOS, these treaties contributed to the peaceful use of regions "beyond the limits of national jurisdiction" with "scientific investigation" as the keystone of international cooperation. In all of these international regimes, common interests were established for "mankind

BOX 12.1   1982 UNITED NATIONS CONVENTION ON THE LAW OF THE SEA

PREAMBLE

The States Parties to this Convention,

Prompted by the desire to settle, in a spirit of mutual understanding and co-operation, all issues relating to the law of the sea and aware of the historic significance of this Convention as an important contribution to the maintenance of peace, justice and progress for all peoples of the world,

Noting that developments since the United Nations Conferences on the Law of the Sea held at Geneva in 1958 and 1960 have accentuated the need for a new and generally acceptable Convention on the law of the sea,

Conscious that the problems of ocean space are closely interrelated and need to be considered as a whole,

Recognizing the desirability of establishing through this Convention, with due regard for the sovereignty of all States, a legal order for the seas and oceans which will facilitate international communication, and will promote the peaceful uses of the seas and oceans, the equitable and efficient utilization of their resources, the conservation of their living resources, and the study, protection and preservation of the marine environment,

Bearing in mind that the achievement of these goals will contribute to the realization of a just and equitable international economic order which takes into account the interests and needs of mankind as a whole and, in particular, the special interests and needs of developing countries, whether coastal or land-locked,

Desiring by this Convention to develop the principles embodied in resolution 2749 (XXV) of 17 December 1970 in which the General Assembly of the United Nations solemnly declared inter alia that the area of the seabed and ocean floor and the subsoil thereof, beyond the limits of national jurisdiction, as well as its resources, are the common heritage of mankind, the exploration and exploitation of which shall be carried out for the benefit of mankind as a whole, irrespective of the geographical location of States,

Believing that the codification and progressive development of the law of the sea achieved in this Convention will contribute to the strengthening of peace, security, co-operation and friendly relations among all nations in conformity with the principles of justice and equal rights and will promote the economic and social advancement of all peoples of the world, in accordance with the Purposes and Principles of the United Nations as set forth in the Charter,

Affirming that matters not regulated by this Convention continue to be governed by the rules and principles of general international law,

Have agreed as follows:

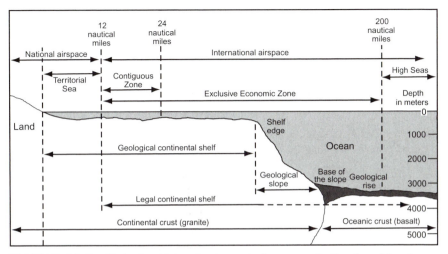

FIGURE 12.2   National and international zones in the ocean, subsoil, and overlying airspace under the 1982 United Nations Convention on the Law of the Sea, which came into force in 1994. The Antarctic Treaty (Article VI) refers to the rights "of any State under international law with regard to the high seas." From the United States Department of State (1995).

as a whole" beyond economic, political, technological, cultural or geographic differences among nations.

Among the three "common spaces" regimes that have been implemented through the United Nations, the 1959 Antarctic Treaty has the longest history of continuously elaborating common interests and cooperative strategies among nations (Antarctic Treaty Searchable Database: 1959–1999 CD-ROM). Moreover, during the past five decades, the Antarctic Treaty System has become uniquely integrated with other international regimes, including conventions on law of the sea, marine pollution, ozone depletion, transboundary wastes, whaling, and other global change processes associated with the sustainable development of humankind (Table 12.1). These international innovations in managing Antarctica for the "progress of all mankind" shine as a bright light in our emerging global society.

"PEACEFUL PURPOSES ONLY"

Just as the first half of the 20th century can be characterized by international antagonism associated with World War I (1914–1918) and then World War II (1939–1945), the second half can be characterized by the expansion of international cooperation (Table 12.1, Fig. 12.1). In perspective, global or regional altercations among nations make Antarctica even more special as the only continent on Earth ever to be used for "peaceful purposes only."

This halo of peace was catalyzed by the International Geophysical Year in

BOX 12.2 1967 TREATY ON PRINCIPLES GOVERNING THE ACTIVITIES OF STATES IN THE EXPLORATION AND USE OF OUTER SPACE, INCLUDING THE MOON AND OTHER CELESTIAL BODIES

PREAMBLE

The States Parties to this Treaty,

Inspired by the great prospects opening up before mankind as a result of man's entry into outer space,

Recognizing the common interest of all mankind in the progress of the exploration and use of outer space for peaceful purposes,

Believing that the exploration and use of outer space should be carried on for the benefit of all peoples irrespective of the degree of their economic or scientific development,

Desiring to contribute to broad international co-operation in the scientific as well as the legal aspects of the exploration and use of outer space for peaceful purposes,

Believing that such co-operation will contribute to the development of mutual understanding and to the strengthening of friendly relations between States and peoples,

Recalling resolution 1962 (XVIII), entitled "Declaration of Legal Principles Governing the Activities of States in the Exploration and Use of Outer Space," which was adopted unanimously by the United Nations General Assembly on 13 December 1963,

Recalling resolution 1884 (XVIII), calling upon States to refrain from placing in orbit around the earth any objects carrying nuclear weapons or any other kinds of weapons of mass destruction or from installing such weapons on celestial bodies, which was adopted unanimously by the United Nations General Assembly on 17 October 1963,

Taking account of United Nations General Assembly resolution 110 (II) of 3 November 1947, which condemned propaganda designed or likely to provoke or encourage any threat to the peace, breach of the peace or act of aggression, and considering that the aforementioned resolution is applicable to outer space,

Convinced that a Treaty on Principles Governing the Activities of States in the Exploration and Use of Outer Space, including the Moon and Other Celestial Bodies, will further the purposes and principles of the Charter of the United Nations,

Have agreed on the following:

Matters of Common Interest

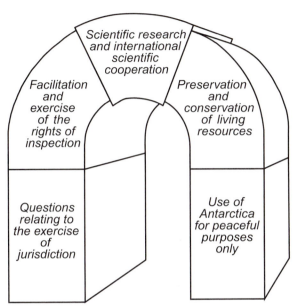

FIGURE 12.3   "Matters of common interest pertaining to Antarctica" that Article IX of the 1959 Antarctic Treaty elaborated as the basis for continuous consultation among nations (Box 5.3). Science is the keystone and common focus among diverse stakeholders, promoting the use of Antarctica for "peaceful purposes only." In the "interest of all mankind," international cooperation in Antarctica provides a global precedent for humanity. Modified from Berkman (1997a).

1957–58, which brought 12 nations together for 18 months as thousands of scientists collaborated in studying the land, ocean, atmosphere, and ice in the Antarctic region (Chapter 4: Awakening Science). These interdisciplinary exchanges fostered international cooperation and facilitated development of the Antarctic Treaty in 1959. The extraordinary feature is that the Antarctic Treaty nations have continuously consulted with each other in a marriage of science and policy that has sustained the cooperative international management of a region beyond the jurisdiction of any nation (Chapter 5: International Stewardship). As noted by Matthew Maury during the 19th century with statesman-like vision:

> Navies are not all for war. Peace has its conquests, science its glories; and no navy can boast of brighter chaplets that those which have been gathered in the fields of geographic exploration and physical research.

From the outset of the Antarctic Treaty System, cooperation extended to the Soviet Union and the United States despite their growing "cold war" differences. Antarctic claimant and nonclaimant nations found common ground. Japan and the United States were collaborating in Antarctica, healing the animus of the previous decade. Even during the Falkland–Malvinas war in 1982, when all diplomatic channels were severed between Great Britain and Argentina, these two nations were meeting in Antarctica to discuss "matters of common interest" regarding the region south of 60° south latitude (Fig. 12.3).

From pollution, ozone depletion, and "greenhouse" warming to the extinction of species and the loss of biodiversity, there is increasing awareness and concern about the extent of human impacts on the global environment (Table 12.1). At the core, these global issues are driven by the geometric growth of the human population and our increasing demand of the Earth's resources at global to local levels (Fig. II). In effect, environmental issues are awakening international discussions about the common future of humankind on a planetary scale (Plates 1 and 8).

As demonstrated by the Antarctic precedent over the past five decades, "international cooperation in scientific investigation" provides a "firm foundation" for nations to unite in managing vast regions of the Earth—perhaps encompassing our entire world one day for "peaceful purposes only." Moreover, like an international language, science engenders communication and education among diverse stakeholders (Fig. V). Across time and space, with vision toward the distant future, science is the keystone for the "progress of all mankind" (Fig. 12.3).

We live in a wondrous world and share in its protection.

CITED REFERENCES

Anderson, J. B., and Bartek, L. R. (1992). Cenozoic glacial history of the Ross Sea revealed by inter-mediate resolution seismic reflection data combined with drill site information. *In* Kennett, J. P., and Warnke, D. A. (eds.), "The Antarctic Paleoenvironment: A Perspective on Global Change," Part One. Antarctic Research Series, Volume 56, pp. 231–263. American Geophysical Union, Washington, D.C.

Arntz, W. E., Gutt, J., and Klages, M. (1997). Antarctic marine biodiversity: an overview. *In* "Antarctic Communities: Species, Structure and Survival," pp. 3–14. Cambridge University Press, Cambridge.

Baron, E. J. (1992). Paleoclimatology. *In* Brown, G. C., Hawkesworth, C. J., and Wilson, R. C. L. (eds.), "Understanding the Earth: A New Synthesis," pp. 485–505. Cambridge University Press, Cambridge.

Baroni, C., and Orombelli, G. (1994). Abandoned penguin rookeries as Holocene paleoclimatic indi-cators in Antarctica. *Geology* **22,** 23–26.

Behrendt, J. C. (1990). Recent geophysical and geological research in Antarctic related to the assess-ment of petroleum resources and potential environmental hazards to their development. *In* Splett-stoesser, J. F. and Dreschhoff, G. A. M. (eds.). "Mineral Resources Potential of Antarctica." Ant-arctic Research Series **51,** pp. 163–174. American Geophysical Union, Washington, D.C.

Berger, A., and Loutre, M. F. (1991). Insolation values for the climate of the last 10 million of years. *Quat. Sci. Rev.* **10,** 297–317.

Berkman, P. A. (1992). The Antarctic marine ecosystem and humankind. *Rev. Aquat. Sci.* **6**(3,4), 295–333.

Berkman, P. A. (1997a). Antarctic Science and Policy: Interdisciplinary Research Education (ASPIRE). Byrd Polar Research Center Report No. 13. The Ohio State University, Columbus.

Berkman, P. A. (1997b). Ecological variability in Antarctic coastal environments: past and present. *In* Battaglia, B., Valencia, J., and Walton, D. W. H. (eds.) Antarctic Environmental Change and Conservation. Cambridge University Press, London. pp. 349–357.

Berkman, P. A. (1998). Indicator species for interpreting environmental variability in the Antarctic coastal zone. *Korean J. Polar Res.* **8**(1), 69–76.

Berkman, P. A., and Forman, S. L. (1996). Pre-bomb radiocarbon and the reservoir correction for calcareous marine species in the Southern Ocean. *Geophys. Res. Lett.* **23,** 633–636.

Berkman, P. A., Foreman, D. W., Mitchell, J. C., and Liptak, R. J. (1992). Scallop shell mineralogy and crystalline characteristics: Proxy records for interpreting Antarctic nearshore marine hydrochemical variability. *In* Elliot, D. H. (ed.), "Contributions to Antarctic Research III," Antarctic Research Series, Vol. 57, pp. 27–38. American Geophysical Union, Washington, D.C.

Berkman, P. A., Andrews, J. T., Björck, S., Colhoun, E. A., Emslie, S. D. Goodwin, I., Hall, B. L., Hart, C. P., Hirakawa, K., Igarashi, A., Ingólfsson, O., López-Martínez, J., Lyons, W. B., Mabin, M. C. G., Quilty, P. G., Taviani, M., and Yoshida, Y. (1998). Circum-Antarctic coastal environmental variability during the Late Quaternary recorded in emerged marine deposits. *Antarctic Sci.* **10**(3), 345–362.

Block, W. (1984). Terrestrial microbiology, invertebrates and ecosystems. *In* Laws, R. M. (ed.), "Antarctic Ecology,". Vol. 1, pp. 163–236. Academic Press, New York.

Bonner, W. N., and Laws, R. M. (1964). Seals and sealing. *In* Priestly, R., Adie, R. J., and Robin, G. DeQ. (eds.), "Antarctic Research," pp. 163–190. Butterworths, London.

Boyd, I. L. (1993). Pup production and distribution of breeding Antarctic fur seals (*Arctocephalus gazella*) at South Georgia. *Antarctic Sci.* **5**(1), 17–24.

Broecker, W. (1987). The biggest chill. *Natural History,* October, pp. 74–81.

Brown, S. G., and Lockyer, C. H. (1984). Whales. *In* Laws, R. M. (ed.), "Antarctic Ecology," Vol. 2, pp. 717–782. Academic Press, New York.

Brownowski, J. (1973). "Ascent of Man." Little Brown, Boston.

Bush, W. M. (ed.) (1982). "Antarctica and International Law: A Collection of Interstate and National Documents," Vols. 1, 2, and 3. Oceana, New York.

Chevrier, M., Vernon, P., and Frenot, Y. (1997). Potential effects of two alien insects on a sub-Antarctic wingless fly in the Kerguelen islands. *In* Battaglia, B., Valencia, J., and Walton, D. W. H. (eds.), "Antarctic Environmental Change and Conservation," pp. 424-432. Cambridge University Press, London.

Cook, G. (1990). "The Future of Antarctica. Exploitation Versus Preservation." Manchester University Press, New York.

Cooper, A. K., Barrett, P. J., Hinz, K., Traube, V., Leitchenkov, G., and Stagg, H. M. J. (1991). Cenozoic prograding sequences of the Antarctic continental margin: a record of glacio-eustatic and tectonic events. *Marine Geol.* **102**, 175–231.

Cooper, A. K., Barker, P. F., and Brancolini, G. (eds.) (1995). "Geology and Seismic Stratigraphy of the Antarctic Margin," Antarctic Research Series, Vol. 68. American Geophysical Union, Washington, D.C.

Darwin, C. (1859). "On the Origin of Species by Means of Natural Selection, or the Preservation of Favoured Races in the Struggle for Life." John Murray, London.

Dietz, R. S., and Holden, J. C. (1976). The breakup of Pangea. *In* Wilson, J. T. (ed.), "Continents Adrift and Continents Aground. Readings from *Scientific American,*" pp. 126–137. W. H. Freeman, San Francisco.

Drewry, D. J. (1983). The surface of the Antarctic Ice Sheet. *In* Drewry, D. J. (ed.), "Glaciological and Geophysical Folio," Sheet 2. Scott Polar Research Institute, Cambridge.

Duxbury, A. C., and Duxbury, A. (1984). "An Introduction to the Worlds Oceans." Addison-Wesley, London.

Earth System Science Committee (1988). "Earth System Science: A Closer View." National Aeronautics and Space Administration, Washington, D.C.

Einstein, A. (1954). "Ideas and Opinions." Bonanza Books, New York.

El-Sayed, S. Z. (1977). "Biological Investigations of Antarctic Marine Systems and Stocks (BIO-MASS)," Vol. 1, "Research Proposals." Scott Polar Research Institute, Cambridge.

Ethridge, D. M., Steele, L. P., Langenfelds, R. L., Francey, R. J., Barnola, J.-M., and Morgan, V. I. (1998). Historical CO_2 records from the Law Dome DE08, DE08–2, and DSS ice cores. *In* "Trends: A Compendium of Data on Global Change. Carbon Dioxide Information Analysis Center, Oak Ridge National Laboratory." U.S. Department of Energy, Oak Ridge. (http://cdiac.esd.ornl.gov/trends/co2/lawdome.html).

Fairbanks, R. G. (1989). A 17,000-yr glacio-eustatic sea level record: Influence of glacial melting rate on the Younger Dryas event and deep-ocean circulation. *Nature* **342**, 637–641.

Fischer, W., and Hureau, J. C. (1985). Food and Agricultural Organization of the United Nations (1977). "The Living Resources of the Southern Ocean," Vols. 1 and 2. United Nations, Rome.

Franklin, B. (1746). "Poor Richard's Almanack." Philadelphia.

Gambell, R. (1985). Birds and mammals—Antarctic whales. *In* Bonner, W. N., and Walton, D. W. H. (eds.), "Antarctica: Key Environments," pp. 223–241. Pergamon Press, New York.

Garrels, R. M., Mackenzie, F. T., and Hunt, C. A. (1975). "Chemical Cycles and the Global Environment. Assessing Human Influences." William Kaufmann, Los Altos, CA.

Goethe, J. W. von (1808). "Faust." J. G. Cotta, Tübingen, Germany.

Greene, S. W., Gressitt, J. L., Koob, D., Llano, G. A., Rudolph, E. D., Singer, R., Steere, W. C., and Ugolini, F. C. (1969). "Terrestrial Life in Antarctica. Antarctic Map Folio Series," Folio 5. American Geographical Society, New York.

Gremmen, N. J. M. (1997). Changes in the vegetation of sub-Antarctic Marion Island resulting from introduced vascular plants. *In* Battaglia, B., Valencia, J., and Walton, D. W. H. (eds.), "Antarctic Environmental Change and Conservation." Cambridge University Press, London, pp. 417–423.

Hardin, G. (1960). The competitive exclusion principle. *Science* **131**, 1292–1297.

Hawking, S. W. (1988). "A Brief History of Time from the Big Bang to Black Holes." Bantam Books, New York.

Hedgpeth, J. W. (1969). "Distribution of Selected Groups of Marine Invertebrates in Waters South of 35°S Latitude," Antarctic Map Folio Series, Folio 11. American Geographical Society, New York.

Heisenberg, W. K. (1958). "Physics and Philosophy." S. Hirzel, Stuttgart.

Heywood, R. B., and Whitaker, T. M. (1984). The marine flora. *In* Laws, R. M. (ed.), "Antarctic Ecology," Vol. 2, pp. 373–420. Academic Press, New York.

Holdgate, M. W. (1984). The use and abuse of polar environmental resources. *Polar Record* **22**, 25–48.

Houghton, L. G., Filho, M., Callander, B. A., Harris, N., Kattenberg, A., and Maskell, K. (1996). "Intergovernmental Panel on Climate Change 1996: Climate Change 1995: The Science of Climate Change." Cambridge University Press, Cambridge.

Huntford, R. (1979). "Scott and Amundsen." G. P. Putnam's Sons, New York.

Huntford, R. (1985). "Shackleton." Fawcett Columbine, New York.

Huxley, T. H. (1868). A liberal education and where to find it. *In* Huxley, T. H. H. (1895). "Collected Essays: III: Science and Education." Appleton, New York.

Imbrie, J., McIntyre, A., and Mix, A. C. (1989). Oceanic response to orbital forcing in the Late Quaternary: observational and experimental strategies. *In* Berger, A., Schneider, S. H., and Duplessy, J.-C. (eds.), "Climate and Geosciences: A Challenge for Science and Society in the 21st Century," pp. 121–164. Kluwer, Boston.

Jacobs, S. S. (1992). Is the Antarctic ice sheet growing? *Nature* **360**, 29–33.

Keeling, C. D., and Whorf, T. P. (2000). Atmospheric CO_2 records from sites in the SIO air sampling network. *In* "Trends: A Compendium of Data on Global Change. Carbon Dioxide Information Analysis Center, Oak Ridge National Laboratory." U. S. Department of Energy, Oak Ridge. (http://cdiac.esd.ornl.gov/trends/co2/sio-mlo.htm).

Kennett, J. P. (1977). Cenozoic evolution of Antarctic glaciation, the Circum-Antarctic Ocean and their impact on global paleoceanography. *J. Geophys. Res.* **82**, 3843–3859.

Kennett, J. P. (1982). "Marine Geology." Prentice-Hall, Englewood Cliffs, N.J.

Kerr, R. A. (1993). The ozone hole reaches a new low. *Science* **262**, 501.

Knox, G. A. (1970). Antarctic marine ecosystems. *In* Holdgate, M. W. (ed.), "Antarctic Ecology," Vol. 1, pp. 69–96. Academic Press, New York.

Laws, R. M. (1977). Seals and whales in the Southern Ocean. *Phil. Trans. Roy. Soc.* (*London*) **B279**, 81–96.

Leader-Williams, N. (1985). The Sub-Antarctic islands—introduced mammals. *In* Bonner, W. N., and Walton, D. W. H. (eds.), "Antarctica: Key Environments," pp. 318–328. Pergammon Press, New York.

Lennon, J. (1971). "Imagine." Apple Records.

Lovelock, J. (1979). "Gaia: A New Look at Life on Earth." Oxford University Press, Oxford.

Lutgens, F. K., and Tarbuck, E. J. (1998). "The Atmosphere: An Introduction to Meteorology." Prentice Hall, New Jersey.

May, R. M. (1979). Ecological interactions in the Southern Ocean. *Nature* **277**, 86–89.

Milankovitch, M. (1938). Astronomische Mittel zur Erforschung der erdgeschichtlichen Klimate. *Handbuch der Geophysik* **9**, 593–698.

Milton, J. (1667). *Paradise Lost,* Book IV. Peter Parker, London.

Mörch, J. A. (1908). Improvements in whaling methods. *Sci. Am.* **94**(5), 75.

National Foreign Assessment Center. (1978). "Polar Regions Atlas." Central Intelligence Agency, Langley, VA.

Parsons, T. R., and Takahashi, M. (1973). "Biological Oceanographic Processes." Pergamon Press, Oxford.

Payne, M. R. (1977). Growth of a fur seal population. *Phil. Trans. Roy. Soc. (London)* **B279**, 67–80.

Petit, J. R., Jouzel, J., Raynaud, D., Barkov, N. I., Barnola, J.-M., Basile, I., Bender, M., Chappellaz, J., Davis, M., Delaygue, G., Delmotte, M., Kotlyakov, V. M., Legrand, M., Lipenkov, V. Y., Lorius, C., Pépin, L., Ritz, C., Saltzman, E., and Stievenard, M. (1999). Climate and atmospheric history of the past 420,000 years from the Vostok ice core, Antarctica. *Nature* **399**, 429–436.

Pickard, G. L., and Emery, W. J. (1982). "Descriptive Physical Oceanography: An Introduction." Pergamon Press, New York.

Picken, G. B. (1985). Marine habitats—benthos. *In* Bonner, W. N., and Walton, D. W. H. (eds.), "Antarctica: Key Environments," pp. 154–172. Pergamon Press, New York.

Ryther, J. H. (1969). Photosynthesis and fish production in the sea. *Science* **166**, 72–76.

Schwerdtfeger, W. (1970). The Climate of the Antarctic. *In* Landsberg, H. E. (ed.), "World Survey of Climatology," Vol. 14, pp. 253–355. Elsevier, New York.

Stommel, H. (1958). The abyssal circulation. *Deep-Sea Res.* **5**, 80–82.

Sumich, J. L. (1996). "An Introduction to the Biology of Marine Life." Wm. C. Brown, Boston.

Tennyson, A. (1842). "Poems," Vols. 1 and 2. W. D. Ticknor, Boston.

Thoreau, H. D. (1848). "Ktaadn." *Union Magazine.*

Thurman, H. V. (1978). "Introductory Oceanography," 2nd ed. Bell and Howell, Columbus.

Tucker, M. E. (1992). Limestones through time. *In* Brown, G. C., Hawkesworth, C. J., and Wilson, R. C. L. (eds.), "Understanding the Earth: A New Synthesis," pp. 347–363. Cambridge University Press, Cambridge.

United States Department of State (1995). "Law of the Sea Convention: Letters of Transmittal and Submittal Commentary," U.S. Department of State Dispatch Supplement, Vol. 6(1). Government Printing Office, Washington, D.C.

Vincent, W. F. (1988). "Microbial Ecosystems of Antarctica." Cambridge University Press, Cambridge.

Webb, P.-N., and Cooper, A. K. (1999). SCAR Antarctic Offshore Stratigraphy Project (ANTOSTRAT). SCAR Report Number 16. Scientific Committee on Antarctic Research, Cambridge.

Winograd, I. J., Coplen, T. B., Landwehr, J. M., Riggs, A. C., Ludwig, K. R., Szabo, B. J., Kolesar, P. T., and Revesz, K. M. (1992). Continuous 500,000-year climate record from vein calcite in Devils Hole, Nevada. *Science* **258**, 255–260.

Wylie, P. J. (1976). The Earth's mantle. *In* Wilson, J. T. (ed.), "Continents Adrift and Continents Aground: Readings from *Scientific American,*" pp. 46–57. W. H. Freeman, San Francisco.

Recommended Resources

CHAPTER 1: GLOBAL DIMENSIONS

Botkin, D. and Keller, E. (1995). "Environmental Science: Earth as a Living Planet." John Wiley and Sons, New York.

Kump, L. R., Kasting, J. F. and Crane, R. G. (1999). "The Earth System." Prentice Hall, Upper Saddle River.

Lovelock, J. (1995). "Gaia: A New Look at Life on Earth." Oxford University Press, Oxford.

INTERNET RESOURCES

Site name	Site address
American Geophysical Union	http://earth.agu.org
Earth View	http://www.fourmilab.ch/cgi-bin/uncgi/Earth/action?opt=-p
Earth Observatory	http://earthobservatory.nasa.gov/
Great Globe Gallery	http://hum.amu.edu.pl/~zbzw/glob
Earth from Space	http://earth.jsc.nasa.gov/
Unit Conversion Factors	http://pump.net/thebasics/unitconvfactors.htm
United Nations Environmental Program	http://www.unep.org
United Nations Population Division	http://www.undp.org/popin
United States Central Intelligence Agency Publications	http://www.odci.gov/cia/publications/factbook
United States National Aeronautics and Space Administration Earth Science Enterprise	http://www.earth.nasa.gov

---

CHAPTER 2: CONCEPTUAL INTEGRATION

Ingram, C. F. (1980). "Fundamentals of Educational Assessment." D. Van Nostrand, New York.
Olsen, S. and Loucks-Horsley (eds.) (2000). "Inquiry and the National Science Education Standards: A Guide for Teaching and Learning." National Research Council, Washington, D.C.
National Academy Press (1999). "Transforming Undergraduate Education in Science, Mathematics, Engineering, and Technology." National Academy of Sciences, Washington, D.C.

INTERNET RESOURCES

Site name	Site address
Antarctic Treaty Searchable Database: 1959–1999	http://webhost.nvi.net/aspire
Earth System Science Education	http://www.usra.edu/esse
Gateway Antarctica—Centre for Antarctic Studies and Research	http://www.anta.canterbury.ac.nz
Glacier	http://www.glacier.rice.edu/
Institute of Antarctic and Southern Ocean Studies	http://www.antcrc.utas.edu.au/iasos.html
Undergraduate Education Resources	http://www.sigmaxi.org/scienceresources/undergradedu.htm
United States Global Change Research Information Office	http://www.gcrio.org/edu/educ.html
University of Aukland's Antarctica as an Educational Resource Website	http://antarctica.org.nz/

CHAPTER 3: *TERRA AUSTRALIS INCOGNITA*

Alexander, C. (1998). "The Endurance: Shackleton's Legendary Antarctic Expedition." Alfred A. Knopf, New York.
Baughman, T. H. (1994). "Before the Heroes Came: Antarctica in the 1890's." University of Nebraska Press, Lincoln.
Byrd, R. E. (1986). "Alone." St. Martin's Press, New York.
Cherry-Gerrard, A. (1997). "The Worst Journey in the World." Carroll & Graf, New York.
Christie, E. W. (1951). "The Antarctic Problem." Allen and Unwin, London.
Lansing, A. (1999). "Endurance: Shackleton's Incredible Voyage." Carroll and Graf, New York.
Mawson, D. (1999). "The Home of the Blizzard: A True Story of Antarctic Survival." St. Martins Press, New York.
National Science Foundation (1989). "Gazetteer of the Antarctic. 4th ed. Names Approved by the United States Board of Geographic Names." National Science Foundation, Washington, D.C.
Reader's Digest (1985). "Antarctica: Great Stories from the Frozen Continent." Reader's Digest, London.

INTERNET RESOURCES

Site name	Site address
Antarctic Heritage	http://www.heritage-antarctica.org
Antarctic Maps	http://www.70south.com/resources/maps
Antarctic Explorers	http://www.south-pole.com/p0000089.htm
Secrets of the Ice—Antarctic Explorers	http://www.secretsoftheice.org/explore/ discovery.html
Shackleton	http://www.pbs.org/wgbh/nova/shackle- ton/1914/

CHAPTER 4: AWAKENING SCIENCE

Fifield, R. (1987). "International Research in the Antarctic." Oxford University Press, New York.
Fogg, G. E. (1992). "A History of Antarctic Science." Cambridge University Press, Cambridge.
Headland, R. K. (1989). "Chronological List of Antarctic Expeditions and Related Historical Events." Cambridge University Press, Cambridge.
Lewis, R. S. (1965). "A Continent for Science." Viking Press, New York.
Walton, D. W. H. (ed.) (1987). "Antarctic Science." Cambridge University Press, Cambridge.

INTERNET RESOURCES

Site name	Site address
Byrd Polar Research Center	http://www-bprc.mps.ohio-state.edu
Cooperative Research Center for Antarctica and Southern Ocean Studies	http://www.antcrc.utas.edu.au/antcrc
International Council for Science	http://www.icsu.org
International Geophysical Year	http://www4.nas.edu/arc.nsf/web/ igyhistory?OpenDocument
Live from Antarctica	http://passport.ivv.nasa.gov/antarctica/
Scientific Committee on Antarctic Research	http://www.scar.org
Scott Polar Research Institute	http://www.spri.cam.ac.uk
United States Antarctic Resource Center	http://usarc.usgs.gov

CHAPTER 5: INTERNATIONAL STEWARDSHIP

Auburn, F. M. (1982). "Antarctic Law and Politics." Indiana University Press, Bloomington.
Beck, P. J. (1986). "International Politics of Antarctica." St. Martin's Press, New York.
Joyner, C. C. and S. K. Chopra (eds.) (1988). "The Antarctic Legal Regime." American Society of International Law, Boston.
National Research Council (1993). "Science and Stewardship in the Antarctic." National Academy Press, Washington, D.C.

Parsons, A. (1987). "Antarctica: The Next Decade. Report of a Study Group." Cambridge University Press, Cambridge.

Peterson, M. J. (1988). "Managing the Frozen South: The Creation and Evolution of the Antarctic Treaty System." University of California Press, Berkeley.

Polar Research Board (1986). "Antarctic Treaty System: An Assessment. Proceedings of a Workshop Held at Beardmore South Field Camp, Antarctica, June 7–13, 1985." National Academy Press, Washington, D.C.

Quigg, P. W. (1983). "A Pole Apart: The Emerging Issues of Antarctica." McGraw-Hill, New York.

Triggs, G. D. (1987). "The Antarctic Treaty Regime: Law, Environment, and Resources." Cambridge University Press, New York.

INTERNET RESOURCES

Site name	Site address
Antarctic National Organizations	http://www.spri.cam.ac.uk/lib/organ/argent.htm#index
Antarctica New Zealand	http://www.antarcticanz.govt.nz
Antarctica Project	http://www.asoc.org
Argentine Antarctic Institute	http://www.dna.gov.ar
Australian Antarctic Division	http://www.antdiv.gov.au
Belgian Antarctic Program	http://www.belspo.be/antar
Brazilian Antarctic Program	http://www.mar.br
British Antarctic Survey	http://www.nerc-bas.ac.uk
Canadian Polar Commission	http://www.polarcom.gc.ca
Chilean Antarctic Institute	http://www.inach.cl
Council of Managers of National Antarctic Programs	http://www.delm.tas.gov.au/comnap
French Polar Institute	http://www.ifremer.fr/ifrtp
Germany—Alfred Wegner Institute	http://www.awi-bremerhaven.de
Italian Antarctic National Research Program	http://www.pnra.it
Japan—National Institute of Polar Research	http://www.nipr.ac.jp
National Antarctic Program Activities	http://www.delm.tas.gov.au/comnap/members.html
Norsk Polarinstitut at the Norwegian Institute of Technology	http://www.npolar.no
Russia—Arctic and Antarctic Research Institute	http://www.aari.nw.ru
Swedish Polar Research Secretariat	http://www.polar.kva.se
United States—Office of Polar Programs	http://www.nsf.gov/od/opp
World Wildlife Fund	http://www.panda.org

CHAPTER 6: SPREADING PLANET

Adie, R. J. (ed.) (1972). "Antarctic Geology and Geophysics." Universitetsforlaget, Oslo.

Brown, G. C., Hawkesworth, C. J. and Wilson, R. C. L. (1992). "Understanding the Earth: A New Synthesis." Cambridge University Press, Cambridge.

Craddock, C. (ed.) (1982). "Antarctic Geoscience." University of Wisconsin Press, Madison.

Kennett, J. P. (1982). "Marine Geology." Prentice Hall, Englewood Cliffs, New Jersey.

INTERNET RESOURCES

Site name	Site address
Antarctic Margin and Seismic Stratigraphy Program	http://www.aist.go.jp/GSJ/dMG/ ANTOSTRAT/Intro.html
Ocean Drilling Program	http://www-odp.tamu.edu
Polar Technology Program	http://www.geotek.sintef.no/poltech
United States National Geophysical Data Center	http://www.ngdc.noaa.gov

CHAPTER 7: FLOWING PLANET

Broecker, W. S. and Peng, T.-H. (1982). "Tracers in the Sea." Eldigio Press, New York.

Deacon, G. E. R. (1984). "The Antarctic Circumpolar Ocean." Cambridge University Press, Cambridge.

Grove, J. M. (1988). "The Little Ice Age." Methuen, London.

Hambrey, M. and Alean J. (1994). "Glaciers." Cambridge University Press, Cambridge.

Hansen, J. E. and Takahashi, T. (eds.) (1984). "Climate Processes and Climate Sensitivity. Geophysical Monographs 29." American Geophysical Union, Washington, D.C.

Harris, C. M. and Stonehouse, B. (eds.) (1991). "Antarctica and Global Climatic Change." Belhaven Press, London.

Smith, W. O. (ed.) (1990). "Polar Oceanography: Part A—Physical Science and Part B—Chemistry, Biology and Geology." Academic Press, New York.

Thurman, H. V. (1978). "Introductory Oceanography. 2nd Edition." Charles E. Merrill, Columbus, Ohio.

Zwally, J. H., Comiso, J. C., Parkinson, C. L., Campbell, W. J., Carsey, F. D., Gloersen, P. (1983). "Antarctic Sea Ice, 1973–1976: Satellite Passive-Microwave Observations." National Aeronautics and Space Administration, Washington, D.C.

INTERNET RESOURCES

Site name	Site address
Antarctic Digital Database	http://www.nerc-bas.ac.uk/public/magic/ add home.html
Center for Astrophysical Research in Antarctica	http://astro.uchicago.edu/cara/
Intergovernmental Panel on Climate Change	http://www.ipcc.ch/index.htm
Iceberg Page	http://uwamrc.ssec.wisc.edu/amrc/ iceberg.html
Jet Propulsion Laboratory Polar Oceanography Group	http://polar.jpl.nasa.gov/
National Snow and Ice Data Center	http://nsidc.org/index.html
Unites States Army Cold Regions Research and Engineering Library	http://www.crrel.usace.army.mil/library/ cold reg.html
West Antarctic Ice Sheet Program	http://igloo.gsfc.nasa.gov/wais
World Climate Research Program	http://www.wmo.ch/web/wcrp/wcrp-home.html

CHAPTER 8: BREATHING PLANET

Hartmann, D. L. (1994). "Global Physical Climatology." Academic Press, San Diego.
King, J. C. and Turner, J. (1997). "Antarctic Meteorology and Climatology." Cambridge University Press, Cambridge.
National Research Council (1989). "Ozone Depletion, Greenhouse Gases, and Climate Change." National Academy Press, Washington, D.C.
Perry, A. H. and Walker, J. M. (1977). "The Ocean-Atmosphere System." Longman, New York.
Schwerdtfeger, W. (1984). "Weather and Climate of the Antarctic. Developments in Atmospheric Science, No. 15." Elsevier, Amsterdam.
Wallace, J. M. and Hobbs, P. V. (1977). "Atmospheric Science: An Introduction." Academic Press, San Diego.

INTERNET RESOURCES

Site name	Site address
Antarctic Automatic Weather Stations	http://uwamrc.ssec.wisc.edu/aws/
Antarctic Meteorology Online	http://www.nbs.ac.uk/public/icd/metlog/
Antarctic Meteorology Research Center	http://uwamrc.ssec.wisc.edu/ amrchome.html
Carbon Dioxide Information Analysis Center	http://cdiac.esd.ornl.gov/home.html
Intergovernmental Panel on Climate Change	http://www.ipcc.ch/
International Geosphere Biosphere Program	http://www.igbp.kva.se/cgi-bin/php/ frameset.php
Wind Chill Calculator	http://www.srh.noaa.gov/ftproot/ssd/html/ windchil.htm

CHAPTER 9: LIVING PLANET

Bonner, W. N. and Walton, D. W. H. (eds.) (1985). "Key Environments: Antarctica." Pergamon Press, Oxford.
Crame, J. A. (ed.) (1989). "Origins and Evolution of the Antarctic Biota. Geological Society Special Publication 47." The Geological Society of London, London.
Eastman, J. T. (1993). "Antarctic Fish Biology: Evolution in a Unique Environment." Academic Press, San Diego.
Friedman, E. I. (ed.) (1993). "Antarctic Microbiology." Wiley, New York.
Kerry, K. R. and Hempel, G. (eds.) (1990). "Antarctic Ecosystems: Ecological Change and Conservation." Springer-Verlag, New York.
Knox, G. A. (1994). "The Biology of the Southern Ocean." Cambridge University Press, Cambridge.
Krebs, C. J. (1978). "Ecology: The Experimental Analysis of Distribution and Abundance." Harper and Row, New York.
Laws, R. M. (ed.) (1982). "Antarctic Ecology. Volumes 1 and 2." Academic Press, San Diego.
Llano, G. A. (ed.) (1977). "Adaptations Within Antarctic Ecosystems." Gulf Publishing Co., Houston.
Siegfried, W. R., Condy, P. R. and Laws, R. M. (eds.) (1985). "Antarctic Nutrient Cycles and Food Webs." Springer-Verlag, Berlin.
Stonehouse, B. (ed.) (1975). "The Biology of Penguins." Macmillan Press, London.

INTERNET RESOURCES

Site name	Site address
Smithsonian Institution Oceanographic Sorting Center	http://www.nmnh.si.edu/iz/usap/
World Wildlife Fund	http://www.panda.org/seachange/fisheries

CHAPTER 10: ECOSYSTEM CONSERVATION

Allen, K. R. (1980). "Conservation and Management of Whales." University of Washington Press, Seattle.

El-Sayed, S. Z. (ed.) (1994). "Southern Ocean Ecology: The BIOMASS Perspective." Cambridge University Press, Cambridge.

Fischer, W. and Hureau, J-C. (1985). "FAO Species Identification Sheets for Fishery Purposes: Southern Ocean. Volumes 1 and 2." Food and Agriculture Organization of the United Nations, Rome.

Hansom, J. D. and Gordon, J. E. (1998) "Antarctic Environments and Resources: A Geographical Perspective." Addison Wesley Longman, Singapore.

Kock, K.-H. (1992). "Antarctic Fish and Fisheries." Cambridge University Press, Cambridge.

Orrego Vicuna, F. (ed.) (1983). "Antarctic Resources Policy: Scientific, Legal and Political Issues." Cambridge University Press, Cambridge.

Parker, B. C. (ed.) (1972). "Conservation Problems in Antarctica." Allen Press, Lawrence, Kansas.

Sahrhage, D. (ed.) (1987). "Antarctic Ocean and Resources Variability." Springer-Verlag, New York.

Sherman, K., Alexander, L. M. and Gold, B. D. (eds.) (1990). "Large Marine Ecosystems: Patterns, Processes and Yields." American Association for the Advancement of Science, Washington, D.C.

Shapley, D. (1985). "The Seventh Continent: Antarctica in a Resource Age." Resources for the Future, Washington, D.C.

INTERNET RESOURCES

Site name	Site address
Convention on the Conservation of Antarctic Marine Living Resources	http://www.ccamlr.org
International Whaling Commission	http://ourworld.compuserve.com/home pages/iwcoffice
United Nations Food and Agriculture Organization	http://www.fao.org

CHAPTER 11: ENVIRONMENTAL PROTECTION

Barnes, J. N. (1982). "Let's Save Antarctica." Greenhouse Publications, Victoria, Australia.

Benninghoff, W. S. and Bonner, W. N. (1985). "Man's Impact on the Antarctic Environment." Scientific Committee on Antarctic Research, Cambridge.

Dewitt, M. J. (1985). "Minerals and Mining in Antarctic Science and Technology, Economics and Politics." Clarendon Press, Oxford.

Elliot, L. M. (1994). "International Environmental Politics: Protecting the Antarctic." St. Martin's Press, New York.

Hall, C. M. and Johnston, M. E. (eds.) (1995). "Polar Tourism: Tourism in the Arctic and Antarctic Regions." Wiley, New York.

Husseiny, A. A. (ed.) (1978). "Iceberg Utilization: Proceedings of the First International Conference and Workshop on Iceberg Utilization for Fresh Water Production, Weather Modification and Other Applications." Pergamon, New York.

May, J. (1988). "The Greenpeace Book of Antarctica: A New View of the Seventh Continent." Macmillan Press, Toronto.

Splettstoesser, J. F. and Dreschhoff, G. A. M. (eds.). (1990). "Mineral Resources Potential of Antarctica. Antarctic Research Series. Volume 51." American Geophysical Union, Washington, D.C.

Strahler, A. N. and Strahler, A. H. (1973). "Environmental Geoscience: Interaction Between Natural Systems and Man." Hamilton Publishing Company, Santa Barbara, CA.

Wolfrum, R. (ed.) (1984). "Antarctic Challenge: Conflicting Interests, Cooperation Environmental Protection, Economic Development." Duncker & Humblot, Berlin.

INTERNET RESOURCES

Site name	Site address
Committee on Environmental Protection	http://www.npolar.no/cep
International Association of Antarctic Tour Operators	http://www.iaato.org

CHAPTER 12: THE SCIENCE KEYSTONE

Bull, H., Kingsbury, B. and Roberts, A. (1995). "Hugo Grotius and International Relations." Clarendon Press, Oxford.

Bush, W. M. (1991). "Antarctica and International Law: A Collection of Inter-State and National Documents. Volumes 1–3." Oceana Publications, New York.

Charney, J. I. (ed.) (1982). "The New Nationalism and the Use of Common Spaces." Allanheld, Osmun, New Jersey.

Francioni, F and T. Scovazzi (eds.) (1996). "International Law for Antarctica." Kluwer Law International, The Hague, London.

Jorgensen-Dahl, A. and Ostreng, W. (eds.) (1991). "The Antarctic Treaty System in World Politics." Macmillan, London.

Kish, J. (1973). "The Law of International Spaces." A. W. Sijthoff, Leiden.

National Research Council (1999). "Our Common Journey: A Transition Toward Sustainability." National Academy Press, Washington, D.C.

Rothwell, D. R. (1996). "Polar Regions and the Development of International Law." Cambridge University Press, Cambridge.

Stokke, O. S. and Vidas, D. (1997). "Governing the Antarctic: The Effectiveness and Legitimacy of the Antarctic Treaty System." Cambridge University Press, Cambridge.

INTERNET RESOURCES

Site name	Site address
International Environmental Treaties	http://sedac.ciesin.org/pidb
Multilateral Treaty Project	http://www.tufts.edu/fletcher/multilaterals.html
Outer Space Treaty	http://www.oosa.unvienna.org/treat/ost/ost.html
United Nations Convention on the Law of the Sea Searchable Database	http://webhost.nvi.net/inspire
United Nations Treaty Collection	http://www.un.org/Depts/Treaty
United Nations General Assembly Documents	http://www.un.org/ga/documents/gadocs.htm

INDEX

ABOUT THE CD-ROM

The CD-ROM contains the Antarctic Treaty Searchable Database: 1959–1999, a replica of the web site (http://webhost.nvi.net/aspire). No further installation is required. Specific information on database operation is located in the "Help" and "FAQ" menus and detailed in the Preface to this volume.

The CD-ROM is compatible with most Windows-based PC systems (tested on Windows 95, 98, 2000, NT 4.0) using Java-enabled MS Internet Explorer or Netscape Web browser software, versions 5.x. It does not support Macintosh systems. Macintosh users unable to access the CD-ROM are advised to use the Antarctic Database online at http://webhost.nvi.net/aspire.

For technical support, contact the Harcourt Technical Support Center at the numbers indicated below. Service is available in English only between the hours of 7 AM and 6 PM US Central Time (15:00 to 02:00 GMT), Mondays through Fridays.

Toll free in the US and Canada	(877) 809-6433
Direct dial	(817) 820-3710
Toll free fax in the US only	(800) 354-1774
Direct fax	(817) 820-5100
E-mail:	tscap@hbtechsupport.com